D1559818

THE FOOD
RETAILING INDUSTRY

THE FOOD RETAILING INDUSTRY

Market Structure, Profits, and Prices

Bruce W. Marion
Willard F. Mueller
Ronald W. Cotterill
Frederick E. Geithman
John R. Schmelzer

PRAEGER PUBLISHERS
Praeger Special Studies

New York • London • Sydney • Toronto

Library of Congress Cataloging in Publication Data

Main entry under title:

The Food retailing industry.

Includes index.
1. Grocery trade--United States. 2. Food
industry and trade--United States. 3. Competition--
United States. I. Marion, Bruce W.
HD9321.56.F66   381'.45'66400973   78-19751
ISBN 0-03-046106-5

PRAEGER PUBLISHERS
PRAEGER SPECIAL STUDIES
383 Madison Avenue, New York, N.Y. 10017, U.S.A.

Published in the United States of America in 1979
by Praeger Publishers,
A Division of Holt, Rinehart and Winston, CBS, Inc.

9   038   987654321

PREFACE

In the fall of 1974 the Joint Economic Committee of the U.S. Congress initiated an investigation of the food retailing industry. Hearings were held and subpoenas were sent to 17 of the nation's largest food chains, requesting data on their sales, profits, and prices on a divisional and metropolitan area basis during the period 1970-74.

Because the committee was not adequately staffed to analyze the volume of data received in response to its subpoenas, the committee chairman, the late Sen. Hubert H. Humphrey, requested the senior authors of this book to prepare a "document on the economics of retailing," analyzing "the relationship between retail concentration in local markets and the level of profits and prices" and other matters relating to the structure and performance of food retailing. A report was subsequently prepared: The Profit and Price Performance of Leading Food Chains, 1970-1974.

The Joint Economic Committee held hearings on the report March 30 and April 5, 1977. At these hearings the Food Marketing Institute, a national trade association whose members are largely food chains, was very critical of the report. Its economist, Dr. Timothy M. Hammonds, characterized the report as "a technical and complex document unfortunately flawed by a multitude of incorrect assumptions and inappropriate manipulations." On the other hand, 26 independent academic economists, whose comments are included in the hearing record, without exception commended the report.

Although this book draws heavily from the report to the Joint Economic Committee, it expands several sections and clarifies others. It also includes two additional chapters: Chapter 2 provides an analysis of the courses of changing concentration, and Chapter 6 examines the policy implications of the study and recommends several policy options that would promote competition in grocery retailing.

This research would not have been possible without the cooperation of the Joint Economic Committee. Research on the competitive performance of any industry requires information that generally is not available to independent researchers. In food retailing, the public financial reports of large food chains represent the consolidation of operations spread over numerous metropolitan areas. Since the metropolitan area is the relevant arena of competition in food retailing, consolidated financial statements hide more than they reveal.

We are indebted to several members of the Joint Economic Committee, especially the late Sen. Hubert H. Humphrey, for inviting us to conduct the study, and the Hon. Gillis W. Long and the Hon. Margaret M. Heckler, cochairpersons of the hearings on the report. Dr. George Tyler of the committee staff provided valuable assistance throughout the study, as did the staff director, John R. Stark.

Ms. Tonya Kins and Ms. Julie Caswell were primarily responsible for organizing and tabulating merger data on food retailing. Ms. Heloisa Scholl and Ms. Judy Peterson did much of the secretarial work for the drafts of this volume. Mr. Michael Von Schneidemesser provided computer assistance in data handling.

The major financial support for the project was provided by the North Central Regional Project, NC 117, "Organization and Control of the U.S. Food System," and the College of Agriculture and Life Sciences, University of Wisconsin. The Joint Economic Committee provided part of the computer costs of the study.

CONTENTS

LIST OF TABLES

LIST OF FIGURES

THE FOOD
RETAILING INDUSTRY

1

OVERVIEW
OF THE FOOD RETAILING INDUSTRY

For the period 1972-74, food prices rose at the most rapid rate in recent history (see Figure 1.1). Consumer response to the increase in food prices resulted in congressional interest in a better understanding of how the U.S. food system operates, and specifically in what factors impact on food prices. In this study we do not attempt to analyze all the factors and industries that may have contributed to the increase in the general level of food prices. Rather, the study focuses on the organization and competitive performance of one vital part of the U.S. food system—the food retailing industry. In particular, it examines the profit and price performance of large U.S. grocery chains to determine whether the competitive environment of these chains has an important influence on their profit and price performance. It first investigates the nature and changing market structure of the industry, and then analyzes the influence of the competitive environment of local markets on retail grocery store prices and profits. These analyses appear in chapters 2-5. This chapter examines some general aspects of the food retailing industry, especially its changing organization, the trends in national and local sales concentration among leading retailers, merger activity, and the levels of gross margins and profits.

In 1977, U.S. consumers spent approximately $180 billion for foods produced on U.S. farms. Payments to U.S. farmers accounted for 31 percent of the total; the remaining 69 percent went to the various intermediary marketing agencies involved between the farm gate and the consumer.[1] (See Figure 1.2.)

Food processors have historically accounted for the largest portion of the "marketing bill." However, their share has declined markedly during recent years while the shares represented by food retailers, wholesalers, and eating places have expanded (Figure 1.3). Between 1958 and 1976 the food processors' share of the "marketing bill" declined by over one-third, to 28.6 percent. Conversely, the share held by food retailers expanded by about one-fifth, to 26.4 percent.[2] During that period modest increases also occurred in the

1

FIGURE 1.1

Consumer Price Index and Food at Home Component, 1960-77
(1967 = 100)

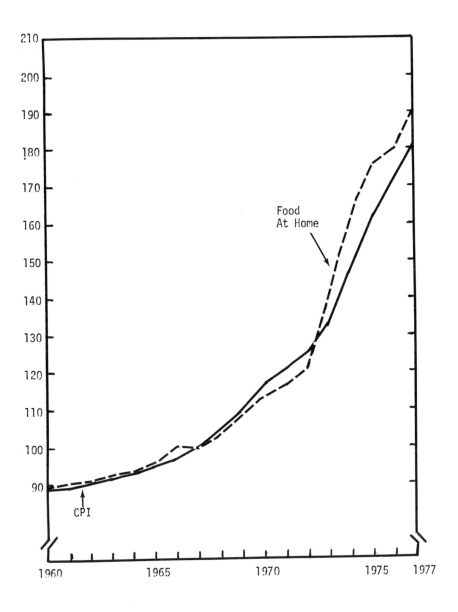

Source: Bureau of Labor Statistics.

2

FIGURE 1.2

Consumer Expenditures, Farm Value, and Marketing Bill, 1958-76

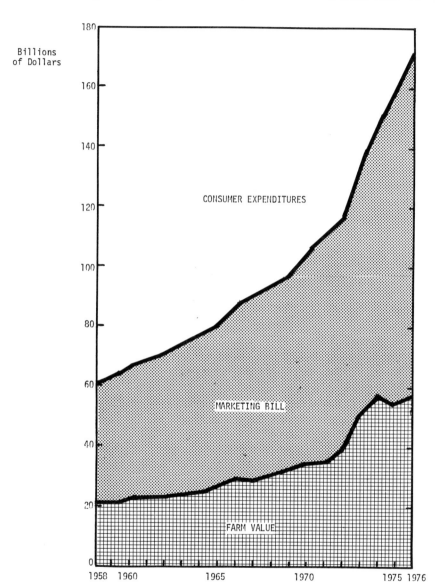

Source: United States Department of Agriculture (USDA), Agri-cultural Statistics, 1972 and 1977 (Washington, D.C.: U.S. Government Printing Office, 1972 and 1977).

FIGURE 1.3

Distribution of Food Marketing Bill, 1958-76
(percent)

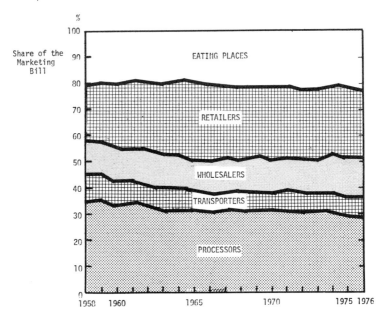

Sources: USDA, Marketing and Transportation Situation, MTS
198 (Washington, D.C.: U.S. Dept. of Agriculture, August 1975),
p. 36; USDA, Developments in Marketing Spreads for Food Products
in 1977, Agricultural Economic Report no. 398 (Washington, D.C.:
U.S. Department of Agriculture, March 1978), p. 13. Revised marketing bill data received from National Economics Analysis Division
(NEAD), USDA, April 1978.

food wholesalers' and eating places' share of the "marketing bill."
Thus, for whatever reasons, those agencies most closely linked with
the consumer have accounted for a steadily increasing portion of the
marketing bill for U.S. farm foods.

Retail food store sales in 1976 were estimated at $141 billion
by the Bureau of the Census, or about one-fifth of all retail sales in
the United States. The vast majority of these food sales—93 percent—
were made by retail grocery stores, while specialty food stores
(such as meat markets and confectionery stores) accounted for the
remaining 7 percent.[3] Progressive Grocer reported higher total food
store sales—$161.3 billion for 1976—with grocery stores accounting
for 94 percent of this total.[4]

The emergence of the grocery store as the primary food retailing unit in the United States can be traced to the introduction of the supermarket in the 1930s. The supermarket, which combined self-service, cash-and-carry and a broad selection of products under one roof revolutionized the U.S. food retailing industry and provided the impetus for fewer but larger retail food stores. This trend has continued to the present. The period 1967-77 is illustrative; over the period the number of grocery stores declined by about one-fifth, from 226,170 to 175,820 establishments. Average real dollar sales per grocery store increased by 52 percent, from $320,000 to $487,000. [5]

In 1977 industry-defined supermarkets made nearly 76 percent of all grocery store sales, although they represented only about 19 percent of all stores. [6] It is important to note that a $1 million store in 1967 would have achieved sales of nearly $2 million in 1977 due to price increases alone. To remove the effects of inflation, the 1967 market share of stores with over $1 million in sales (61.3 percent) can be compared with the 1977 market share of stores with over $2 million in sales (64.2 percent). [7] These numbers suggest modest increases in supermarket concentration relative to those using current dollars over the 1967-77 period. If one uses a $2 million supermarket definition, corporate chains operated two-thirds of the supermarkets in 1977 and had annual sales of about $4.6 million per supermarket. Independent grocers operated the remaining one-third of the supermarkets and 95 percent of the smaller grocery stores (annual sales less than $2 million), excluding convenience stores. [8] Thus, although independently owned and operated grocery stores accounted for 49 percent of total grocery store sales in 1977, their share in the important supermarket "submarket" was only one-third.

RETAIL GROCERY CHAINS

Large retail grocery chains rank among the nation's leading retailers. In 1976 the largest grocery chain (Safeway) had domestic food store sales in excess of $8 billion, and the 17 largest grocery chains each reported sales exceeding $1 billion. [9] These and other chains have become the dominant institutional force in food retailing.

Retail grocery chains have grown in relative importance since they became commonplace in the 1930s. Between 1948 and 1972 the chains' share of grocery store sales rose from 34 to 57 percent. [10] (See Figure 1.4.) The share held by smaller chains (operating 11 to 100 stores) increased from 7.0 percent to 17.4 percent during this period; large chains (operators of more than 100 stores) accounted for 27.4 percent of grocery store sales in 1948 and 39.6 percent in 1972.

FIGURE 1.4

Distribution of Grocery Store Sales by Size of Firm, 1948-72

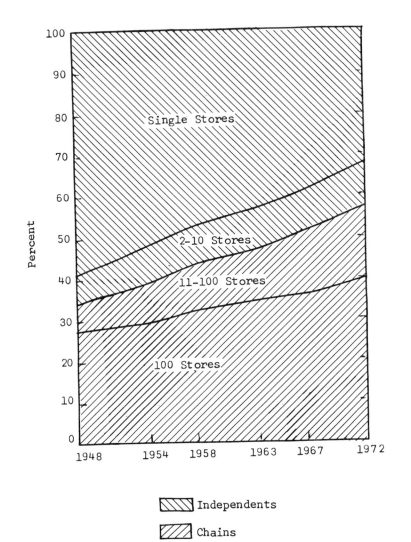

Source: U.S. Bureau of the Census, Census of Retail Trade
1958, 1963, 1967, 1962 (Washington, D.C.: U.S. Government Printing Office).

TABLE 1.1

Market Share of the 20 Largest Grocery Chains, 1948-76
(percent)

Rank	Share of Grocery Store Sales						
	1948	1954	1958	1963	1967	1972	1976
A&P	10.7	11.3	11.1	9.4	8.3	6.6	5.1
1-4	20.1	20.9	21.7	20.0	19.0	18.1	18.7
5-8	3.6	4.5	5.8	6.6	6.7	7.1	7.4
1-8	23.7	25.4	27.5	26.6	25.7	25.2	26.1
9-20	3.2	4.5	6.6	7.4	8.7	11.9	11.5
1-20	26.9	29.9	34.1	34.0	34.4	37.1	37.6
Top 20 excluding A&P	16.2	18.7	23.0	24.6	26.1	30.5	32.5

Note: National Tea and Loblaw were treated as a single entity and their sales were combined accordingly. This adjustment placed National Tea-Loblaw fourth among the largest grocery chains in both 1963 and 1967 and ninth among the chains in 1972.

Sources: 1948-63 estimates based upon Census Bureau Data as reported in National Commission on Food Marketing, Organization and Competition in Food Retailing, Tech. Study no. 7 (Washington, D.C.: U.S. Government Printing Office, June 1966), p. 513, App. Table 15. Estimates for 1967 are based upon Federal Trade Commission, 1969 Food Retailing Survey (unpublished) and U.S. Bureau of the Census, 1967 Census of Business, Retail Trade (Washington, D.C.: U.S. Government Printing Office). Estimates for 1972 are based on data supplied by leading retail food chains and U.S. Bureau of the Census, Census of Retail Trade, 1972, Subject Series, Establishment and Firm Size, RC72-S-1 and Census of Retail Trade, 1972, Merchandise Line Sales, RC72-6 (Washington, D.C.: U.S. Government Printing Office, 1975). Estimates for 1976 are from American Institute of Food Distribution, Weekly Digest, vol. 84, no. 25 (Fair Lawn, N.J.: American Institute of Food Distribution, June 18, 1977).

FIGURE 1.5

Percentage of Grocery Store Sales Made by the 4, 8, and 20 Largest Retail Grocery Chains, 1948–76

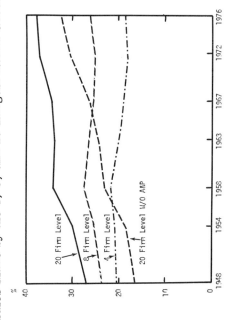

Sources: 1948–63 estimates based upon Census Bureau Data as reported in National Commission on Food Marketing, Organization and Competition in Food Retailing, Tech. Study no. 7 (Washington, D.C.: U.S. Government Printing Office, June 1966), p. 513, App. Table 15. Estimates for 1967 are based upon Federal Trade Commission, 1969 Food Retailing Survey (unpublished) and U.S. Bureau of the Census, 1967 Census of Business, Retail Trade (Washington, D.C.: U.S. Government Printing Office). Estimates for 1972 are based on data supplied by leading retail food chains and U.S. Bureau of the Census, Census of Retail Trade, 1972, Subject Series, Establishment and Firm Size, RC72–S–1 and Census of Retail Trade, 1972, Merchandise Line Sales, RC72–6 (Washington, D.C.: U.S. Government Printing Office, 1975). Estimates for 1976 are from American Institute of Food Distribution, Weekly Digest, vol. 84, no. 25 (Fair Lawn, N.J.: American Institute of Food Distribution, June 18, 1977).

Table 1.1 indicates the share of U.S. grocery store sales held by the 20 largest chains from 1948 through 1976. One of the most dramatic changes was A&P's decline from 11.3 percent of the nation's grocery sales in 1954 to 5.1 percent in 1976. The remaining three of the four largest chains realized a steady increase in market share from 9.4 percent in 1948 to 13.6 percent in 1976. The most rapid growth during this period occurred among the fifth through eighth and nine through twentieth largest chains, which doubled and tripled their market shares, respectively.* (See Table 1.1 and Figure 1.5.) The 20 largest chains increased their market share from 26.9 to 37.6 percent; without A&P, however, the other 19 largest chains grew from 16.2 to 32.5 percent of U.S. grocery store sales.

---

*The 1972 Census Bureau concentration figures were adjusted to make them more comparable with concentration figures for earlier years. Since the late 1960s discount stores with food departments have grown in importance. Since census collects data on an establishment rather than a company basis, in those cases where a discount store is classified as a department store (SIC 531), the total sales are credited to department store sales and to the company operating the nonfood portion of the discount store. This poses problems in those instances where the food department is operated by a separate firm. Since large grocery chains frequently operate food departments within discount stores, their grocery store sales calculated by the Bureau of the Census would be understated, as would the total sales for all grocery stores (SIC 541). This results in an understatement of 4-, 8-, and 20-firm concentration figures.

Since data provided by companies as part of this study indicated their total sales from grocery stores, these figures were used to calculate national concentration ratios for 1972. Total grocery store sales in the United States, as reported by the Bureau of the Census, were adjusted by adding the grocery sales occurring in department stores, as reported in its report on merchandise line sales. These adjustments resulted in the concentration figure shown in Table 1.1 for 1972, whereas the 1972 Census of Retail Trade reports 4-, 8-, and 20-firm concentration ratios of 17.5, 24.4, and 34.7.

The 1972 concentration figures in Table 1.1 also differ from other published reports in which the total company sales of the 4, 8, and 20 largest grocery chains were used in the calculations instead of the grocery store sales of these firms. An estimated 5-10 percent of the sales of these companies stem from nongrocery store operations. Use of total company sales therefore overstates the level of concentration.

Nearly all large chains have performed the wholesaling function for their own stores for many years. Some chains are also integrated into food processing. However, except for certain commodities—especially fluid milk—where substantial increases in vertical integration by chains have occurred,[11] the available evidence suggests no strong overall trend toward either integration or disintegration by food chains (see Table A.6).

Many grocery chains have diversified since the late 1960s into other types of retailing, such as drugstores and general merchandise stores. However, in 1973 grocery store sales still accounted for over 90 percent of the domestic sales of the largest 20 chains.[12]

INDEPENDENT RETAILERS

Although chains have significantly increased their share of total grocery store sales since the late 1920s, independent food retailers[*] continue to be an important factor in grocery retailing. In 1976 they accounted for 44 percent of grocery store sales in the United States.[13]

One of the primary factors that has contributed to the survival of independent food retailers has been the increase in the proportion that have affiliated with cooperative or voluntary wholesale organizations.[†] In 1972 affiliated independents did 86 percent of all independent grocery store sales (38 percent of U.S. grocery store sales), while unaffiliated independents accounted for only 14 percent. Average store sales for affiliated independents were $680,000, over eight times larger than the $75,000 per store average for their unaffiliated counterparts.[14]

Although the number of stores operated by chains in 1972 was more than double the number operated in 1954, the opposite was true for independent grocers. Unaffiliated independents experienced a 57 percent decrease in store numbers during this period, while the

---

[*]An independent is defined as an operator of fewer than 11 grocery stores.

[†]Independents may be affiliated with either voluntary or cooperative groups. Cooperative retailers (generally independents) are stockholder members of cooperative wholesale buying groups, such as Certified Grocers and Associated Grocery. Voluntary group retailers are affiliated with voluntary merchandising groups sponsored by wholesalers and operate under a common name, such as IGA, Red and White, Super Value, and Clover Farm.

TABLE 1.2

Share of General-Line Wholesale Grocery Sales, by Type of Organization,
1948-72
(percent)

Type of Business	Share of Sales in					
	1948	1954	1958	1963	1967	1972
Affiliated						
Voluntary groups						
4 Largest	2.2	5.2	7.4	9.7	11.2	14.9
8 Largest	3.8	9.2	11.8	13.6	n.a.	21.2
All voluntaries	n.a.	n.a.	38.5	45.7	47.4	29.9[*]
Cooperative groups						
4 Largest	3.2	5.2	7.9	8.5	10.6	8.3
8 Largest	4.2	7.3	10.6	12.4	n.a.	12.2
All cooperatives	n.a.	n.a.	25.4	24.8	26.4	32.2
Nonaffiliated	n.a.	n.a.	36.1	29.5	26.2	37.9[*]
Total	n.a.	n.a.	100.0	100.0	100.0	100.0

n.a. = Not available.

[*]Although these figures appear to be in error, staff members in charge of the census of wholesale trade were unable either to find an error or to explain the drastic changes in 1972. Progressive Grocer reports that wholesale grocery sales in 1977 were distributed as follows: 53 percent to voluntary wholesalers, 28 percent to cooperative wholesalers, and 19 percent to unaffiliated wholesalers. "45th Annual Report of the Grocery Industry," Progressive Grocer, vol. 57, no. 4 (New York: Progressive Grocer, April 1978), p. 127.

Sources: Data for 1948, 1954, 1958, and 1963 are from National Commission on Food Marketing, Organization and Competition in Food Retailing, Technical Study no. 7 (Washington, D.C.: U.S. Government Printing Office, June 1966), App. Table 17, p. 514. Data for 1967 were estimated from issues of U.S. Bureau of the Census, Monthly Wholesale Trade (Washington, D.C.: U.S. Government Printing Office). Data for 1972 are from Bureau of the Census, Wholesale Trade (Washington, D.C.: U.S. Government Printing Office).

FIGURE 1.6

Percentage of General-Line Wholesale Grocery Sales Made by the
Four and Eight Largest Voluntary and Cooperative Groups, 1948-72

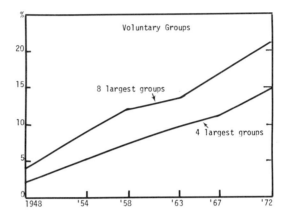

Note: Census estimates of the percentage of general-line
wholesale grocery sales made by the eight largest voluntary and the
eight largest cooperative wholesalers were not available for 1967.

Sources: Data for 1948, 1954, 1958, and 1963 are from National
Commission on Food Marketing, Organization and Competition in
Food Retailing, Technical Study no. 7 (Washington, D.C.: U.S. Gov-
ernment Printing Office, June 1966), App. Table 17, p. 514. Data
for 1967 were estimated from issues of U.S. Bureau of the Census,
Monthly Wholesale Trade (Washington, D.C.: U.S. Government
Printing Office). Data for 1972 are from Bureau of the Census,
Wholesale Trade (Washington, D.C.: U.S. Government Printing
Office).

number of stores operated by affiliated independents declined by
about 35 percent.[15] The slower rate of decrease in store numbers
among affiliated independents was due, in part, to the movement of
unaffiliated independents to the affiliated category.

Affiliated independents are served by various types of food
wholesalers. Concentration in grocery wholesaling has increased
markedly since 1948 (Table 1.2). The eight largest voluntary wholesalers and the eight largest cooperative wholesalers accounted for
33 percent of U.S. sales by general-line grocery wholesalers in
1972, more than four times their share in 1948. Voluntary wholesalers have grown more consistently and rapidly than their cooperative counterparts (Figure 1.6).

FIGURE 1.6 (continued)

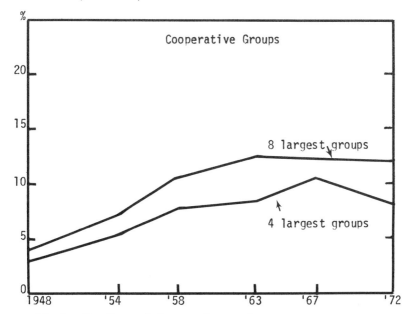

The implications of the trend toward greater concentration in grocery wholesaling are not clear. To the extent that the growth of large wholesalers stems from or leads to the ability to supply their retail customers in ways that make them more effective competitors with grocery chains, the trend may enhance competition at the retail level. Several of the large grocery wholesalers have been active in acquiring other wholesalers. Data are not available on the rate of growth of wholesalers of different sizes, excluding the impact of mergers.

From the standpoint of competition among wholesalers, changes in the concentration of grocery wholesaling at the state or standard metropolitan statistical area (SMSA) level are more relevant than national concentration trends. While data are not available for these smaller geographic areas, it is apparent that independent retailers in many areas have relatively few wholesalers from whom to choose. At least in part this occurs because voluntary and cooperative wholesalers often operate under exclusive territorial arrangements that prohibit their seeking the patronage of retailers located outside their territories.

Taken together with the increasing share of grocery sales held by the 20 largest chains, the above data indicate a continued trend toward greater concentration in grocery procurement. The National Commission on Food Marketing expressed concern about concentration in procurement in 1966:

Concentration of purchasing power by food retailers is especially significant. The increasing market orientation of the food industry and changes in the organization of buying have transferred market power from processors and manufacturers to retailers. Prospective developments in the industry are likely to further enhance their position. Increasing concentration of purchases restricts the alternatives open to suppliers, stimulates compensating concentration on their part, and weakens the effectiveness of competition as a self-regulating device throughout the industry.[16]

This trend has not abated.

LOCAL MARKET CONCENTRATION

While the level and trends of concentration at the national level are useful in indicating the rate of growth of large chains and the potential degree of market power in procurement, the performance of food retailers as sellers is largely determined by the structure of local markets. Food retailing, unlike many industries, is highly localized; and competition for customers is limited to a small geographic area. Thus, the level and trends of local market concentration are especially important in analyzing competitive behavior in food retailing.

The level of local market concentration in food retailing is significant for two reasons. First, the level of concentration within a market is likely to influence the competitive conduct and strategies of the firms operating in that market. Second, changes in local market concentration may serve as a proxy for changes in other market structure variables that are more difficult to measure. For example, changes in market concentration may indicate changes in the entry barriers facing new firms: increasing concentration suggests that barriers to entry are high or increasing, while decreasing concentration may indicate the reverse.

Local market concentration followed a persistent upward trend between 1954 and 1972. (This was a continuation of a trend already under way between 1948 and 1954.)* For a sample of 194

---

*Although the National Commission on Food Marketing was unable to obtain concentration data for 1948 because the Bureau of the Census had destroyed the basic data, available information

SMSAs,* the four largest firms in each SMSA controlled 45.1 percent of grocery store sales in 1954, on average. By 1972 the unweighted average share held by the largest four firms had increased 7.0 percentage points, to 52.1 percent (Table 1.3).†

The trends in concentration were similar for SMSAs with populations both greater and less than 500,000, although the rate of increase was slightly different between these groups. Four-firm concentration (CR_4) in SMSAs with 1970 populations greater than 500,000 increased nearly 10 percent (4.6 percentage points), while concentration in smaller SMSAs increased over 17 percent (8.0 percentage points) from 1954 to 1972. Concentration increased most in SMSAs that had relatively low concentration in 1954 (CR_4 less than 50). The average local market concentration in those SMSAs increased from 40.6 to 50.0 percent over the period. The only significant reduction in average market concentration occurred in those

---

indicates that a sizable increase in four-firm concentration occurred between 1948 and 1954. For example, the largest chains in 11 metropolitan areas increased their average share from 25.7 percent to 32.5 percent. Additionally, in seven small Midwest cities the average four-firm concentration increased from 45.6 percent to 54.2 percent (8.6 percentage points) over the period. Federal Trade Commission, The Structure and Competitive Behavior of Food Retailing (Washington, D.C.: U.S. Government Printing Office, June 1966), pp. 6-7.

*These are SMSAs for which CR_4 data are available for each census year between 1954 and 1972. The geographic definition of 109 of these was changed over the period.

†The data indicate that markets that did not experience a change in definition increased more sharply in concentration than did SMSAs that were redefined. Definitions changed for 109 of the 194 sample SMSAs between 1954 and 1972; for this subset of markets, average concentration increased from 45.4 percent to 50.2 percent, significantly less than the average increase in concentration (44.8 to 53.9 percent) for the remaining 85 SMSAs. The relative magnitude of the definitional change also had a discernible influence on concentration. Those SMSAs (70 in all) in which the definitional change resulted in more than a 10 percent addition to grocery store sales experienced an increase in concentration from 45.4 percent to 49.0 percent. The 7.9 percent (3.6 percentage point) increase in four-firm concentration in those markets was substantially less than the 19.2 percent (8.6 percentage point) increase in concentration in SMSAs whose definitions either remained the same or, if changed, resulted in less than 10 percent increase in total grocery store sales (Table A.7).

TABLE 1.3

Average Four-Firm Concentration for 194 SMSAs Classified by 1954 Four-Firm Concentration Level, 1954–72

Market Size and Level of Four-Firm Concentration Level in 1954	No. of SMSAs	Four-Firm Concentration					Average 1972 Market Sales (thousand dollars)[a]
		1954	1958	1963	1967	1972	
SMSAs over 500,000[b]							
CR_4 less than 40	17	35.3	39.7	40.8	41.5	46.4	803,505
40.0–49.9	21	45.4	49.2	49.4	47.5	49.2	568,975
50.0–59.9	18	53.5	55.6	54.1	54.2	53.0	725,802
60.0 and over	2	69.7	68.7	67.9	67.3	75.0	524,411
Total and average	58	45.8	49.1	49.0	48.5	50.4	684,850
SMSAs under 500,000[b]							
CR_4 less than 40	44	34.8	41.8	42.6	45.6	46.8	112,654
40.0–49.9	54	45.2	49.0	51.0	52.7	54.1	107,092
50.0–59.9	30	54.0	57.1	57.4	56.1	57.1	107,916
60.0 and over	8	64.0	63.9	62.4	60.3	61.7	111,216
Total and average	136	44.9	49.3	50.4	51.6	52.9	109,639
Average all SMSAs		45.1	49.2	50.0	50.7	52.1	281,610

[a] Grocery store sales for establishments with payroll.
[b] Population in 1970.
Sources: 1954–63, National Commission on Food Marketing, Organization and Competition in Food Retailing, Tech. Study no. 7 (Washington, D.C.: U.S. Government Printing Office, June 1966), pp. 44–51; Tables 2–6. This was a special tabulation by the Bureau of the Census for the Federal Trade Commission and the U.S. Department of Agriculture.

SMSAs in which the four-firm concentration ratio exceeded 60 in 1954 and that had populations in 1970 that were less than 500,000; these SMSAs experienced a decline of 2.3 percentage points in average CR_4 over the period.

The shift toward higher levels of local market concentration is further illustrated by the changes in the percentage distribution of SMSAs classified by four-firm concentration. For the identical sample of 194 SMSAs, the percentage of markets with CR_4 below 50 percent declined from 70.2 in 1954 to 44.9 in 1972, while the percentage of markets with CR_4 of 50 or more expanded from 29.8 to 55.1 (Figure 1.7). Especially significant was the increase in the proportion of highly concentrated markets (CR_4 over 60); they rose from 5.1 percent to 24.7 percent of the sample of SMSAs examined.

The upward trend in concentration has continued since 1972. On the basis of the best and most recent data available, four-firm concentration increased an average of 3.4 percentage points between 1972-73 and 1975-76 in the 135 metropolitan areas for which comparable data are available. This is a larger increase than that reported by the Census Bureau for 1967-72, suggesting an acceleration in market concentration since 1972. The average four-firm concentration ratios in 135 metropolitan areas for 1972-73 and 1975-76 are shown below.[*]

	Number of Metropolitan Areas	Average 4-Firm Concentration	
		1972-73	1975-76
Level of 4-firm concentration in 1972-73 (percent)			
30-39.9	14	35.5	38.5
40-49.9	51	45.4	49.4
50-59.9	42	53.9	59.3
60-69.9	22	64.8	63.1
70 and over	6	73.4	77.4
Total	135	51.4	54.8

[*]Data were calculated from 1974 Grocery Distribution Guide and 1977 Grocery Distribution Guide (Wellesley Hills, Mass.: Metro Market Studies, 1974 and 1977 respectively). It should be noted that the data developed by this source do not cover a calendar year. For example, the 1977 Grocery Distribution Guide provides market share estimates for 1975-76.

FIGURE 1.7

Percentage Distribution of SMSAs by Level of Concentration for Identical Sample of 194 SMSAs, 1954 and 1972

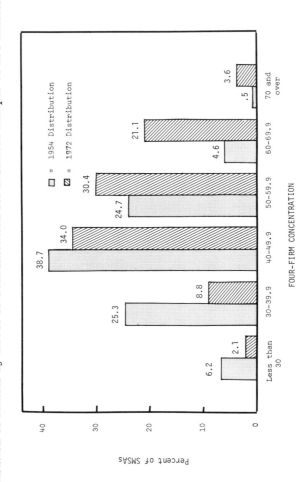

Note: The sample is limited to those SMSAs for which the Bureau of the Census calculated four-firm concentration ratios in both 1954 and 1972.

Sources: Bureau of the Census, 1972 Census of Retail Trade; this was a special tabulation for the Federal Trade Commission and the U.S. Department of Agriculture.

18

A number of countervailing forces are working to change the level of concentration in local markets. These are examined in Chapter 2. The analysis is restricted to the period 1967-75 because information on horizontal mergers was not available for earlier years.

IMPACT OF MERGERS ON STRUCTURE
OF GROCERY RETAILING

The period 1949-75 witnessed considerable merger activity involving food retailers. There were 1,016 recorded acquisitions representing total sales of $13.0 billion (Table 1.4). During the first 15 years of this period, mergers contributed significantly to national concentration. From 1949 to 1964 the 20 largest chains of 1963 acquired retail grocery firms with sales exceeding $3 billion. This represented about 70 percent of all acquired retail grocery sales. A National Commission on Food Marketing study concluded that, in the absence of mergers by the 20 largest chains of 1963, the share of national sales held by these chains would have increased by less than 1 percent between 1948 and 1963. [17]

Commencing in the mid-1960s, public policy toward mergers by large food chains changed the pattern, if not the tempo, of mergers in food retailing. [18] On June 10, 1965, Grand Union entered into a consent decree with the Federal Trade Commission (FTC) that required Grand Union to dispose of certain acquired stores and to make no further horizontal acquisitions for ten years without the prior approval of the FTC. On December 21, 1965, the commission entered into a consent agreement that required Consolidated Foods to divest itself of food stores with combined sales of about $200 million. [19] On March 3, 1966, the FTC, reversing a hearing examiner's decision, issued a decision finding that several mergers by National Tea violated Section 7 of the Clayton Act; it then ordered that National Tea make no further food store acquisitions for a period of ten years without the prior approval of the Commission. Finally, on January 3, 1967, the commission issued an enforcement policy statement with respect to mergers in food retailing. [20] This statement made it clear that acquisitions by chains with annual sales exceeding $500 million would be subject to investigation and possible challenge, except when the acquired retailer was very small. In 1965 there were ten chains with annual sales over $500 million.

These various legal actions, reinforced with the 1967 enforcement policy statement, had an important impact on mergers in the industry. They did not stop all mergers, nor was this the intent. In its policy statement the FTC recognized that very likely "market

TABLE 1.4

Acquisitions of Food Retailers, 1949-75
(dollars in millions)

Year	By All Acquirers		By 20 Leading Food Chains[a]			By 10 Leading Food Chains[a]		
	Number of Acquisitions	Sales of Acquired	Number of Acquisitions	Sales of Acquired	Percent of Total Acquired Sales	Number of Acquisitions	Sales of Acquired	Percent of Total Acquired Sales
1949	5	$ 66	1	$ 47	71	1	$ 47	71
1950	5	4	2	3	75	1	1	25
1951	12	28	6	25	89	5	19	68
1952	10	71	5	55	77	4	53	75
1953	13	88	4	77	88	2	61	69
1954	24	76	7	37	50	4	31	41
1955	55	559	23	465	83	15	267	48
1956	69	450	32	310	69	20	141	31
1957	52	319	20	194	61	14	170	53
1958	74	517	41	361	70	27	261	50
1959	63	319	34	136	43	14	24	8
1960	44	307	25	201	65	10	36	12
1961	50	518	30	407	79	16	292	56
1962	53	306	24	179	58	14	157	51

1963	51	568	27	463	82	16	416	73
1964	41	312	16	188	60	8	153	49
1965	28	558	5	61	11	3	35	6
1966[b]	40	539	6	110	20	3	73	14
1967	33	1,350	3	21[c]	2[d]	0	0[c]	0[d]
1968	51	1,155	12	314[c]	(12)27[d]	6	199[c]	(2)17[d]
1969	45	715	14	41	8	6	13	3
1970	36	688	9	74	11	5	22	3
1971	27	435[e]	2	28	6	2	28	6
1972	59	1,069[e]	6	242[e]	20	1	3	(f)
1973	27	206[e]	13	29[e]	14	3	11	5
1974	18	1,591[e]	4	30	2	3	14	1
1975[g]	29	255	5	99	39	3	84	35
Total	1,014	12,879	376	4,197	32	206	2,611	20

Notes:

[a] For 1949-66, data are for largest chains of 1963. Subsequent data are for largest chains in 1975.

[b] The FTC merger notification program did not require reports from food distributors until June 1967.

[c] Includes Lucky's acquisition of Eagle Stores, with estimated sales of $175,000,000.

[d] Percent excluding Lucky's acquisition of Eagle Stores, which was approved by the FTC.

[e] Sales data not available for one firm in this category.

[f] Less than 1 percent.

[g] Data for 1975 not complete, since premerger notification data were available only for the first months of 1975.

Sources: Data from 1949-66 are from the Federal Trade Commission as reported in Willard F. Mueller, The Celler-Kefauver Act: Sixteen Years of Enforcement, report to the Antitrust Subcommittee on the Judiciary, House of Representatives (Washington, D.C.: U.S. Government Printing Office, Oct. 16, 1967). Data for 1967-75 from FTC merger notification reports supplied the joint Economic Committee; and from secondary sources such as Moody's Manual, various years, Supermarket News, various issues, and Weekly Digest, various issues. FTC data reported 185 retail acquisitions with combined sales of $4.455 billion. Secondary sources reported 142 retail acquisitions with combined sales of $2.954 billion. Of this latter total, eight acquisitions had combined sales of $1.265 billion. These large acquisitions involved the acquisition of large food retailers by large firms not involved in food retailing. The FTC notification program did not require reporting these mergers.

21

forces will continue to create an environment conducive to mergers in the industry."[21] While recognizing that personal and financial reasons might dictate further mergers, the commission concluded:

> . . . whereas mergers by retail firms with annual sales in excess of $500 million may contribute to further concentration of buying power, in addition to any adverse effect that they may have at the retail selling level, it is unlikely that the prohibition of mergers by such companies would have an adverse effect on efficiency. Moreover, insofar as economies of scale require fairly large-scale operations, the goal of promoting efficiency might be better achieved by channeling mergers away from the largest firms to those whose efficiency would be enhanced by further growth.[22]

During 1967-75 merger activity by the top ten chains (all with sales exceeding $500 million) was sharply lower than during 1955-64, the decade prior to FTC action. These chains acquired food retailers with sales of about $374 million, which was only about 5 percent of the sales of all food retailers acquired during the period. Moreover, the only sizable acquisition by the top 10 was Lucky's acquisition of Eagle Stores in 1968, which was made with the approval of the FTC as part of a consent decree with Consolidated Foods.[23] If this acquisition is assumed to have involved annual sales of $175 million, the other 28 acquisitions made by the top 10 chains since 1967 had combined sales of only $115 million, for an average of only $4 million per acquisition. This is a marked contrast with previous years. From 1955 to 1964, these chains averaged 15 acquisitions per year, with $12.4 million the average size of acquisition.

Merger activity by the eleventh through twentieth largest food chains (all of which had sales exceeding $500 million in 1975) also declined after 1967, although less sharply than that of the ten largest chains. Total sales acquired per year by these chains dropped from about $100 million during 1955-64 to about $50 million during 1965-75.

The 1965-67 FTC actions toward mergers by large grocery chains occurred on the eve of the great merger movement that swept American industry during 1967-71, and has continued at a relatively high plateau through the late 1970s.[24] Total merger activity in food retailing peaked during the first two years of this period (1967 and 1968), dropped to a level similar to 1955-66 during the next three years, and then peaked again in 1972 and 1974 (Table 1.4). In total, merger activity during 1967-75 increased over prior periods. The effect of the FTC enforcement policy was to channel this accelerated merger activity away from the top 20 chains, not to stop it.

Table 1.5 breaks down the acquisitions by type of acquirer and by type of merger for the period 1967-75. It shows that the largest share of all acquisitions (measured by sales) was conglomerate in nature—that is, the acquiring firm was not engaged in food retailing. Conglomerate acquirers made 12 acquisitions with total sales of $3.0 billion, which represented 41 percent of total acquired sales.[*]

Food retailers other than the top 20 were the second most active group of acquirers, making acquisitions with combined sales of $2,685 million (36 percent of the total). Wholesalers acquired 83 food retailers with combined sales of $808 million (10 percent), and the remaining 12 percent were acquired by the top 20 chains.

In looking at the types of mergers, 29 percent of acquired sales involved horizontal mergers (between firms operating in the same market). Over half of these involved retailers other than the top 20. Market extension mergers (between food retailers operating in different local markets) were somewhat more numerous than horizontal mergers. Again, the most active acquirers were retailers other than the top 20.

Post-1967 merger activity affected the structure of the market in several ways. Conglomerate mergers did not have an immediate impact on concentration at either the local or the national level. But, as will be shown in Chapter 2, when other things are held constant, market concentration tends to rise in metropolitan areas that conglomerate firms or large food chains enter by acquiring established food retailers.[25]

The horizontal and market extension acquisitions of food retailers increased somewhat the level of concentration on a national basis. Between 1967 and 1975 the top 20 chains of 1975 made horizontal and market extension mergers with combined sales of $881 million. Over this period the top 20 chains of each year increased their market share from 34.4 percent of total U.S. grocery store sales to 37.0 percent. If we subtract the acquisitions from their growth, these chains' share of total grocery store sales would have risen to about 36.4 percent in 1975. Thus, the direct contribution of mergers accounted for only about one-fourth of the increase in these chains' market share over the period. As discussed in Chapter 2, mergers may also have an indirect effect on an acquiring firm's share.

---

[*]Some of these acquirers were in other lines of distribution, in which case they are product extension conglomerate mergers. The largest conglomerate acquisitions are shown in Table A.8.

TABLE 1.5

Food Retailer and Wholesaler Acquisitions, by Type of Acquiring Firm, 1967–75 (sales in million dollars)

| | Acquired Grocery Retailers, by Type of Acquisition | | | | | | | | Acquired Food Wholesalers | |
| | Total | | Horizontal | | Market Extension | | | | | |
Nature of Acquiring Firm	No.	Sales	No.	Sales	No.	Sales	No.	Sales	No.	Sales
Food retailers										
Top 10	29	$372	17	$104	12	$268			—	—
Top 20	68	$876	42	$337*	26	$539			1	$45
Other retailers	164	$2,690	105	$1,282*	59	$1,408			13	$105
Food wholesalers	83	$808	71	$540	12	$268			25	$996
Conglomerate	12	$3,035	—	—	—	—			—	—
Total	327	$7,409	218	$2,159	97	$2,215			39	$1,146

*Sales data not available for one firm in this category.

Notes: FTC data reported 211 acquisitions of grocery retailers and wholesalers with combined sales of $5,494 million; secondary sources reported an additional 155 acquisitions with combined sales of $3,601 million. Of the latter total, eight acquisitions had combined sales of $1,256 million. These large acquisitions involved the merger of large food retailers and large firms not involved in food retailing. The FTC merger notification program did not require reporting these mergers.

Sources: Federal Trade Commission merger notification reports submitted to Joint Economic Committee; secondary sources such as Moody's Industrial Manual, Supermarket News, and Weekly Digest.

During 1967–75 the overall direct impact of horizontal mergers on concentration in local markets was quite small. All retailers, including the top 20, made horizontal acquisitions with sales of $2,159 million.* This was equal to only 2.3 percent of national grocery store sales in 1972. Thus, horizontal mergers increased local concentration by an average of just over 2 percent. This is not to imply, of course, that average concentration among the top four firms in SMSAs was increased by this percentage, since most acquisitions were by smaller firms, which are less likely to be among the top four firms in an SMSA than are large chains.

The impact of horizontal mergers in some SMSAs was quite substantial, however. Tables A.9 and A.10 show the market shares of the acquiring and acquired firms in the SMSAs in which both firms operated. Table A.9 covers only acquisitions by the 20 largest grocery chains of 1975. Table A.10 indicates the nature of acquisitions where the acquiring retailers were smaller than the top 20, and where the acquired grocery retailer had sales in excess of $10 million. Most of the 74 acquisitions shown in these tables involved small market shares; in only 25 cases did the acquired firm hold over 2 percent of SMSA sales. In only 10 cases did the acquiring firm hold a market share of 10 percent or more and the acquired firm over 1 percent.

In sum, the pattern of the merger movement in grocery retailing changed drastically after 1964. Whereas total acquisitions of grocery retailers actually increased substantially (as measured by acquired sales) after the FTC actions aimed at the largest chains, the top ten chains virtually ceased making acquisitions beginning in 1965. Although the change has been less dramatic, the tempo of mergers by the eleventh through twentieth largest chains has also slowed since 1964. The result very probably has been to slow the trend toward national sales concentration among the largest chains.†

---

*Actually, the volume of horizontal mergers was larger than this because many of the grocery store acquisitions by wholesalers were horizontal, either because the acquiring wholesalers operated grocery stores of their own in the SMSA and/or, as was true of most wholesaler acquisitions, the acquiring wholesalers had affiliated retailers that operated in the same SMSA as the acquired grocery retailers. Additionally, eight horizontal acquisitions with combined sales of $54 million occurred outside SMSAs. In four cases the acquiring firm made 10 percent or more of the sales in the county where the acquisition occurred and the acquired firm made 5 percent or more of such sales.

†Our data do not include 1976–78, a period during which the 20 largest chains have increased rapidly their merger activity. See Chapter 6 for a discussion of recent mergers involving large chains.

As shown earlier, the leading chains (excluding A&P) have continued to expand their share of national sales rapidly; whereas between 1948 and 1967 their share expanded by ten percentage points (0.53 percentage points per year), between 1967 and 1975 their share grew by six percentage points (0.75 percentage points per year). Thus, the trend toward concentration in national sales has continued despite a rather strict merger policy in food retailing.

CONDITIONS OF ENTRY

Whereas market concentration measures the number and size distribution of firms actually competing within a market, the conditions of entry indicate the constraints that potential competitors face and must overcome before they can become established within a market. The extent to which barriers to entry exist is indicated by the cost or selling advantage that established firms hold relative to entering firms.[26]

In food retailing the most relevant conditions of entry are at the local market level. At this level entry is relatively unrestricted for independent entrepreneurs who operate one or two stores and are affiliated with a viable voluntary or cooperative wholesaler. The situation is substantially different, however, for new entrants interested in establishing a number of competitively viable stores. The factors making the latter type of entry difficult include the following:

- The real and pecuniary advertising and promotional economies of multistore firms that are well-established in the market, especially when any of these firms hold large market positions
- The enterprise differentiation or consumer franchise held by firms already established in the market
- The scarcity and resulting difficulty of obtaining preferred new store sites, especially in shopping centers whose operators prefer to accept as tenants supermarkets that are already well-known in the market
- The disadvantages new firms face in the cost of supplying and supervising new stores that may be a considerable distance from their existing warehouses. This generally dictates that chains establish, in a relatively short time, a sufficient number of stores in a community to be supplied efficiently.

The advertising advantages of large, established firms are of particular significance and stem from a combination of real and pecuniary scale economies. Real scale economies in advertising accrue to established chains with a large local market share. Since

advertising expenditures are spread over large sales volumes, adver·
tising expenses per dollar of sales are lower. Additionally, the advertising allowances of food retailers may increase more rapidly
than advertising expenditures as a firm moves from a small share
of a market to a large share.* As a result, net advertising expenses
as a percent of sales are often significantly lower for firms with
large market shares.

Pecuniary scale economies accrue from the inverse relationship that exists between the total volume of company advertising and
the advertising rates charged by the media. Large, established
firms in a market often realize volume discounts from newspapers
that cannot be achieved by a new entrant or small-scale competitors.†

Taken in total, the factors cited above likely pose significant
barriers to the entry of grocery chains into most local markets.
They are probably more difficult for small chains to overcome than
for large chains like those included in this study.‡

---

*Advertising allowances, in order to be legal, must be propor-
tional to sales volume. However, firms with large market shares
may use only a portion of their advertising allowances to pay for the
required ads. The remainder may then be used to support advertising
of store brands, perishables, and other products. In some cases the
total advertising allowances received by retailers have been found to
exceed their total advertising expenditures.

†For example, the newspaper advertising rates in a medium-
size midwestern SMSA result in a situation in which a firm that runs
one full-page ad per week pays 10 percent more per page than a firm
that runs four pages per week.

‡As used in this context, "entry" refers to expansion into a
market through internal firm growth so that industry capacity is increased. By this definition "entry" into a market requires building
new stores. A sample of 180 SMSAs was examined to determine the
extent to which the 17 chains moved in and out of markets by various
means between 1966 and 1974. It was not possible to determine
whether expansion into new markets was by acquisition of existing
stores or by internal growth ("market entry"). During this eight-year
period 104 (58 percent) of the SMSAs were moved into by one or more
of the 17 chains. In 16 SMSAs there were offsetting departures by
one of these chains. Chains most often moved into SMSAs that had
relatively low CR_4s in 1967. Whereas 57 percent of the 86 SMSAs
with CR_4 of less than 50 percent were moved into by one of these
chains, this was true for only 41.5 percent of the 94 SMSAs with CR_4s
of 50 or more. Size of SMSA seemed to have no bearing on the markets into which these chains chose to move.

TRENDS IN GROSS MARGINS, EXPENSES, AND PROFITS

Gross margin—the difference between what retailers pay for merchandise and what they sell it for—represents the cost to consumers of the retailing function. When the operating expenses of retailers are deducted from their gross margins, the result is net operating profit. All three—gross margins, operating expenses, and net operating profits—are key indicators of food retailer performance. Typically, all three are measured as a percent of sales. However, net profits are also calculated as a percent of owners' equity and total assets.

Two sources provide annual statistics on the operating results of food retailers. The FMI Operations Review, published by Food Marketing Institute (prior to 1977, the SMI Figure Exchange), provides the typical operating ratios for a large sample of chain and independent supermarkets;[*] the Cornell University publication Operating Results of Food Chains provides weighted mean values of the operating results of a sample of food chains. Since the SMI/FMI data are likely more representative of the entire spectrum of the retail grocery industry, this source will be relied upon more heavily in the following discussion than the Cornell data, which are more representative of large grocery chain operations.

During the decade prior to the mid-1960s, retail gross margins increased steadily as a percent of sales. The National Commission on Food Marketing noted that gross margins in food retailing increased about 14 percent over the period 1954-63.[27] During the next nine years gross margins stabilized at about 18.2 percent.[†] In 1973 the SMI median gross margin dropped abruptly to 17.4 percent, about 0.8 percentage point lower than the average gross margin over the period 1965-72 (Figure 1.8 and Table A.2). The lower gross margin

_____

[*]The Super Market Institute (SMI) and the National Association of Food Chains (NAFC) merged in January 1977 to form the Food Marketing Institute (FMI). The SMI Figure Exchange is now the FMI Operations Review.

[†]SMI/FMI reports "store door gross margin"—that is, the cost of merchandise includes a charge for warehouse and delivery. The Cornell studies report firm gross margins, from which warehouse and delivery expenses have not been deducted. The Cornell data indicate a drop in gross margins between 1967 and 1968; thereafter the data follow a pattern similar to the SMI/FMI gross margins but are 3 to 4 percentage points higher than the SMI/FMI figures due to computational differences.

FIGURE 1.8

Trends in Retail Grocery Gross Margins, Selected Operating Expenses, and Net Operating Profits, 1965–77

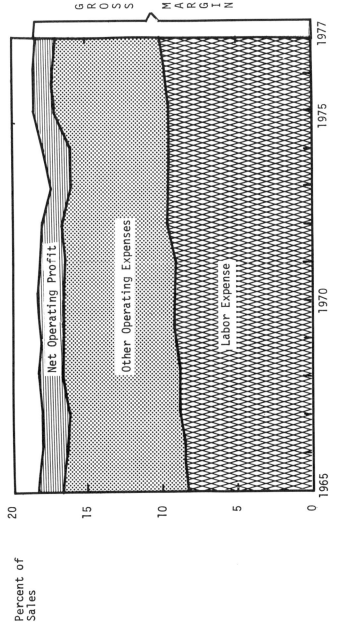

Source: Super Market Institute, Figure Exchange; Food Marketing Institute, Operations Review.

FIGURE 1.9

After Tax Return on Stockholder Equity, Weighted Average
for Leading Grocery Chains, 1963-76

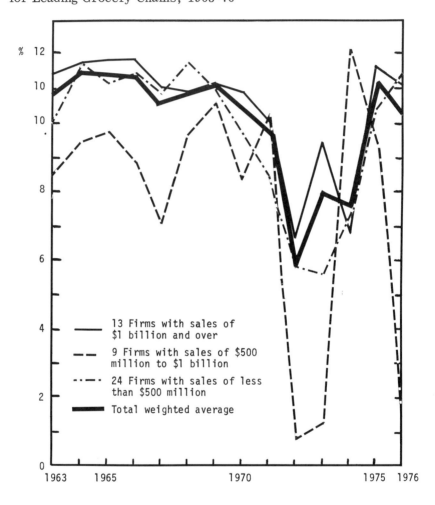

Source: Federal Trade Commission, Economic Report on Food
Chain Profits, Report no. R-6-15-23 (Washington, D.C.: U.S. Government Printing Office, July 1975), as amended in Table A.4.

during 1973 may reflect rapid inflation at the wholesale level and perhaps the price-depressing effects of the A&P WEO program. Gross margins rebounded to 18.6 in 1975, a level maintained in the succeeding two years.

Operating expenses were relatively stable during 1965-74, ranging from 16.1 percent to 16.7 percent of sales. Labor expense, the most important expense category, however, increased by more than 1.0 percentage point over this period (labor increased by 0.5 percentage point between 1971 and 1972), while other operating expenses as a percent of sales declined slightly (Table A.2). Since 1974 store expenses have increased from 16.1 to 17.2 percent of sales.

The combination of relatively stable gross margins and expenses during 1965-71 led to relatively stable net operating profits. The SMI Figure Exchange indicates that net operating profits declined slightly, from 1.8 percent to 1.6 percent of sales over the period. A low of 1.3 percent was realized in 1972 and 1973, a period during which both price controls and the A&P WEO program were in full force (Figure 1.8). Steadily increasing operating expenses thereafter have left net operating profit at about 1.3 percent.

The profitability of grocery chains has shown much greater variability from the mid-60s to the mid-70s than that reflected in the SMI/FMI data. The Cornell studies indicate that pretax profits declined from 2.4 percent of sales in 1965-66 to 0.94 percent in 1972-73 (Table A.3). Although chain profits recovered somewhat to 1.25 percent of sales in 1974-75, they declined slightly to 1.12 percent of sales in 1976-77.

The trend in average (weighted) after-tax return on stockholder equity for 46 of the largest grocery chains reveals much the same pattern as return on sales (Figure 1.9). Between 1964 and 1971 returns declined gradually from 11.5 percent to 9.9 percent of stockholder equity, and then dropped precipitously to 5.8 percent in 1972. Profits rebounded in 1973 to 8.0 percent, continued at about the same level during 1974, and then increased to an average of 10.7 percent during 1975 and 1976. Although the unweighted average return on stockholder equity generally followed a similar pattern for both large and medium-size chains, the medium-size chains experienced a somewhat more severe decline in return on stockholder equity*

---

*Bohack and Penn Fruit were excluded from the sample in 1974 and 1975, respectively, after filing for bankruptcy. Big Bear was acquired in 1976, so financial data were no longer available. Loblaw was also excluded in 1975 because of difficulty in breaking out U.S.

and also recovered more slowly than their larger counterparts (see Table A.4).

By nearly all indicators, 1972-74 was an unusual period for retail grocery firms. With rapidly rising farm and wholesale food prices, price and wage controls, and desperate actions by one of the industry giants, A&P, the early 1970s presented a combination of shocks that resulted in short-run disequilibrium in the industry.* For some of the least profitable companies, the stresses of this period placed them on the brink of, or pushed them into, bankruptcy. Some of the more profitable companies, however, particularly in the West and South, weathered this period with relatively little adverse effect on their profits. Thus, it appears that one of the net effects of the events of the early 1970s was to strengthen the relative position of healthy companies and weaken the competitive viability of marginal food retailers.

---

sales and profit data. Thus, simple averages shown understate the true losses in the under-$500 million category during 1974-76.

*Rapid inflation creates problems in interpreting the operating results of an industry. For example, from 1967 to 1974 the following occurred:

- Retail prices of food consumed at home increased 62.4 percent
- Retail grocery store sales increased 68.3 percent
- Grocery store dollars of gross margin increased 60.9 percent
- Grocery store dollars of labor expense increased 85.9 percent
- Grocery store dollars of net operating profit increased 40.2 percent

Although the percent gross margin and percent net profit declined during this period, the dollars of gross margin and net profit realized increased substantially. With rapid increases in the prices retailers both paid and charged for merchandise, dollar sales increased more rapidly than total assets in 1972-74. Merchandise inventory increased from 37 percent of total assets for all chains in 1972-73 to 43 percent in 1974-75.

After a period of rapid inflation, one would expect established firms to have asset valuations somewhat lower than those of new firms. This likely results in a calculated return on net worth for established firms that is somewhat higher than the return that would be realized by a new firm, all other factors assumed equal.

NOTES

1. U.S. Department of Agriculture (USDA), Marketing and Transportation Situation, MTS 198, Economic Research Service (August 1975), p. 36; USDA, Developments in Marketing Spreads for Food Products in 1977, Agricultural Economic Report no. 398 (March 1978).

2. Revised "marketing bill" data were received from National Economic Analysis Division, USDA, April 1978.

3. Bureau of the Census, Monthly Retail Trade, Sales and Accounts Receivable (Washington, D.C.: U.S. Government Printing Office, December 1976).

4. "45th Annual Report of the Grocery Industry," Progressive Grocer (April 1978): 49.

5. Ibid., p. 55. For comparative purposes, 1977 sales were expressed in 1967 dollars, using the food-at-home component of the CPI for 1977.

6. Ibid., p. 50, defines a supermarket as any grocery store, chain or independent, with annual sales of $1 million or more. For percentage of total grocery store sales, see ibid., p. 52.

7. U.S. Bureau of the Census, Census of Business, 1967, vol. 1.1, Retail Trade Subject Reports (1971), pp. 2-15; "45th Annual Report of the Grocery Industry," p. 52. Using current dollars, the average grocery store size nearly doubled between 1967 and 1977.

The 1972 Census Bureau data for establishments operated the entire year indicated that establishments with sales of $1 million or more accounted for 72.2 percent of total sales, whereas Progressive Grocer data for 1972 show $1 million or more establishments accounting for 67.4 percent of total grocery sales. Bureau of the Census, Retail Trade, Establishment and Firm Size, RC72-S-1 (September 1975), pp. 1-11; "40th Annual Report of the Grocery Industry," Progressive Grocer (April 1973): 97.

8. "45th Annual Report of the Grocery Industry," pp. 50, 52.

9. American Institute of Food Distribution, Weekly Digest 84, no. 25 (June 18, 1977).

10. Census estimates for 1972-76 indicate that chains' share of grocery store sales remained stable at 56 percent. See Bureau of the Census, Annual Retail Trade Report (1972-75); Monthly Retail Trade, Sales, and Accounts Receivable, p. 10.

11. Federal Trade Commission, Economic Report on the Dairy Industry (Washington, D.C.: U.S. Government Printing Office, March 1973).

12. Estimated from subpoenaed data plus company annual reports, Moody's Industrial Manual, and other public sources.

13. Bureau of the Census, Monthly Retail Trade, loc. cit.

14. "45th Annual Report of the Grocery Industry," p. 55.

15. Ibid.

16. National Commission on Food Marketing, Food from Farmer to Consumer (Washington, D.C.: U.S. Government Printing Office, June 1966), p. 106.

17. Federal Trade Commission, The Structure and Competitive Behavior of Food Retailing (June 1966), p. 114.

18. Willard F. Mueller, The Celler-Kefauver Act: Sixteen Years of Enforcement, report to the Antitrust Subcommittee of the Committee of the Judiciary, House of Representatives (Washington, D.C.: U.S. Government Printing Office, October 16, 1967), pp. 21-22.

19. Ibid.

20. Federal Trade Commission, Enforcement Policy with Respect to Mergers in the Food Distribution Industries, January 3, 1967.

21. Ibid., p. 4.

22. Ibid., p. 7.

23. Mueller, op. cit., p. 21.

24. See Federal Trade Commission, Statistical Report on Mergers and Acquisitions (Washington, D.C.: U.S. Government Printing Office, October 1975).

25. For a discussion of the various ways in which conglomerate mergers may adversely affect competition, see Federal Trade Commission, Economic Report on Corporate Mergers (Washington, D.C.: U.S. Government Printing Office, 1969), chs. 4, 6.

26. Joe S. Bain, Barriers to New Competition (Cambridge, Mass.: Harvard University Press, 1956).

27. National Commission on Food Marketing, Organization and Competition in Food Retailing, pp. 217-19.

2
CAUSES OF INCREASING CONCENTRATION

Chapter I showed that there has been a persistent upward trend in concentration in grocery retailing. Here we shall examine various factors hypothesized to play a role in restructuring local markets.

CONGLOMERATE POWER

The analysis especially examines the restructuring effects of large retail grocery chains and other large corporations that enter food retailing. Because such corporations are large and operate in many markets, they possess what Corwin Edwards describes as conglomerate power.[1] This power is an extension of the traditional power, conferred by oligopoly, to exercise a degree of control over price because a few firms control most sales in a market. The unique characteristic of the conglomerate firm is that it operates across more than one product or geographic market. Such multi-market operations reduce the vulnerability of the conglomerate to the competitive forces in any one market because its livelihood derives from its business in all the markets in which it operates. Fritz Machlup believes that "Even if the [conglomerate] concern, on the strength of its own share in the market in which it buys or sells, should have no great influence over prices and other items, it may acquire such influence as an adjunct of the power generated by sheer bigness."[2] Most important for our purposes is the conglomerate firm's capacity to restructure markets because it possesses greater power than some of its rivals. Edwards states the case eloquently:

> In encounters with small enterprises it can buy scarce
> materials and attractive sites, inventions, and facilities;
> preempt the services of the most expensive technicians
> and executives; and acquire reserves of materials for
> the future. It can absorb losses that would consume the

TABLE 2.1

Competitive Interface between 17 Large Grocery Chains, 1966 and 1974

	A&P	Acme	Albert-son's	Allied	First Na-tional	Fisher	Food Fair	Giant	Grand Union	Jewel	Kroger	Lucky	Na-tional Tea	Safe-way	Super-mar-ket Gen-eral	Stop & Shop	Winn-Dixie	Competi-tive Inter-face (1966 and 1974)	Percent Change (1966-74)	SMSAs 1966	SMSAs 1974	Net Change (1966-74)	Percent Change (1966-74)
A&P		30 (35)	2 (2)	48 (16)	20 (24)	9 (5)	38 (37)	2 (2)	24 (22)	17 (11)	60 (69)	9 (7)	24 (28)	16 (18)	16 (8)	21 (19)	37 (34)	373 (355)	+11.3	147	142	-5	-3.4
Acme	30 (35)		10 (1)	5 (2)	4 (6)	6 (0)	19 (18)	2 (2)	13 (11)	0 (0)	6 (6)	13 (2)	7 (8)	17 (9)	8 (8)	5 (0)	0 (0)	145 (108)	+34.3	36	44	+8	+22.2
Albert-son's	2 (2)	10 (1)		3 (0)	0 (0)	3 (0)	1 (0)	0 (0)	0 (0)	1 (1)	4 (1)	12 (4)	1 (0)	27 (11)	0 (0)	0 (0)	0 (0)	64 (20)	+220.0	11	29	+18	+163.6
Allied	48 (16)	5 (2)	3 (0)		0 (0)	7 (0)	5 (0)	0 (0)	3 (0)	3 (2)	39 (16)	4 (0)	9 (2)	10 (7)	0 (0)	0 (0)	17 (2)	153 (47)	+225.5	24	56	+32	+133.3
First Na-tional	20 (24)	4 (6)	0 (0)	0 (0)		0 (0)	7 (12)	0 (0)	12 (14)	7 (4)	0 (0)	0 (0)	0 (0)	0 (0)	9 (5)	20 (17)	0 (0)	79 (82)	-3.7	24	21	-3	-12.5
Fisher	9 (3)	6 (0)	3 (0)	7 (0)	0 (0)		0 (0)	0 (0)	0 (0)	1 (0)	11 (3)	4 (0)	0 (2)	5 (0)	0 (0)	0 (0)	0 (0)	46 (8)	+475.0	3	14	+11	+266.7
Food Fair	38 (37)	19 (18)	1 (0)	5 (0)	7 (12)	0 (0)		2 (2)	17 (12)	0 (1)	0 (1)	1 (0)	2 (1)	7 (6)	13 (8)	9 (7)	14 (8)	136 (113)	+20.4	37	40	+3	+8.1

36

Chain																Total	% chg				% chg
Giant	2 (2)	2 (2)	0 (0)	0 (0)	0 (0)	0 (0)	0 (0)	1 (1)	2 (2)	0 (0)	0 (1)	1 (0)	0 (0)	0 (0)	0 (0)	10 (10)	0	2	2	0	0
Grand Union	24 (22)	13 (11)	0 (0)	3 (0)	12 (14)	0 (0)	17 (12)	1 (1)	0 (1)	1 (1)	0 (1)	1 (0)	5 (5)	8 (4)	13 (7)	99 (79)	+25.3	22	26	+4	+18.2
Jewel	17 (11)	0 (0)	1 (1)	3 (2)	7 (4)	1 (0)	0 (0)	0 (0)	1 (1)	6 (7)	6 (7)	4 (1)	0 (0)	8 (5)	0 (0)	57 (38)	+50.0	13	20	+7	+53.8
Kroger	60 (69)	6 (6)	4 (1)	39 (16)	0 (0)	11 (3)	0 (1)	0 (1)	0 (1)	4 (1)	4 (3)	4 (3)	9 (21)	0 (0)	17 (16)	166 (151)	+9.9	71	65	-6	-8.5
Lucky	9 (7)	13 (2)	11 (4)	4 (0)	0 (0)	4 (0)	1 (0)	1 (0)	1 (0)	4 (1)	4 (3)	17 (12)	7 (4)	0 (0)	0 (0)	77 (33)	+133.3	16	25	+9	+56.3
National Tea[a]	24 (28)	7 (8)	1 (0)	9 (2)	0 (0)	0 (2)	2 (2)	0 (0)	5 (5)	7 (3)	9 (21)	7 (4)	0 (0)	0 (0)	2 (2)	77 (78)	-1.3	33	28	-5	-15.2
Safeway	16 (18)	17 (9)	27 (11)	10 (7)	0 (0)	5 (0)	7 (6)	2 (2)	1 (1)	2 (2)	10 (6)	17 (12)	1 (2)	1 (1)	0 (0)	116 (77)	+50.6	57	62	+5	+8.5
Supermarket General[b]	16 (8)	8 (8)	0 (0)	0 (0)	9 (5)	0 (0)	13 (8)	0 (0)	8 (4)	0 (0)	0 (0)	0 (0)	0 (0)	10 (0)	0 (0)	64 (33)	+93.9	8	16	+8	+100.0
Stop & Shop	21 (19)	5 (0)	0 (0)	0 (0)	20 (17)	0 (0)	9 (7)	0 (0)	13 (7)	8 (5)	0 (0)	1 (1)	0 (0)	1 (1)	10 (0)	87 (56)	+55.4	19	23	+4	+21.1
Winn-Dixie	37 (34)	0 (0)	0 (0)	17 (2)	0 (0)	0 (0)	14 (8)	0 (0)	0 (0)	0 (0)	17 (16)	0 (0)	2 (2)	0 (0)	0 (0)	87 (62)	+40.3	34	38	+4	+11.8

Notes: Table based on 199 SMSAs. 1966 markets in parentheses.

a National Tea includes Loblaw stores in 1966 and 1974.

b Supermarkets General operated under Shoprite logo prior to 1969.

Sources: 1967 Grocery Distribution Guide and 1975 Grocery Distribution Guide (Wellesley Hills, Mass.: Metro Market Studies, 1967 and 1974); Supermarket News (1968–69; 1975).

> entire capital of a smaller rival . . . moment by moment
> the big company can outbid, outspend, or outlose the small
> one; and from a series of such momentary advantages it
> derives an advantage in attaining its large aggregate
> results. [3]

Any advantage accruing from sheer size is magnified if in some of its markets the conglomerate enjoys the power resulting from market dominance or oligopolistic market structures. The excess profits generated in oligopolistic markets can be employed to achieve market power in additional markets. Once conglomerates enjoy substantial power, says Edwin G. Nourse, there may be no natural market forces that contain their further expansion: "There are no demonstrable or discernible limits at which such concentration of economic power, once fully underway, would automatically cease."[4]

Large food chains possess the requisite characteristics of conglomerates: they are large in absolute terms and operate across many separate geographic markets.

Table 2.1 shows the number of SMSAs in which 17 leading chains operated in 1966 and 1974. All but three chains operated in more than ten SMSAs in 1966, and between 1966 and 1974 most substantially increased the number of SMSAs in which they operated. This increase was accomplished by both internal expansion (entry by building new stores) and market extension mergers.[*] The numbers shown in Table 2.1 understate the multimarket character of these large chains because the table covers only 199 of the 263 SMSAs.[†] Moreover, about 25 percent of grocery store sales are made outside of SMSAs.

Table 2.1 measures another dimension of potential conglomerate power, the extent to which large chains meet one another as actual

---

[*]Lucky's acquisition of Consolidated Foods' Eagle Division, the consolidation of two Wakefern Co-op members to form Supermarkets General Corp., and Fisher Inc.'s acquisition of Dominick's (Chicago area), Shopping Bag (Los Angeles area), and Kantor Markets (Cincinnati area) were the major food retailing acquisitions by the 17 chains between 1966 and 1974.

[†]The Bureau of the Census tabulates information for SMSAs, which typically include at least one county (or other political subdivisions of states) and often several. They frequently encompass cities that are not within the same economic market—that is, where the firms in one city in an SMSA do not compete directly with firms located in other cities within that SMSA.

and potential competitors. According to the conglomerate theory, when large conglomerate firms meet one another as actual and potential competitors in many markets, they tend to compete less aggressively, lest aggressive behavior in one market trigger a retaliatory response in another. [5] Although we have not tested this hypothesis in the present study, there is evidence that multimarket contacts may lessen competition in food retailing as well as in other industries. [6] Moreover, in its National Tea decision the FTC found that "As these leading chains pursue their parallel policies of geographic expansion, they inevitably meet each other in a number of cities. The result is frequently a market completely dominated by three or four chains."[7] The commission further found that when markets became dominated by a few large chains, the quality of competition was affected, so that "hard" competition was likely to give way to "soft" competition. [8]

Conglomerate power resulting from sheer size and multimarket operations is magnified if in some of its markets the conglomerate enjoys the power resulting from oligopolistic market structures. Table 3.3 shows that 14 leading chains held market shares of 10 percent or more in 45 percent of the metropolitan areas and 15 percent or more in about 25 percent of these areas. Additionally, at least some of the markets occupied by individual chains are highly concentrated. As shown in Chapter 3, a chain's profits are significantly higher in concentrated markets and/or in markets where it holds large market shares. Thus, in at least some markets the typical large chain enjoys above-normal profits that enable it to engage in cross-subsidization to enhance or maintain its market position in other markets. The hypothesis advanced here is that the conglomerate characteristics of large chains provide a potential advantage over smaller rivals, so that as a group large chains tend to increase concentration or prevent its erosion.

This is not to say that all large chains always enjoy an advantage that enables them to better their smaller rivals. Nor does conglomerate power always protect a large chain from loss of market share, as the recent history of A&P vividly demonstrates. However, even A&P has been the beneficiary of its conglomerate power. Although it is generally acknowledged to have performed poorly in recent years because of its failure to adjust to the changing market environment, A&P nonetheless has used the resources from its profitable markets to subsidize its survival in markets where it has been unprofitable for years. Certainly, had each of A&P's divisions been forced to survive on its own, as would a single-market retailer, many A&P divisions would have been forced to withdraw from their markets. Thus, A&P stands as a monument of a conglomerate firm with many inefficient operations that have survived because of its conglomerate power. Although A&P is the most notable example, some other large chains also have not been able to maintain their position—for instance, National Tea after it was stopped from growing by merger in the 1960s. These are exceptions, however, to the general rule that large chains continue to expand despite temporary adversities.*

MARKET RESTRUCTURING

Before turning to a statistical test of the hypothesis that large chains not only possess market power but also use it to restructure markets, we shall sketch the process by which such restructuring occurs when such firms enter new markets de novo or by acquisition.

The effect on concentration of mergers between direct competitors (horizontal mergers) is quite obvious. If one of the firms involved is a leading firm, four-firm concentration will increase immediately. But the impact is less obvious when grocery retailers in different geographic markets merge or when a large firm not involved in food retailing acquires a grocery retailer. Both types of mergers may be characterized as conglomerate mergers, since the acquired firm does not operate in the same market as the acquiring firm. There is no immediate impact on the acquired firm's share, since the merger merely involves a change in ownership. The long-run result may be to decrease, increase, or have no effect on concentration.

There is a body of literature that reasons that when the acquired firm holds a relatively modest market position, its acquisition (a so-called toehold acquisition) by a powerful conglomerate will erode concentration. This theory assumes that the new conglomerate entrant will strengthen the acquired firm's ability to compete with the leaders, thereby resulting in an erosion of the latter's market share.[9] According to this theory, such mergers may have the same salutary effect believed to result when large firms enter a market de novo by building new facilities. But the assumed deconcentrating impact of conglomerate toehold acquisitions or de novo entry requires very special assumptions, especially concerning the character of the entering firm and of the firms already in the market. If the acquiring firm is a

---

*There are frequent trade references to the advantages associated with multimarket operations. For example, the president of Pic-n-Pay (with 1977 sales of $383 million) gave as a reason for his company's merger with First National Stores (with 1977 sales of $966 million) that his experience during an intensive price war "taught us that we were very vulnerable to have all our stores in one area." Wall Street Journal, August 22, 1978, p. 31.

conglomerate possessing the power discussed above, its entry carries with it the potential for industry restructuring.

In the late 1950s John M. Blair emphasized the crucial importance of distinguishing between the types of market structures in which conglomerate mergers occur. [10] When a large conglomerate firm enters by merger a highly concentrated industry composed entirely of other, equally powerful conglomerates, it is not possible to predict whether the conglomerate's entry will promote or retard competition. If it engages in cross-subsidization, its rivals will be able to match its price-reducing or cost-enhancing strategies dollar for dollar. Then the outcome is indeterminate because one conglomerate has merely replaced another. But when a conglomerate enters a highly concentrated market de novo it is reasonable to expect an erosion in the position of the leading firms.

But even de novo entry may have anticompetitive consequences when a powerful conglomerate enters an industry (or market) composed of "single-line" (or "single market") firms. As Blair put it, "The danger to competition posed by cross-subsidization, whether actual or anticipated, is at a maximum in unconcentrated industries populated largely by single-line firms." [11] He added, however, that "cross-subsidization may appear as a danger to single-line producers in oligopolistic as well as unconcentrated industries. . . ." [12] The key here is that "What had been a 'symmetrical' oligopoly, with each of the oligopolists having about the same position, might be transformed into an 'asymmetrical' oligopoly, with the new entrant assuming a position of dominance and leadership." [13]

Conglomerate entry into new markets thus may adversely affect competition even when it does not involve acquiring an industry leader The more relevant consideration is the nature of the firms in the acquired firm's market—that is, whether they too are conglomerates or are firms depending exclusively or largely on a single market for their livelihood.

Existing retail grocery markets consist of a mix of large conglomerate, regional, and essentially local retailers. When a conglomerate enters such markets, it has both the capacity and the incentive to engage in cross-subsidization to expand its position. But as its market share grows, the market leaders will not stand idly by and forsake their positions to the conglomerate intruder. Large conglomerates and the strongest local chains already in the market are likely to respond to preserve their positions. In the escalating price and nonprice rivalry triggered by the entering conglomerate's strategies, the largest firms likely will fare better than the smaller firms caught in the struggle for survival.

Large chains possess financial and marketing resources beyond the grasp of smaller retailers. Financial institutions cannot be expected to lend funds to smaller retailers to support advertising and other costly strategies essential to success during periods of structural turmoil caused by conglomerate entry. On the other hand, large food chains can support a variety of costly advertising, pricing, and other competitive tactics tailored to each community in which the firm does business.

The resulting competitive advantages of the large chain should not be misconstrued as economies of scale. They do not arise from its scale of operations in a target market; rather, they derive from the broad reach of the conglomerate's presence, which includes some markets where it reaps the rewards of oligopoly.

The large conglomerate invests in market restructuring strategies because it believes doing so will ultimately pay off in larger market shares and profits. Recent studies have shown that a firm's market share is a key determinant of its profitability.[14] As shown in Chapter 3, this is true in food retailing: a chain's profits in a metropolitan market are positively correlated with its share in that market. Thus, not only does the powerful conglomerate chain have the ability to engage in market share-enhancing strategies, but it also has a strong profit incentive to do so.

National Tea in Detroit

Case study evidence supports the above characterization of the likely result of large chain entry, even when such entry is not entirely successful. An FTC study documents the effects of National Tea's entry into the Detroit market in 1952.[15] It entered by acquiring C. F. Smith Co., which had only about 2.0 percent of sales in Detroit. Between 1953 and 1959, National Tea engaged in massive promotional outlays, doubling expenditures on advertising and trading stamps (as a percent of sales). Whereas its newspaper advertising initially was greater than that of two of the market leaders, all leading chains expanded their promotional outlays, so that by 1959 all but one of the top four were spending more than National Tea. The share of grocery store advertising done by all retailers other than the top five (National Tea was fifth) fell from 32 percent in 1955 to 5 percent in 1959.

The costs of National Tea's subsidized expansion in Detroit were substantial both to itself and to smaller retailers. It incurred losses reaching $2.4 million and $1.5 million, respectively, during 1958 and 1959, an average of 2.9 percent of sales. (No information is available after 1959.) Although its total sales increased, National's market share in Detroit rose modestly—from 2.8 percent in 1954 to 3.9 percent in 1958. On the other hand, the top four chains' share grew from 38.5 percent in 1954 to 49.9 percent in 1958, and to 52.1

percent in 1963. This was a much greater increase than occurred in other large cities over the period.

Thus, while National's subsidized expansion did not give it a large market share by 1958, its entry triggered a response by the leading established firms, which were unwilling to give up market share. Although the leading firms also likely earned subnormal profits during the period, the hardest-hit were the smaller, single-market retailers that could not respond in kind. As a result, between 1954 and 1963 the market share held by retailers other than the top five fell from 59 percent to 44 percent—about one-fourth in just nine years.

National's subsidized expansion was disrupted by an antitrust case in 1959 challenging the C. F. Smith and all other mergers made by National during the 1950s. This may well have caused National to abort its plans for further subsidized expansion, since the practice was a central theory of the FTC case.[16] In any event, National ultimately sold its Detroit operation. There is no way of knowing whether the outcome would have been different if National's mergers had not been challenged by the FTC. But the Detroit case and other instances where National subsidized its expansion illustrate the capacity and willingness of large chains to pursue cross-subsidization policies to increase their share in a market.

Safeway in Houston

A more recent example of the consequences of a conglomerate chain's de novo entry is Safeway's entry into the Houston market in 1970. At the time the leading chains and their respective shares were Weingarten, 22 percent; Kroger, 9 percent; and Rice Foods, 9 percent.[17] Weingarten is a regional chain and Rice a local chain.

During the mid-1970s retailers in Houston became locked in an intensive competitive struggle. As in Detroit, the intensified competition often assumed nonprice forms. In 1976, Supermarket News reported, "Competition here currently is taking the form of a war of words, with most of the chains showing major increases in advertising lineage during the first four months this year."[18] Safeway's, Kroger's, and Lucky's aggressive expansion, especially Safeway's, cut into Weingarten's and Rice's market shares and their profits.[19] Supermarket News quoted a "knowledgeable source" as observing: "Safeway doesn't just want to move in and share a market: it wants to take over."[20]

According to Supermarket News, "By 1977, Safeway and Kroger [had] increased their market shares [each with 14 percent], primarily at the expense of J. Weingarten, Inc., the largest locally based chain, which is struggling to hold its razor-thin and ever diminishing lead [18 percent share]."[21] One local chain, Lewis and Coke Super Markets, filed for bankruptcy; and Rice Food Markets and Handy Andy "appear to be retrenching, as victims of competition. Smaller independents, though retaining influence in their own neighborhoods, also are fighting off the dominance of larger chains."[22]

Among Safeway's strategies has been an increase in store hours, which "has forced many operators into 12- or 14-hour, 7 days-a-week schedules."[23] This results in increased operating costs. Additionally, costs in the Houston market have escalated because "food operators as a group are spending more on newspaper advertising."[24] The overall pattern in Houston appears to be one of declining shares for the leading regional and local chains as they yield ground before the large multimarket chains.

Data in Table 3.4 illustrate that cross-subsidization is common among large chains. Six of the 14 large chains in this table operated one or more of their divisions at a loss during 1970-74. Doubtless many more divisions operated at a loss during at least one year in the period.

The preceding demonstrates that large grocery chains are conglomerate corporations with the capacity and incentive to increase their market shares individually, and that, given the structure of retail grocery markets, such individual pursuit of greater market shares tends to increase the share held by the leading chains. In this setting we expect that large chains will tend to increase concentration in markets where they already operate, as well as in markets that they enter either de novo or by merger. We now turn to a statistical test of this hypothesis.

MODEL SPECIFICATION

Dependent Variable

Change in Four-Firm Concentration (CHCR) and (PCHCR)

The change between 1967 and 1975 in four-firm concentration in an SMSA can be measured by the absolute percentage point change (CHCR) and the percentage change (PCHCR). These are alternative measures of changes in local concentration, one measuring absolute and the other proportional change. The changes in four-firm concentration (CR_4) were examined for the years between 1967 and 1975 because complete merger data were available for this period.[*]

---

[*]As noted in Chapter 1, the FTC provided merger data for this period to the Joint Economic Committee. Bureau of the Census

Independent Variables

Horizontal Mergers (HM and PHM)

HM measures the market share held (in the year of acquisition) by grocery retailers acquired during 1968-75 by the top four firms in an SMSA. PHM is the same as HM except that it is expressed as a percentage of CR_4 in 1967. Since the identity of the top four firms can change over the period, the definition of HM must be more specific. Choosing the top firms at the beginning or end of the period is not an appropriate measure of horizontal merger activity in light of the model's purpose. The model predicts changes in four-firm concentration, not the rise or decline of a particular set of firms. Therefore, HM was constructed using the acquisitions by the top four firms in the year prior to each acquisition. Also, when mergers between firms below the top four created a combined firm larger than the fourth-largest firm, HM is equal to the net percentage point increase in CR_4 caused by the merger.

When one of the four leading firms in a market acquires a smaller firm, the immediate effect is to increase CR_4 by the share held by the acquired firm. Although the longer-term effect on CR_4 could be either greater or less than the immediate effect, HM and PHM are predicted to have positive impacts on $CHCR_4$, but we are unable to predict whether the coefficient is more or less than 1.

Number of Large Food Chains in SMSA in 1967 (NFC)

The number of large food chains in an SMSA in 1967 is a basic indicator of the market's conglomerate structure. Defining which firms are conglomerates is necessarily somewhat arbitrary, because there is no precise threshold at which a firm attains conglomerate power. All chains, except A&P, were included in NFC if their sales exceeded $500 million in 1972. A&P is separated from other large chains and is introduced as a separate variable in the model. The $500 million cutoff was adopted because such chains were multimarket firms in 1967, with substantial potential to engage in cross-subsidization. There were 22 supermarket chains that qualified as conglomerate food retailers under this definition. NFC is included in the analysis to test the hypothesis that the large absolute size and multimarket operations of such chains confer special power on them.

---

estimates of 1967 CR_4 and a projection of 1972 census CR_4 to 1975 were employed to construct the dependent variables. The projection was based upon Metro Market Studies data. It was possible to make reliable estimates for 86 SMSAs.

Such conglomerate-derived power permits chains to engage in competitive strategies not available to smaller food retailers. They are better able to rebuff entry, to outspend and outlast smaller rivals in price and nonprice wars, and generally to pursue strategies to maintain and enhance market share that are not open to nonconglomerate firms.

As discussed earlier, this hypothesis does not require that every large chain continually increase its market position but, rather, that there exist a general tendency for conglomerate chains as a group to increase their combined market share. We therefore predict that the greater the number of large chains occupying an SMSA in 1967, the greater the increase in market concentration between 1967 and 1975.

Large Food Chain Entry de Novo (EDN, EDN-72, EDN-74)

Three measures are used to test hypotheses regarding the effects of de novo entry by large food chains: EDN indicates the number of chains that entered an SMSA between 1967 and 1974; EDN-72 indicates the number that entered between 1967 and 1972; and EDN-74 indicates the number that entered in 1973 and 1974. The sample contains 53 instances of entry into 38 SMSAs between 1967 and 1974. As explained earlier, EDN is hypothesized to be positively related to change in concentration. When EDN-72 and EDN-74 are specified instead of EDN, we expect both to be positively related to change in concentration, although EDN-72 should have more impact than EDN-74.

Conglomerate Entry by Merger (CEM)

This variable measures the number of large food chains and large nonfood corporations that entered an SMSA during 1968-72 by merger. Large food chains are defined as those having sales exceeding $500 million in 1967.* Large nonfood corporations are defined as firms with assets of $100 million or more.† The reason for combining

---

*Allied Stores' entries involving stores located in K-Mart stores were not counted as de novo because they involved predictably limited entry, and therefore did not trigger the same kind of retaliatory responses as did entry on an actual or potentially larger scale.

†Large food chains' sales-to-asset ratios are usually five or more to one, hence the $100 million cutoff. Brown & Williamson's acquisition of Kohl's in 1972 is an example of nonfood conglomerate entry by merger. Kohl's is a regional chain located primarily in

these two types of conglomerate mergers is that there were only ten mergers in nine SMSAs by nonfood chains. The combined variable (CEM) has 31 instances of entry by merger in 23 SMSAs; therefore it is less susceptible to the influence of a single acquisition.[*] Moreover, conglomerate entry by merger is not split between pre- and post-1972 variables because all mergers occurred prior to 1973. As in the case of entry de novo, CEM is hypothesized to have a positive impact on change in concentration.

Large Food Chain Exit (FEX)

The exit variable (FEX) indicates the number of large food chains that left an SMSA between 1967 and 1974. Because the FTC and Department of Justice merger guidelines generally preclude the sale of stores by exiting chains to large competing chains, exit by large chains tends to strengthen the position of smaller retailers.[†] Exit also diminishes the conglomerate presence in the markets. However, exit may also be an indication of a firm's failure to keep pace with the advancing market shares of other conglomerates, and therefore may not be associated with decreasing concentration. Because of the conflicting possibilities, no direction is hypothesized for the relationship between FEX and change in concentration.

Market Share of A&P in 1967 (SAP)

A&P has had a poor profit performance record since the 1960s and has steadily lost market share. Although the company possesses conglomerate-derived power that has enabled some unprofitable

---

Wisconsin, and had sales of $205 million in 1972. In the same year that it was acquired, Kohl's embarked on an expensive and sophisticated advertising program that is strikingly similar to the glossy magazine advertisements of cigarette corporations. "Kohl's Ad Philosophy Leads to Wisconsin Success," Supermarket News, August 2, 1976, p. 8.

[*]An analysis based on a larger but less reliable sample introduced each type of acquirer as a separate independent variable. This analysis found each type of acquirer to be statistically significant at the 1 percent level. Ronald W. Cotterill, Marketing Structure, Performance and Market Restructuring (Ph.D. diss., University of Wisconsin, 1977), p. 120.

[†]As discussed in Chapter 6, there have been notable exceptions in which the antitrust agencies have permitted large exiting chains to sell their stores to other large chains within the SMSA.

divisions to survive, this power has not been sufficient to offset totally the poor management of A&P. Although the avowed purpose of its 1972 WEO program was to check the erosion of the company's profits and market position, it failed to do so. In 1967, A&P was one of the top four firms in most of the markets in which it operated. Because of its exceptionally poor performance during the period examined, we hypothesize that the larger A&P's presence in an SMSA in 1967 (as measured by its market share, SAP), the greater the likelihood that CR_4 decreased between 1967 and 1975. A negative relationship is therefore hypothesized.

Four-Firm Concentration Ratio in 1967 (ICR_4)

This variable measures the initial level of concentration (CR_4 in 1967) for the period examined (1967-75). Previous empirical studies tested the hypothesis that change in concentration is negatively related to initial concentration. These studies cited G. Stigler as providing an underlying economic rationale.[25] Stigler theorized that leading firms in concentrated industries may choose to maximize long-run profits by raising prices in a way that will not forestall all entry, thereby permitting the expansion of fringe firms and enhancing the attractiveness of entry that erodes concentration.

Another hypothesis explains this relationship in food retailing in terms of economies of scale. The existence of scale economies (real and pecuniary) in advertising create declining long-run average costs at the market level for multistore firms (see Chapter 1). If these advantages are substantial, we would expect them to exert influence in markets when few firms are of a size that enables them to enjoy most of these scale advantages. Other things being the same, the impact on concentration would be greatest in the least concentrated markets, because there fewer firms than in concentrated markets would be of minimum optimum size. Thus, we expect this factor to cause greater increases in concentration in less concentrated markets than in highly concentrated ones. This would result in a negative relationship between ICR_4 and $CHCR_4$, not because highly concentrated markets are eroding but because competitive markets are becoming more concentrated. ICR_4 is therefore hypothesized to be negatively related to changes in CR_4.

Market Growth (MG)

Market growth is defined as the percentage increase in deflated grocery store sales in each SMSA between 1967 and 1972, as reported by the Bureau of the Census. When market demand is growing slowly, the "displacement problem" faced by new entrants and small firms is an important deterrent to their growth in market share. On the

other hand, when market demand is growing rapidly, new and established small firms face a less difficult displacement problem because
less of their growth need be at the expense of leading firms. This
leads to the expectation that entering and fringe firms make a disproportionately large share of the expanding sales in rapidly growing
markets, with the result that CR_4 declines. MG is therefore hypothesized to be negatively related to changes in CR_4.

Market Size (MS)

Market size is defined as the 1972 sales of grocery stores with
payroll for each SMSA as reported by the Bureau of the Census. MS
is introduced as a control variable. It is not clear how MS might
influence changes in CR_4 in grocery retailing. Because consumers
in inner cities have less mobility than do those in other areas, and
for other reasons, small stores often thrive despite their higher
costs. This would suggest a negative relationship between MS and
change in CR_4.

EMPIRICAL RESULTS

The basic model to predict the absolute change in four-firm
concentration between 1967 and 1975 is summarized in the following
equation. The hypothesized signs for the coefficients are indicated
below the equation. The explanatory variables and hypotheses for
predicting percent change are identical, except that PHM is substi-
tuted for HM.

$$CHCR_4 = \beta_0 + \beta_1 HM + \beta_2 NFC + \beta_3 EDN + \beta_4 CEM + \beta_5 SAP +$$

$$\beta_1 > 0 \quad \beta_2 > 0 \quad \beta_3 > 0 \quad \beta_4 > 0 \quad \beta_5 < 0$$

$$\beta_6 FEX + \beta_7 ICR_4 + \beta_8 MG + \beta_9 MS$$

$$\beta_6 \lessgtr 0 \quad \beta_7 < 0 \quad \beta_8 < 0 \quad \beta_9 < 0$$

The above model was tested by multiple-regression analysis
of the absolute and percentage change in four-firm SMSA concentration in 86 SMSAs between 1967 and 1975. Preliminary estimation
efforts indicated the presence of heteroskedasticity: When ordered
by market size, the variance of the regression residuals increased
as market size decreased. An intuitive explanation for this phenomenon is that an external shock of a given absolute magnitude will
produce a larger variation in the concentration in smaller cities
than in large ones. If, for example, the sales of the top four firms

TABLE 2.2

Multiple-Regression Equations Predicting the Change in Four-Firm Concentration between 1967 and 1975, 86 SMSAs

						Independent Variables								
Dependent Variable	Inter-cept	Horizontal Mergers (HM)	Percent Horizontal Mergers (PHM)	Number of Large Food Chains (NFC)	Large Food Chain Entry de Novo 1967-74 (EDN)	Large Food Chain Entry de Novo 1967-72 (EDN-72)	Large Food Chain Entry de Novo 1973-74 (EDN-74)	Large Food Chain Exit (FEX)	Conglomerate Merger (CEM)	Market Share of A&P in 1967 (SAP)	4-Firm Concentration Ratio (ICR₄)	Market Growth 1967-72 (MG)	Market Size (MS)	F ratio
Absolute Change														
1a CHCR₄ Percent	2.368	1.470 (2.470)[a]		2.381 (3.103)[a]	2.751 (2.750)[a]				3.344 (3.456)[a]		-.128 (1.456)[c]	-.028 (.516)	-2.469 (2.122)[b]	12.454[a]
1b CHCR₄ Percent	4.097	1.369 (2.322)[b]		2.165 (2.829)[a]	2.189 (2.125)[b]				3.044 (3.128)[a]	-.253 (1.855)[b]	-.090 (1.014)	-.054 (.977)	-2.155 (1.848)[b]	11.728[a]
1c CHCR₄ Percent	1.801	1.398 (2.326)[b]		1.883 (2.335)[b]	2.224 (2.151)[b]			1.737 (1.225)	2.845 (2.670)[a]	-.232 (1.713)[b]	-.051 (.553)	-.045 (.817)	-2.019 (1.574)[c]	10.031[a]
1d CHCR₄ Percent	1.256	1.334 (2.146)[b]		1.836 (2.238)		2.483 (2.274)[b]	.356 (.162)	1.563 (1.067)	2.981 (2.640)[a]	-.251 (1.854)[b]	-.029 (.092)	-.044 (.788)	-1.929 (1.355)[c]	8.617[a]

50

Relative Change

Eq	Dep. var		(1)	(2)	(3)	(4)	(5)	(6)	(7)	(8)	(9)	(10)	F
2a	PCHCR₄	17.424	1.437 (2.763)[a]	4.655 (2.824)[a]	7.702 (3.530)[a]			6.203 (3.520)[a]		-.503 (2.546)[a]	-.078 (.643)	-4.736 (2.050)[b]	16.820[a]
	Percent													
2b	PCHCR₄	19.438	1.370 (2.637)[a]	4.349 (2.627)[a]	6.640 (2.969)[a]			5.197 (3.028)[a]	-.511 (1.666)[c]	-.400 (2.005)[b]	-.129 (1.048)	-4.108 (1.876)[b]	21.123[a]
	Percent													
2c	PCHCR₄	14.391	1.442 (2.706)[a]	4.045 (2.304)[b]	6.486 (2.865)[a]	2.513 (.794)		5.367 (2.514)[a]	-.484 (1.583)[c]	-.314 (1.539)[c]	-.114 (.925)	3.933 (1.592)[c]	12.545[a]
	Percent													
2d	PCHCR₄	13.385	1.403 (2.583)[a]	4.091 (2.310)[b]	7.042 (2.966)[a]	1.809 (.547)	2.011 (.412)	5.909 (2.595)[a]	-.521 (1.707)[c]	-.281 (1.377)[c]	-.106 (.856)	-3.989 (1.509)[c]	12.580[a]
	Percent													

Notes: The reported regressions are weighted to correct heteroskedasticity. The error term's variance is larger in small cities. The variance, σ^2, is estimated from the regression residuals by assuming the following function form: $\sigma^2 = \beta_0 + \beta_1 LN(MS)$. LN(MS) is the natural logarithm of market size. Representative size for β_0 and β_1 in equations 1a–1d are 22 and –13; in equations 2a–2d they are 100 and –85, 2-tail t-tests for significance were used on EDN and FEX; 1-tail t-tests were used for all other independent variables.

[a]Significance level is 1 percent.
[b]Significance level is 5 percent.
[c]Significance level is 10 percent.
Source: Compiled by the authors.

51

decline by $3 million because a fire destroys a store, the CR_4 declines 3 percent in a market with $100 million sales but only 0.3 percent in a market with $1 billion in sales.

Table 2.2 displays the generalized least-squares coefficient estimates and statistics for several different models. Each of the equations reported is statistically significant at the 1 percent level based upon an F-test. Equation 1a is the simplest model.

Horizontal mergers (HM) has the hypothesized positive sign and is significant at the 1 percent level. Importantly, the coefficient is greater than 1, which means that the impact on concentration was greater than the share of the market acquired. If one of the top four firms acquired 1 percent of the market, CR_4 increased by about 1.5 percent by 1975.

The number of large food chains (NFC) operating in an SMSA in 1967 also has the hypothesized positive sign and is statistically significant at the 1 percent level. This means that the larger the number of large food chains operating in a market in 1967, the greater the increase in CR_4 between 1967 and 1975.

Both large chain entry de novo (EDN) and conglomerate entry by merger (CEM) have the predicted positive signs and are statistically significant at the 1 percent level. This indicates that concentration increased when large chains entered these markets de novo or by merger, and when large outside corporations entered by merger.

Initial concentration (ICR_4) has the predicted sign but is only marginally significant. Market growth (MG) is not statistically significant. Market size (MS) has a positive sign and is statistically significant at the 5 percent level.

Equation 1b contains the same explanatory variables as equation 1a, except that the market share of A&P in 1967 (SAP) is introduced. It has the hypothesized negative sign and is significant at the 5 percent level. If A&P had a 10 percent market share in 1967, $CHCR_4$ was 3.72 percentage points lower than if A&P were not in the market. Whereas the presence of other large food chains (NFC) had a positive impact on $CHCR_4$, A&P's presence had a negative effect. Clearly, A&P's behavior during the recent past differed significantly from that of other large food chains. The inclusion of SAP in the model generally reduces the total values for other variables and eliminates ICR_4 as a significant variable.

Large food chain exit (FEX), which is introduced in equation 1c, has a positive sign; however, it is not statistically significant. Thus, during the period examined, exit by large food chains conferred no measurable competitive advantage to either leading or fringe firms.

Equation 1d tests the dynamics that are associated with entry de novo by substituting EDN-72 and EDN-74 for EDN. As hypothesized, pre-1973 entry (EDN-72) has a larger positive impact on $CHCR_4$ and is statistically significant at the 1 percent level. Post-1972 entry (EDN-74) has a positive sign but is not statistically significant. Since all cases of conglomerate entry by merger (CEM) occurred between 1967 and 1972, the coefficient on CEM is comparable to that on EDN-72. The concentrating effect of entry de novo was slightly less than entry by merger (2.3 points versus 2.6 points), but the difference was not significant.

Equations 2a-2d are identical to equations 1a-1d except that the dependent variable, change in CR_4, is expressed as a percentage change rather than as a change in percentage points. The results are generally the same as those of earlier models, although they are statistically somewhat more robust. The only variables to change in significance are SAP, which is significant at the 10 percent level rather than 5 percent, and ICR_4, which is consistently significant in the latter three models.

The most important findings of the analysis are the consistently significant effects of NFC, EDN, and CEM, which provide strong confirmation of the hypothesis that large conglomerate firms not only possess the power to restructure markets but also, during the period examined, they succeeded in doing so. The finding that acquisitions (many of which might be classed as toehold) by conglomerates increase concentration may surprise many, but is consistent with Stephen Rhodes's findings in banking.[26] Perhaps more surprising to many is the finding that even de novo entry by large chains tends to increase CR_4 in SMSAs. This finding must be interpreted cautiously, however, since it does not test the hypothesis that de novo entry will erode concentration in highly concentrated markets. There were in the sample relatively few instances of de novo entry into highly concentrated markets. Indeed, the de novo entry markets had a four-firm concentration of only 42.8 percent in 1972, which was significantly below the average four-firm concentration of 52.4 percent for all SMSAs. In sum, our findings support the hypothesis that de novo entry by large chains in low-to-moderately concentrated markets tends to increase concentration, but leaves unanswered the question of their impact on highly concentrated markets. However, for our sample of de novo entry experience during 1967-72, the net effect of such entry was to increase concentration.

The findings of this chapter are disturbing. They strongly suggest that the growing presence of large chains in markets tends to accelerate market concentration. These findings support the gloomy statement of E. G. Nourse that "there are no demonstrable or discernible limits at which [conglomerate-induced] concentration of economic power, once fully underway, would automatically cease."[27] We do not believe this gloomy prediction is inevitable in grocery retailing. Options do exist to prevent all markets from becoming highly concentrated and to improve the competitive performance of markets that already are concentrated. As discussed in Chapter 6, this will require vigorous and innovative enforcement of existing antitrust laws as well as complementary programs to stimulate more effective competition.

NOTES

1. Corwin Edwards, "Conglomerate Bigness as a Source of Power," in George J. Stigler, ed., Business Concentration and Price Policy (Princeton: National Bureau of Economic Research, 1955).

2. Fritz Machlup, The Political Economy of Monopoly (Baltimore: Johns Hopkins Press, 1952), p. 112.

3. Edwards, op. cit., pp. 334-35.

4. E. G. Nourse, "Government Discipline of Private Economic Power," in Senate Judiciary Committee, Subcommittee on Antitrust and Monopoly, Administered Prices: A Compendium on Public Policy (Washington, D.C.: U.S. Government Printing Office, 1963), p. 255.

5. Corwin Edwards first identified this problem in his "Conglomerate Bigness as a Source of Power."

6. Federal Trade Commission, Report on Corporate Mergers (Washington, D.C.: U.S. Government Printing Office, 1969), pp. 468-70. An empirical study in the banking industry found a similar relationship. Arnold A. Heggestad and Stephen A. Rhoades, "Multimarket Interdependence and Local Market Competition," Review of Economics and Statistics, forthcoming.

7. National Tea, Docket no. 7453, Final Decision and Order (1966), p. 7.

8. Ibid., p. 8.

9. J. S. Campbell and W. G. Shepherd, "Leading Firm Mergers," Antitrust Bulletin 13 (Winter 1968): 1361-82.

10. John M. Blair, "The Conglomerate Merger in Economics and Law," Georgetown Law Journal 46 (Summer 1958): 672-700.

11. John M. Blair, Economic Concentration (New York: Harcourt Brace Jovanovich, 1972), p. 51.

12. Ibid., p. 53.

13. Blair, "The Conglomerate Merger . . .," p. 693.

14. R. D. Buzzell, B. T. Gale, and R. Sultan, "Market Share—a Key to Profitability," Harvard Business Review 53 (January-February 1975): 95-105.

15. The following is from National Commission on Food Marketing, Organization and Competition in Food Retailing, Technical Study no. 7 (Washington, D.C.: U.S. Government Printing Office, June 1966), pp. 379-83.

16. In the Matter of National Tea, Docket no. 7453 (1959). The FTC decision in this matter found National's merger violated Section 7 of the Clayton Act. Opinion of the Commission, March 4, 1966. The commission's Final Order prohibited National from making acquisitions for ten years.

17. 1971 Grocery Distribution Guide (Wellesley Hills, Mass.: Metro Market Studies, 1971).

18. "Texas Retailers Scramble for $1.5 Billion Market," Supermarket News, Market Profiles, 1976, August 16, 1976, p. 28.

19. "Independents' Share Slips in Chain-Dominated City," Supermarket News, Market Profiles, 1977, August 15, 1977, p. 69.

20. Ibid.

21. "Militant Labor, Price War, Supermarket Openings Reflect Growing Pains of Space Age, Texas Capital," Supermarket News, Market Profiles 1978, August 14, 1978, p. 40. Weingarten's incurred losses of $3,225,000 for the 40 weeks ending April 8, 1978, compared with losses of $1,615,000 for the similar period in 1977.

22. Ibid.

23. Ibid.

24. Ibid., p. 41.

25. G. Stigler, The Theory of Price (New York: Macmillan, 1952), p. 252, cited in W. F. Mueller and L. G. Hamm, "Trends in Industrial Market Concentration, 1942 to 1970," Review of Economics and Statistics 56 (November 1974): 514-15.

26. Stephen Rhoades, "The Impact of Foothold Acquisitions on Bank Market Structure," Antitrust Bulletin 22 (Spring 1977): 119-29. Rhoades, a senior economist with the Federal Reserve Board, tested the hypothesis that "foothold" acquisitions tend to reduce concentration. Using multiple-regression analysis, he examined various factors influencing changes in concentration in commercial banking in 112 metropolitan areas between 1966 and 1973. Although Rhoades interpreted his results as not supporting the foothold theory, his statistical findings not only failed to support the foothold theory but also actually supported the contrary theory that foothold acquisitions by bank holding companies increase concentration.

27. Nourse, op. cit., p. 255.

3

PROFIT PERFORMANCE
OF LARGE FOOD RETAILERS

The performance of an industry has many dimensions, including its pricing and profit behavior, operating efficiency, progressiveness, and responsiveness to the preferences and needs of customers.[*] We will analyze only the profit and pricing dimensions. These are particularly important because both bear on the critical issue of the price consumers pay business firms for performing the food retailing function.

In attempting to identify the factors that influence the price levels and profitability of food chains, this study draws heavily on the framework of industrial organization theory. This theory holds that the structure of a market has an important influence on the business conduct of firms in that market and, in turn, on market performance.[1] Market structure elements that are considered of particular importance are the number and size distribution of firms in the market (as measured by market concentration and relative firm size), the conditions of entry (the ease or difficulty with which new firms can enter the market), and the degree of product differentiation (the extent to which customers prefer the products of one seller over those of others).

Past empirical studies in various industries have provided compelling evidence concerning the effect of these three elements of market structure on the average profits of firms in a market.[2] This evidence supports the proposition that as concentration, entry barriers, and product differentiation in an industry increase—

---

[*]Economists use the term "performance" to mean "the strategic end results of the market conduct of sellers and buyers . . . this is the crucial indicator of how well the market activity of firms has contributed to the enhancement of general material welfare." Joe S. Bain, Industrial Organization (New York: Wiley, 1968), p. 372.

particularly beyond a certain threshold level—industry prices and profits also increase.

Industrial organization theory is concerned primarily with the behavior of industries—that is, the combined behavior of groups of firms. Since there is always variance in the behavior among the firms composing an industry, the theory loses explanatory power in examining the performance of individual firms. Because the data in this study are for individual firms rather than for groups of firms in various markets, the study undertakes the more difficult task of explaining the prices and profits of individual firms.[3]

In any analysis of industry behavior, defining the "relevant" product and geographic market within which competition occurs is essential. This market is determined largely by the extent to which buyers perceive alternative firms as close substitutes. In food retailing at least two product markets can be defined. The first includes those stores, largely supermarkets, that consumers perceive as close substitute sources for their major weekly food purchases. The second includes those stores, such as convenience stores and small grocery stores, that are close substitute sources for "fill-in" shopping. Supermarkets, small grocery stores, convenience stores, and specialty food markets offer distinct combinations of products, services, and prices. The supermarket submarket is clearly the most important, accounting for 67 percent of all food store sales and 72 percent of all grocery store sales in 1972. Because of their dominant role, supermarkets set the competitive tone in most markets.

The product mix and gross margins of supermarkets and convenience stores support the contention that they operate in different submarkets. Studies by Progressive Grocer indicate that convenience stores generally do not carry fresh produce or meat, and derive 60 percent of their sales from six product categories: tobacco, beer, soft drinks, milk, magazines and newspapers, and candy.[4] The same categories represent only 15 percent of a typical supermarket's sales. The value of the average transaction in supermarkets is about five times that in convenience stores. Gross margins are about 50 percent higher in convenience stores than in supermarkets (28.5 percent vs. 19.3 percent).[5] These differences suggest that the cross elasticity of demand between supermarkets and convenience stores is low and that these stores operate in separate product submarkets.

The price and profit data obtained from the 17 chains in this study are for their supermarket operations. Therefore, measures of the competitive environment of the supermarket submarket are expected to be most appropriate for explaining chain prices and profits. Unfortunately, concentration and market share data for the supermarket submarket are not available for much of our analysis.

Therefore, structural data for the grocery store "market" were used along with a variable to adjust for the differences in grocery store and supermarket structural measures.

The geographic scope of a market can be determined by examining the spatial characteristics of buying behavior. For example, if consumers regularly purchase a product from firms throughout the country, the selling firms compete in a <u>national</u> market. This is not the case in food retailing. Consumers generally purchase their groceries within a few miles of home. Competition in the food retailing-consumer market is essentially local in nature, often involving quite small communities. In this study SMSAs defined by the Bureau of the Census are used as the relevant markets for analysis. In many cases the SMSA is an excessively broad definition of the geographic market within which competition occurs in the retail sale of grocery products. SMSAs often are made up of two or more counties and several population centers. Where an SMSA embraces a number of distinct population centers, concentration ratios computed on an SMSA basis generally understate the concentration level occurring in individual population centers. However, SMSAs are the smallest geographic areas for which concentration data are available, and therefore are used as "markets" in this study.

Since data were not available on the barriers to entry into various SMSAs, this analysis examines only two market structure variables: the four-firm concentration ratio (the sum of the market shares of the largest four firms) and the market shares of individual companies. The latter variable, at least to some extent, also measures the degree of differentiation enjoyed by individual firms, and therefore also serves as a proxy for one source of entry barriers. One aspect of the study also examines the impact of entry barriers on the profits of individual firms entering a market.

In relating firm prices and profits to firm market share and the four-firm concentration ratio, alternative interpretations should be recognized. A positive and significant relationship between firm profits in a market and firm market share may be due to higher prices, lower costs, or both. Costs in food retailing are particularly susceptible to variations in the utilization of store facilities. For example, a National Commission on Food Marketing study found that a 20 percent increase in sales per square foot of selling space reduced store operating costs per dollar of sales by one percentage point (about a 6 percent reduction).[6] The same study found that firms with high market shares generally realized higher sales per square foot and, hence, lower store costs.[7] Firms with high market shares also had somewhat higher gross margins and net margins.

In addition to its influence on store operating costs, a high market share may bring economies in advertising, physical distribution, and other headquarters operations. Thus, costs per dollar of sales would be expected to decline as firm market share increases. Unless prices are dropped to reflect lower costs, a positive relationship between profits and market share would follow.

Industrial organization theory also suggests a positive relationship between profits and firm market power (for which market share is one measure). However, in this case the cause of higher profits is hypothesized to be monopolistic selling or monopsonistic purchasing practices, not lower real costs. Monopolistic sellers can charge higher prices, and monopsonistic buyers may induce discriminatory low prices from input suppliers.[*]

Another study for the National Commission on Food Marketing, which analyzed a large chain operating in several markets, found a strong positive relationship between market share and the pretax profits in different markets.[8] A weaker positive relationship was found between market share and percent of gross margins. Market share and operating costs per dollar of sales had a moderate negative relationship; market share and net advertising costs per dollar of sales also were negatively correlated. These findings lend support to the above discussion of expected relationships between market structure and profit performance of food store chains. However, they deal only indirectly with the influence of market position on price levels. Gross margins are directly influenced by price levels, but are not a perfect proxy for prices because they are also influenced by procurement costs (which might be lower in high-market-share markets as a result of real economies in large-volume procurement and/or greater bargaining power), the type of specials offered (a dominant firm may be able to maintain its market position without offering deep-cut specials), and the amount of marketing loss (shrinkage, mark-downs, and throw-outs). Thus, although the above study found a modest positive relationship between market share and percent of gross margin, one cannot conclude that this was necessarily due to differences in prices.

---

[*]There is evidence that on occasion the largest chains in a market have been able to buy fluid milk and bread products at lower prices than those paid by other retailers. See FTC, Economic Report on Food Retailing (Washington, D. C.: U. S. Government Printing Office, January 1966), pp. 181-202. Recently an FTC administrative law judge found A&P guilty of knowingly inducing discriminatory prices in the purchase of milk and other dairy products sold in the stores of its Chicago division. FTC News, October 9, 1975, pp. 1-2.

TABLE 3.1

Company Sales and Net Income for 17
Large Retail Food Chains, 1974

Firm	Total Sales[a] (thousand dollars)	Net Income[b] (thousand dollars)	Net Income as percent of Sales	Net Income[b] as percent of Stockholder Equity
Safeway	$8,185,190	$79,205	1.0%	11.4%
A&P	6,874,611	(157,071)	-2.3	-35.4[c]
Kroger	4,782,449	45,239	.9	10.8
Winn Dixie	2,962,165	55,552	1.9	19.1
Acme	2,734,710	19,321	.7	9.0
Lucky	2,701,771	41,446	1.5	20.5
Jewel	2,598,913	30,230	1.2	10.6
Food Fair	2,380,561	8,926	.4	6.4
Grand Union	1,562,736	9,504	.6	6.2
Supermkt. Genl.	1,498,475	2,673	.2	3.7
National Tea	1,403,815	(2,635)	-.2	-3.5
Stop & Shop	1,223,791	11,992	1.0	14.7
Fisher Foods	1,124,404	12,581	1.1	18.9
Albertson's	1,046,105	11,702	1.1	19.3
Allied	1,044,404	(3,426)	-.3	-8.5
First. Nat'l.	934,803	5,708	.6	8.9
Giant	741,043	6,979	.9	10.6
Total	43,843,746	177,926		
Average	2,579,044	10,466	.6	6.3

[a] Includes sales from all company operations.
[b] After-tax provisions.
[c] In fiscal year 1974 (ended February 2, 1975) A&P provided $200 million for the cost of closing store facilities. The $200 million write-off offset the company's $33.4 million operating profit for the year and resulted in a net after-tax loss of $157 million.

Source: Company annual reports.

The present study examines the relationship between the structure of markets and both price levels and profits. The results should provide useful insights into this important and controversial subject.

FOOD CHAINS INCLUDED IN THE STUDY

In 1974 the 17 retail grocery chains included in this study all ranked among the 20 largest U.S. grocery firms (see Table 3.1). All 17 had 1974 company sales in excess of $700 million, and 15 of the firms had sales greater than $1 billion. The average company sales of these chains was $2.6 billion. They operated over 12,700 grocery stores during 1974, which represented about 6 percent of the total number of grocery stores in the United States and about 52 percent of the total number of chain stores (excluding convenience stores) in operation during the year.[9] Their combined sales were $43.8 billion, which represented 69 percent of all chain food store sales and 37 percent of total food store sales.[10]

Although many of these 17 chains have diversified into other business activities, their food retailing operations provided over 90 percent of their total revenue in 1974. Thus, the profitability of these firms was largely dependent upon their food retailing operations. The average after-tax profits of the 17 chains in 1974 was 0.6 percent return on sales and 6.3 percent return on stockholder equity. The return on stockholder equity varied greatly, ranging from -35.4 percent for A&P to 20.5 percent for Lucky.

PROFIT PERFORMANCE, 1970-74

The Joint Economic Committee requested quarterly sales and net profit data from the 17 large chains for 1970-73, and for the first three quarters of 1974. Data were requested for each retail operating division and for each SMSA over 500,000 in population. Company responses provided comparable data for 114 divisions of 14 companies. Six companies also furnished sales and net profit data for their operations in 50 large SMSAs. The division and SMSA data series were analyzed separately.

The sales and profit data examined are for grocery store operations only. Nonfood store operations, such as drugstores or general merchandise stores, and manufacturing operations were excluded.

Table 3.2 summarizes the annual profit-to-sales ratios for the supermarket divisions of the 14 chains for each of the five years examined. The average pretax profit rate for all firms was highest

TABLE 3.2

Pretax Profits of Grocery Store Operations as a Percent of Sales, 14 Leading Grocery Chains, 1970-74

Firm	1970	1971	1972	1973	1974
			Year		
A	1.30^a	.56	-2.11	-.49	$.81^b$
B	2.56^a	2.31	2.51	2.06	2.77^c
C	-1.08	-.31	-.10	-.03	$-.83^b$
D	3.28	2.38	1.28	1.22	1.26^b
E	1.84	2.84	1.98	1.19	2.50^b
F	1.50^a	1.11	-.06	-.34	$.80^c$
G	3.25	3.16	2.97	2.61	2.64^b
H	1.17	.85	-.43	-.26	$.63^b$
I	2.74	2.49	2.03	1.92	2.19^c
J	.66	.63	$-.98^d$	-1.65	$-.26^b$
K	2.77	2.74	2.55	2.13	2.76^b
L	-.34	-.12	.13	1.08	1.57^c
M	2.04	1.73	.59	1.35	1.85^c
N	4.17	4.00	3.67	3.74	4.00^b
Simple average	1.85	1.74	1.01	1.04	1.62

Notes: Pretax rates of return shown above represent only the profits in the domestic supermarket divisions of the 14 companies. The data are adjusted to approximate a calendar year. Extraordinary gains or losses have not been included in calculating the rates of return.

[a] Based on last three quarters of calendar 1970.
[b] Based on first three quarters of calendar 1974.
[c] Based on first two quarters of calendar 1974.
[d] Data for only three quarters.
Source: Company data provided to the Joint Economic Committee. Three additional firms (O, P, and Q) are not included because the profit data furnished were not comparable with those of the other firms or were not furnished for all five years.

in 1970 at 1.85 percent of sales, reached its nadir in 1972 at 1.01 percent, and rebounded to 1.62 percent in 1974. Firms G and N consistently achieved the highest return on sales. Six of the chains (firms A, C, F, H, J, and L) experienced losses in at least two of the five years.

Table 3.2 reveals considerable variation in chain profits during 1970-74. Factors contributing to this variation were the switch in inventory accounting procedures, food price inflation, wage-price controls, and A&P's price-cutting campaign, "Where Economy Originates" (WEO).

During periods of inflation, the switch from first-in-first-out (FIFO) to last-in-first-out (LIFO) inventory accounting procedures lowers the amount of reported profits for the year in which the change is made. During 1974 four of the firms studied made the switch, so the reported profit figures for 1974 are understated relative to preceding years.*

Wage-price controls appear to have had a definite impact on the profitability of large food chains.† Since price controls and WEO occurred during the same period, chains that competed with A&P

---

*Acme, Giant, Safeway, and Winn-Dixie changed from FIFO to LIFO in 1974. See FTC, Staff Economic Report on Food Chain Profits, Report no. R-6-15-23 (Washington, D.C.: U.S. Government Printing Office, July 1975), for a discussion of the impact of this change in accounting procedure on retailers' profits. Also see note to Table A.5 in this report.

†Phase I of wage-price controls froze retail prices at their August 15, 1971, level for the following 90 days. From November 15, 1971, to January 11, 1973, Phase II price controls permitted a food retailer to increase prices to reflect increased costs, so long as his profit margin did not increase over that which prevailed during a designated base period. Compliance was mandatory and enforced by the Internal Revenue Service. Phase III was in effect from January 11, 1973, to September 12, 1973. For most industries Phase III meant self-administration of the Phase II gross margin rule and voluntary compliance. Food retailing was an exception; Phase III was simply the extension of Phase II. In addition, consumer concern about high meat prices led the president to establish a ceiling on retail meat prices at their March 29, 1973, level for 5.5 months. (During Phase II all retail food prices increased 5.2 percent, but red meat went up 11.8 percent.) Cost of Living Council, Phase III Regulation, Questions and Answers (Washington, D.C.: U.S. Government Printing Office, 1973). For food retailers Phase IV, which

TABLE 3.3

Distribution of Market Shares, 14 Food Chains in 153 SMSAs, 1972

Market Share	Safeway	A&P	Kroger	Winn-Dixie	Lucky	Jewel	Grand Union	Supermkt. Gen'l.	Nat'l. Tea	Stop & Shop	Fisher	Albertson's	Allied	Giant	Total No.	Total Per-cent
0–4.9	5	13	26	1	6	4	7	4	6	3	6	11	9	1	102	24.3
5–9.9	4	49	20	4	8	4	5	6	8	2	5	4	4	–	123	29.4
10–14.9	8	33	12	9	3	2	4	2	7	4	1	2	3	1	91	21.7
15–19.9	14	14	7	4	3	1	1	1	2	3	–	2	1	–	53	12.6
20–24.9	6	3	7	5	1	–	–	–	2	1	1	–	–	–	25	6.0
25–29.9	6	1	2	4	3	1	–	–	–	–	–	–	–	1	18	4.3
30	4	–	1	–	2	–	–	–	–	–	–	–	–	–	7	1.7
Total SMSAs	47	113	75	27	26	12	17	13	23	13	13	20	17	3	419	100.0
Average Share	17.2	9.9	9.0	16.2	12.9	8.6	7.2	7.1	8.9	11.2	6.8	6.6	6.3	14.9		

Source: 1973 Grocery Distribution Guide (Wellesley Hills, Mass.: Metro Market Studies, 1973).

were exposed to both shocks simultaneously. In 1972 and 1973 most firms had lower profit rates than during 1970 and 1971. Even the West Coast firms, which were less exposed to WEO, had profit rates below their previous levels. However, in 1974 (after mandatory price control) the profit rates for many chains rebounded nearly to the 1970 level.

For firms east of the Rockies, A&P's WEO program may have contributed to chain profit variability during 1970-74. A&P began converting its stores to food discounting operations in late 1971. The conversion involved discontinuing trading stamps, promotional games, and other nonprice competition strategies at the same time that prices were sharply reduced. A&P's gross margins allegedly contracted from the traditional level of 20 percent to 13 percent.[11] At the time A&P was debt-free and had substantial cash reserves. The immediate impact was a 9 percent expansion in first quarter 1972 sales and a $30 million loss.

WEO, however, elicited response from competitors, who lowered prices, extended store hours, and employed a variety of nonprice competitive tactics.[12] A&P's attempt to expand sales failed. Consumers increased their patronage of A&P during the low-price phase of WEO, but as A&P raised prices to regain profitability, many consumers returned to competing retailers who had larger and more attractive stores and better product selection.

Wage-price controls, changes in accounting procedures, and WEO were the extraordinary factors that influenced profits during this period. Although such factors are important in the short run, preoccupation with such relatively random events may mask more fundamental local market forces that determine the long-run profit margins of chains. In general, a firm's rate of profit is determined by the interaction of management decisions with the competitive market environment in which the firm operates.

Two fundamental indicators of a firm's competitive market environment are the four-firm concentration ratio and the firm's market share. Figure 1.7 shows that the concentration ratio for SMSAs varies considerably. In 1972, 10.9 percent of the 194 SMSAs examined had concentration ratios less than 40 percent, and 24.7 percent had ratios greater than 60 percent. Table 3.3 summarizes the variation in estimated market shares of the respondent companies. Safeway and Winn-Dixie had the highest average market shares in

---

began on September 13, 1973, decontrolled meat prices and involved largely self-administration of the gross margin rule and voluntary compliance. Phase IV ended on April 30, 1974.

TABLE 3.4

Frequency Distribution of Average Divisional Profit-Sales Ratios, 14 Leading Grocery Chains, 1970–74

Average Divisional 1970–74 Profit-Sales Ratio (percent)	Number of Divisions														
	A	B	C	D	E	F	G	H	I	J	K	L	M*	N	Total
–3 and less	1	–	–	–	–	–	–	–	–	–	–	–	–	–	1
–2.9 to –2.0	2	–	1	–	–	–	–	–	–	1	–	–	–	–	4
–1.9 to –1.0	10	–	–	–	–	–	–	2	–	1	–	–	–	–	13
–.9 to 0	6	–	1	–	–	3	–	4	–	3	–	1	1	–	19
.1 to 1.0	3	3	2	–	–	2	–	2	–	1	–	1	1	–	15
1.1 to 2.0	4	–	–	1	1	1	1	2	–	2	4	–	–	2	18
2.1 to 3.0	3	–	1	2	–	–	1	2	3	–	6	1	3	–	22
3.1 to 4.0	–	3	–	–	–	–	1	1	–	–	6	–	–	4	15
4.1 and over	–	2	–	–	–	–	1	–	–	–	2	–	–	3	8
Total	29	8	5	3	1	6	4	13	3	8	18	3	5	9	115

* Divisions were redefined in 1970. Hence, average profits during 1971–74 were used.

Source: Company data supplied to Joint Economic Committee.

1972: 17.2 and 16.2 percent, respectively. Allied Markets had the lowest: 6.3 percent. A&P was the most geographically dispersed company, operating in 113 of the 153 SMSAs examined. Giant operated in only three SMSAs. The larger companies enjoyed somewhat higher average market shares.

Table 3.4 reveals that there is not only substantial interfirm variation in profit rates but also considerable intrafirm variation. For example, during 1970-74, chain A had one division with an average profit-sales ratio below -3 percent, three above 2 percent, and the remaining 25 divisions distributed rather evenly in between. Although other chains' divisions were on average more profitable than chain A, all the chains shown in Table 3.4 experienced considerable intrafirm variation. Clearly, there were strong factors besides management and operating characteristics influencing the profitability of individual divisions of each company.

We hypothesize that firm prices and profits in a market are heavily influenced by the structure of that market. The following section of this report involves two tests of the profit portion of this hypothesis. One test employs SMSA data; the second uses division data. (Chapter 4 tests the relationship between market structure and prices.)

VARIABLES USED IN PROFIT AND PRICE ANALYSES

Market Structure Variables

Four-Firm Concentration Ratio (CR_4)

The four-firm concentration ratio is the sum of the market shares of the top four firms in a market. It can be used to measure either buyer or seller concentration. In this study it measures seller concentration. For the most part it is used to measure grocery store concentration; in a few instances it is also used to measure supermarket concentration. The degree of market concentration is used as an index of market power because it strongly influences the intensity and ways that firms compete with one another.[13] When a few sellers control most sales in a market, they tend to behave interdependently rather than as independent competitors. Such interdependence tends to lead to implicit or explicit forms of collusion to enhance profits by maintaining prices above the competitive level. Economic theory does not predict the precise level at which concentration results in an elevation of prices and profits. It does predict, however, that after some threshold level of concentration is reached, further increases in concentration result in greater interdependence among rivals and, hence, in higher prices and profit rates. Although the precise nature of this relationship must be determined empirically, we expect that CR_4 will be positively related to both prices and profits.

This rationale led us to explore a class of S-shaped functional relationships in addition to a simple linear relationship between CR_4 and profits (prices). This class is generated by the nonlinear transformation of the partial relationship between concentration and profits (prices)

$$P = \beta \frac{(CR_4 + a)^3}{1 - 3(CR_4 + a) + 3(CR_4 + a)^2}$$

where $0 \leq CR_4 \leq 1$; β is a parameter estimated by linear least-squares regression; (a) is an unestimated parameter that shifts the inflection of the S-curve and, hence, its location in concentration-profits (prices) space. The formula $I = .5 - a$ determines the inflection point (I) of the curve.[*] Figure 3.1 illustrates the general form of this function and its location in concentration-profit (price) space for different values of (a). Given a limited range of CR_4, the relevant portion of the S-curve for different values of (a) is indicated by solid lines. In this illustration we have not allowed the curve to elongate or contract vertically—that is, β is held constant. For different estimated values of β, the S-function can vary in slope and in its vertical expanse. The profit and price models were estimated for various preset values of (a) to determine the value of (a) in each model that minimized the standard error of the regression.

In interpreting the observed statistical significance of four-firm concentration, it should be recalled that often an SMSA does not accurately reflect the actual relevant geographic area of competition. Although this error tends to understate CR_4 in most markets, the error is not uniform across markets, thereby tending to bias the statistical results toward zero. That is, were it not for errors in

---

[*]The following condition must hold for all values of CR_4 in a sample to restrict the class of functions to those consistent with the theoretical concepts mentioned above:

$$0 > CR_4 + a < 1.00$$

If $CR_4 + a > 1.00$, the resulting curve rises, flattens, and then rises at the highest levels of concentration. There is no theoretical basis for this functional form. Thus, the values of (a) were constrained to the range $-.3$ to $.2$ for our samples.

FIGURE 3.1

Examples of the S-function for Different Values
of the Shift Parameter

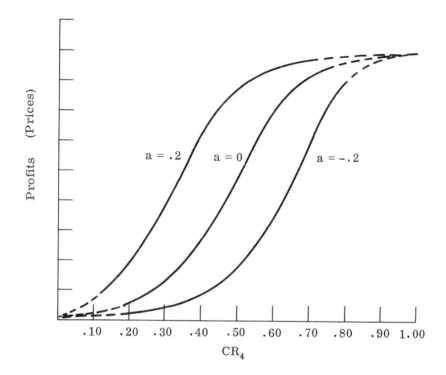

Source: Compiled by the authors.

defining relevant markets, the level of statistical significance very
probably would be higher than those actually reported for CR_4 in the
various equations.

Firm Market Share (FMS)

This variable measures the percent of a market's sales held
by a particular firm.[14] Other things being the same, as a firm
obtains a higher market share, it becomes a more dominant force
in the market. Firms with large market shares enjoy a degree of
discretion in pricing and other decisions that are likely to result in
higher price and profit levels. In addition, store-level and company
overhead expenses may be lower for a chain with a high market
share.

Of considerable importance in food retailing is the existence of enterprise differentiation* and advertising cost advantages conferred on the dominant firm because it can engage in larger-scale advertising. A National Commission on Food Marketing study concluded:

> Because advertising is one of the leading forms of nonprice competition in this industry, the retailer with the largest local advertising budget may have a pronounced advantage over its rivals. This advantage will be reflected in increased demand for the retailer's products and services, as well as lower per-unit advertising cost.[15]

The study then identifies the various ways in which a firm with a strong market position may be able to influence its profit margins. These include the following:[16]

- Charge higher prices
- Offer fewer specials with sharply reduced prices, thereby selling a greater percentage of high-margin items
- Provide fewer services to customers, thereby reducing operating costs
- Operate stores nearer capacity, thereby capturing the lower costs associated with high store utilization

The various factors associated with a leading position in a market give dominant grocery retailers an advantage over both smaller rivals and potential entrants. Thus, in those markets where a dominant firm exists, high entry barriers also are likely and give dominant firms some freedom to engage in noncompetitive behavior without attracting new competitors.[17]

On the basis of the above, we hypothesize that, other things remaining the same, the greater a firm's market share, the higher its prices and its profit margins.

---

*The term "enterprise differentiation" is used instead of the more familiar "product differentiation" to avoid confusion. The "product" of food retailers can be viewed as the bundle of merchandise, service, store facilities, location, and other nonprice factors that influence consumer store selection decisions. Thus, enterprise differentiation is simply a broad interpretation of product differentiation.

Relative Firm Market Share (RFMS)

Relative firm market share (RFMS) is an alternative to FMS as a means of measuring firm dominance vis-a-vis leading rivals. A firm's relative market share is the ratio of its market share to the four-firm concentration ratio. Whereas FMS measures a firm's absolute share of the entire market, RFMS measures a firm's size relative to the leading firms in a market. We believe RFMS is preferable to FMS because a firm's discretion in pricing and its cost advantage or disadvantage depend largely on its relative position in the market. Market share is more directly related to the realization of absolute scale economies in a particular market. Relative market share measures relative scale economies that may exist— that is, the cost advantage that one firm has relative to its major competitors. RFMS is also a superior measure of the degree of enterprise differentiation among firms in a market.[18]

A simple numerical example illustrates the difference between FMS and RFMS. A firm with a 15 percent market share in a market where the next three firms each hold 5 percent of the market would be expected to enjoy a much stronger competitive position than if each of the other three firms also held 15 percent of the market. While the market share for the firm is identical in the above two examples, its relative market share is .5 in the first case and .25 in the second. Because RFMS measures the relative competitive position of a firm in a market, it is more appropriate than FMS in cross-sectional analyses involving many markets.

RFMS also has the statistical virtue that it is not highly correlated with CR_4, whereas FMS is. As FMS increases, CR_4 is constrained to be larger than FMS. Therefore, FMS and CR_4 will, on average, be correlated in a random sample drawn from the population.* Unlike FMS, relative market share does not constrain CR_4; therefore, specifying it jointly with CR_4 does not introduce multicollinearity into the model.

We hypothesize that this variable, like FMS, will be positively related to both price levels and profits.

---

*The proof is as follows: $\eta_{xy} \neq 0$ if and only if Cov XY $\neq 0$; define Z = X - Y, then $\eta_{xz} \neq 0$ if and only if Cov XZ $\neq 0$, but Cov XY = Cov X(x - y) = Var X - Cov XY, and hence Cov XZ = 0 only if Var X = Cov XY. This is true only if Y = X + k, where k is some constant. For a study that uses CR_4 - FMS as an explanatory variable, see William Shepherd, "The Elements of Market Structure," Review of Economics and Statistics 54 (February 1972): 25-38.

Mean Store Size (SS)

Mean store size (SS) measures the average sales per grocery store with payroll in each SMSA in 1972. This variable was included in the regression models to adjust for differences in the importance of supermarkets vis-a-vis small stores in various SMSAs. As indicated earlier, the supermarket submarket is the relevant market within which the chains in this study compete. However, data on supermarket CR_4 and RFMS were not available at the time of this study. Therefore, four-firm concentration and firm market shares within the grocery store market were used. (When supermarket concentration ratios for some markets became available after the completion of our analysis, several of the profit regressions were re-run using these ratios. The results are reported in Table B.15.)

Mean store size provides a surrogate measure of the importance of supermarkets in different markets. In markets with many small stores, the Census Bureau's CR_4 (based upon all grocery stores) will be a poorer measure of supermarket concentration than it will be in SMSAs in which small stores are a minor element. Thus, the understatement of CR_4 will be inversely related to SS. Insofar as SS corrects partially for such understatements, we hypothesize that it will be negatively related to both profits and prices.

Other Independent Variables

Market Growth (MG)

Market growth (MG) is defined as the percentage change from 1967 to 1972 in deflated grocery store sales in each SMSA as reported by the Census Bureau. Market growth is thus a measure of the growth in demand.[*] Its influence depends, in part, on the rate at which grocery store capacity expands. If capacity expansion lags behind market growth, as we expect, excess demand is likely to exist in the market, resulting in higher utilization of existing facilities. Since higher utilization of existing facilities is expected to lower retailing costs per dollar of sales, profits in excess-demand markets would tend to be higher even if prices are not increased.

---

[*]Comparable geographic areas were used in estimating the growth in market demand over 1967-72. For those SMSAs whose definition changed between 1967 and 1972, the 1967 grocery store sales were adjusted to reflect the definitional change before computing market growth.

The influence of excess demand on price levels is less clear. Excess demand is frequently expected to lead to higher prices as interested buyers "bid up" the available supply. However, it is also easier to enter rapidly growing markets. Established firms may elect not to increase prices and maximize short-run profits, lest they encourage entry. Indeed, they may lower prices to forestall entry. If average retailing costs decline with excess capacity, as expected, retailers may be able to charge lower prices in rapidly growing markets in order to forestall entry and to maintain or expand market share while still realizing profits that are comparable with or greater than the profits in slower-growing markets.

The expected influence of market growth is therefore mixed. Although we hypothesize a positive relationship to profits, we are unable to hypothesize an expected relationship between market growth and price levels.

Market Size (MS)

Market size (MS) is defined as the 1972 sales of grocery stores with payroll for each SMSA as reported by the Census Bureau. The size of a market is expected to influence the profits and prices of retail operations in two ways. Very large SMSAs, such as New York, Los Angeles, and Chicago, are actually made up of several smaller economic markets. For example, consumers in southern Chicago or the central city are not likely to travel to the suburbs to buy groceries. To the extent that retail grocery firms hold stronger market positions in certain parts of an SMSA and weaker positions (or are not present) in others, our structural variables do not accurately reflect actual market structure in the relevant submarkets. In these cases, market share and concentration figures will be understated. Since this problem of market fragmentation increases with the size of the SMSA, MS is expected to explain some of the differences in profits that concentration or market share would explain if they were properly measured. On the basis of this rationale, market size is expected to be positively related to profits and price levels.

A large market also allows for larger total sales by retail firms and the potential for greater economies of scale in warehousing, physical distribution, supervision, and advertising. These factors would tend to result in somewhat lower prices in large markets, other things remaining the same.

Thus, market size is included as an adjustment for CR_4 and RFMS, as well as a proxy for the level of costs in markets of different sizes. We hypothesize a positive relationship between market size and profits; because market size may influence price levels in contrary directions, we are unable to predict the net relationship between market size and price levels.

Impact of A&P (API)

The impact of A&P (API) was included in the analysis to measure A&P's presence as a competitor in a market or geographic area. It is measured by a binary variable. A value of 1 indicates that A&P operates in that SMSA, and 0 indicates that A&P is not present. In the divisional analysis this variable is aggregated, as are other explanatory variables, to conform with divisional profit-sales data.

A&P was singled out as a particularly important competitor because of its precipitous decline in market share in many markets prior to and during the period being studied, and because of the WEO program launched in 1972. The aggressive price competition provided by WEO is expected to have had a negative impact on the profits of firms competing with A&P in 1972 and, to a lesser extent, in 1973. In the remaining years (1970, 1971, 1974) A&P appears to have been a "weak" competitor whose presence likely enhanced the profits of competing firms.

Thus, we hypothesize a positive relationship between API and profits during 1970, 1971, and 1974, and a negative relationship during 1972 and 1973. For the entire period a positive relationship is expected. API was not included in the price models because price data were for October 1974, when the WEO program was essentially over.

A&P Company (APC)

In the division profit analysis, the API variable discussed above does not distinguish between the self-inflicted effect of WEO and inferior operations on A&P's profits and their impact on the profits of A&P's competitors. To overcome this problem, an A&P binary variable (APC) was specified in which A&P divisions were given a value of 1 and other chain divisions a value of 0.

This variable enables analysis of the direct impact of A&P's WEO program on its own profitability, as opposed to its impact on the profits of chains in direct competition with A&P. This variable also was included to reflect the fact that for over a decade A&P has had profit rates well below the industry average. Although the various market and other variables discussed above may explain differences in the profitability of A&P's various divisions, other forces unique to A&P are responsible for its persistently lower average profit rate.

For these reasons we hypothesize that APC will have a negative sign in both the five-year average and in the annual profit models. However, the absolute value of the coefficient should attain a peak in the annual regressions in 1972 to reflect the lower profits that A&P divisions experienced during the height of the WEO program.

Firm Growth (FG)

Industrial organization theory attempts to predict the performance of groups of firms or entire industries. As such, it deals with the average performance that would be expected with different industry structures. The performance of individual firms is expected to deviate from the central tendencies predicted by this theory. Because the present analysis deals with differences in the profits of individual grocery chains, we expect that part of the variation in individual chain profits is attributable to reasons unrelated to the structure of the markets in which they operate.

Perhaps the main such nonstructural variable influencing profits is the caliber of management. We would expect managerial differences to be reflected in the past and current success of a chain in achieving operating efficiencies and in developing a unique store image and consumer preference for its services. Insofar as a chain is more successful in the above respects than are its rivals, we would expect such success to be reflected in higher growth rates. We therefore have incorporated a firm growth (FG) variable as a proxy for the relative success of a chain (whether due to managerial superiority, successful product differentiation, or good luck). For each chain this variable measures the internal growth (excluding mergers) in the company's total grocery store sales between 1970 and 1973.[*] All division and SMSA observations for a company have the same value—for example, 55 percent for Winn-Dixie. We hypothesize that this variable will be positively related to a chain's profits.

It is possible that this variable reflects some underlying structural variables. Specifically, if a firm holds a more dominant relative market position (RFMS) than do other chains, and/or it operates in more highly concentrated markets than do other chains, it has a greater financial capability for growth. Hence a firm's observed growth rate may be due in part to the structural characteristics of the markets in which it operates.

Entry (E)

Entry (E) is included to identify and measure the profit impact of the act of entry on entering firms. Since the barriers to entry for

---

[*]These years were chosen rather than 1970–74 because grocery store sales data were not reported for all four quarters in 1974.

any market are expected to affect the "cost" of entry, this variable is specified accordingly. E has a value of 0 for established firms in a market. For firms that entered a market between 1967 and 1970, E is equal to the 1972 four-firm concentration ratio for the SMSA.

Entering a new market is more difficult than expanding operations in established markets because of the barriers to entry that exist in many markets. Joe Bain says a barrier to entry exists if ". . . any one or a few firms in a [market] can obtain some long-term strategic advantage over all actual and potential competitors."[19]

There are three major barriers to entry in grocery retailing that give the leading firms in a market long-term strategic advantages. First, it is highly probable that these firms have control over many of the preferred sites for new supermarkets in their market.[20] Since these sites are an essential resource for supermarket operations, their control strongly influences entry.

Second, leading established firms enjoy considerable sales promotion and enterprise differentiation advantages over entering firms. Not only can leading firms spread current advertising expenditures over a larger sales volume, but they also may have established consumer loyalties based upon their past merchandising efforts and spatial distribution of stores.

Finally, as the number of firms in a market declines and their share of the market increases, the probability increases that an entering firm will be in direct competition with the established market leaders. The entering firms then confront a more serious displacement problem. They must either risk incurring losses as they try to capture (at the expense of existing firms) a sufficient share of the market to operate efficiently, or settle for a smaller share than is required to operate at an efficient scale.

As concentration in a market increases, entry barriers are expected to increase. High entry barriers are more difficult and costly to overcome than low entry barriers. Thus, the act of entry is expected to have a negative influence on the profits of entering firms; further, the magnitude of this negative influence is expected to be directly related to the four-firm concentration ratio, which influences the height of entry barriers.

Market Rivalry (MR)

In many industries, including grocery retailing, firms engage in temporary competitive strategies designed to improve their position vis-a-vis their rivals. In these circumstances, rivalry among chains is more intense than would be expected on the basis of a given configuration of structural and control variables. When such rivalry is intense, it usually is accompanied by lower prices and often leads to changes in the market shares of firms in the market. We therefore

have used the 1972-74 changes in the market shares of the four leading firms of 1974 as a proxy of short-run market rivalry (MR).* We
expect MR to be negatively associated with grocery prices; that is,
the greater the change in the leading firms' market shares (whether
up or down) the lower grocery store prices will be in the SMSA
affected.

Union Wage Rate (WR)

Labor expense is the most important operating expense of food
retailing firms, accounting for nearly 60 percent of total expenses
in 1974. Data are not available on the labor expenses per dollar of
sales in different markets, either for all food retailers or for the
chains included in this study. Data on the union wage rates (WR) for
meat cutters, grocery clerks, and checkers are available, and are
used as a proxy variable for labor expense in our analysis. Although
labor productivity and the mix of full-time and part-time employees
may vary across markets, resulting in union wage rate being an
imperfect proxy for labor expense, we expect WR to reflect the
major source of variation in labor expense in different markets.[21]

All else being equal, union wage rate is expected to be directly
related to labor expenses in metropolitan areas and, hence, to
grocery prices. A positive relationship is therefore hypothesized
between wage rate and prices. There is no a priori basis for expected
wage rate to be related to profits. For this reason the variable is
not included in the profit models.

---

*We emphasize that MR is designed to capture the short-run
effect on prices of the intensity of rivalry among leading chains.
This differs from the finding of Arnold A. Heggestad and Stephen A.
Rhoades that the intensity of rivalry is negatively related to the level
of market concentration. "Concentration and Firm Stability in Commercial Banking," Review of Economics and Statistics 58 (1976):
443-52. Their study provides an explanation for the general tendency
of prices and profits to be positively associated with market concentration, because as rivalry decreases at higher levels of concentration, prices tend to rise above competitive levels. We would expect
a similar relationship between concentration and rivalry in the long
run in food retailing. Since in this study we are attempting to explain
grocery prices at only one point in time, temporary market turbu-
lence, if unaccounted for, can cloud the underlying structure-price
relationships. Our market rivalry variable (MR) attempts to explain
why, in the short run, prices depart from those we could expect to
occur at various levels of market concentration (CR_4).

Dependent Profit Variable

Profit-Sales (P/S)

The profit-sales ratio (P/S) for a firm in a market (division or SMSA) is defined as the net profits before taxes, divided by the firm's sales in that market. Alternative profit measures, such as return on assets or stockholders' equity, were not employed in this analysis because data on asset or stockholder equity at the division or SMSA level were unavailable. The profit-sales ratio, although lacking in comparability with other industries, is an accurate measure of relative profitability of firms within an industry.[*]

Profit Models

Division and SMSA profit-sales ratios were examined using the following basic models:

(1)   Division $P/S = \alpha_0 + \alpha_1 RFMS + \alpha_2 CR_4 + \alpha_3 FG + \alpha_4 MG + \alpha_5 MS + \alpha_6 APC + \alpha_7 A$

   Hypothesis: $\alpha_1 > 0$ $\alpha_2 > 0$ $\alpha_3 > 0$ $\alpha_4 > 0$ $\alpha_5 > 0$ $\alpha_6 < 0$ $\alpha_7 >$

(2)   SMSA $P/S = \beta_0 + \beta_1 RFMS + \beta_2 CR_4 + \beta_3 SS + \beta_4 E + \beta_5 FG + \beta_6 MG + \beta_7 MS + \beta_8 AI$

   Hypothesis: $\beta_1 > 0$ $\beta_2 > 0$ $\beta_3 < 0$ $\beta_4 < 0$ $\beta_5 > 0$ $\beta_6 > 0$ $\beta_7 > 0$ $\beta_8 >$

where

   P/S = division or SMSA profit-sales ratio
   RFMS = 1972 relative firm market share
   CR_4 = 1972 four-firm concentration ratio—a curvilinear form of
       this variable (CCR_4) was used in several models
   SS = 1972 mean sales per grocery store within an SMSA
   E = entry conditions in SMSAs that sample firms entered be-
       tween 1967 and 1970; the 1972 CR_4 in these markets is used
       as an estimate of entry barriers

---

[*]We have included only those chains that appear to use similar accounting procedures in developing their profit-sales ratios. However, it is impossible to determine whether identical procedures were used in all cases. Insofar as differences exist among the chains in our sample, this would tend to bias our results toward zero—that is, it would reduce the observed levels of significance of our models.

FG = firm growth as measured by the percentage increase in a
   company's grocery store sales between 1970 and 1973
MG = 1967-72 percentage real growth in total grocery store sales
   in a division or SMSA
MS = 1972 market size (dollar grocery store sales)
APC = binary identifying A&P divisions
API = variable used to indicate the presence or absence of A&P
   in a market.

RESULTS OF PROFIT ANALYSIS

As noted above, during 1970-74 there was considerable variation in the profitability of various chains as well as among the
divisions of individual chains. In addition, profitability varied considerably from one year to the next.

Two data sets were used to explore the relationships between
chain profitability and various market structure and other variables.
The first set of data consisted of pretax profit-sales ratios and other
data for six chains in 50 SMSAs. There were 72 observations because,
in some instances, more than one of the firms operated in an SMSA.
The second data set consisted of pretax profit-sales ratios and other
data for 96 divisions of 12 food chains.* Because data on the market
structure and control variables included in the profit models were
available on an SMSA basis, the first data set does not involve aggregating these variables to a divisional basis.† For this reason the

---

*The divisional sample is identical to the one shown in Table
3.4 with a few exceptions. Firms C and M were excluded because of
the lack of division definitions. An additional nine divisions were
not included either because they involved entry into a new SMSA or
because they did not contain an SMSA. The end result of these dele-
tions is a sample with 96 observations.

†Data on the independent variables were not available for the
entire areas served by various company divisions. Thus, in order
to relate division profits to the structure of the market(s) and other
market characteristics within each division, weighted independent
variables were computed. The weighted values were based upon the
characteristics of the SMSAs within each division. The CR_4, RFMS,
MS, MG, and API values for each SMSA were multiplied by the sales
of the firm in that SMSA. The sum of these values over all SMSAs
within a division was then divided by the total sales of the division
in the SMSAs to obtain the appropriate weighted value for each

regression analysis of SMSA profits may be more discriminating than the analysis of division profits in identifying the impact of various factors on firm profitability.

SMSA Profit Analysis

This analysis examines the statistical relationship between the dependent variable P/S (a firm's profit-sales ratio in each SMSA) and the various independent variables identified above. Pretax P/S were available for each year during 1970-74, whereas the explanatory variables (except market growth and firm growth) were constructed for 1972. Although use of a single year for CR_4 and other independent explanatory variables may introduce some errors into the results, we believe this does not seriously bias the findings because structural variables tend to be quite stable over short periods.[22]

The hypothesized relationship between market structure and profit rates is assumed to be long-run. Short-terms factors, such as temporary price wars, local strikes, depressed local business conditions, and price controls, may distort this relationship in some or in all areas in a particular year. The most common method of controlling for such short-term disturbances is to average the data

---

variable. For example, if a division has annual sales of $100 million and $75 million are derived from the two SMSAs in the division, a weighted CR_4 for the division would be computed as follows:

	(1) CR_4	(2) Sales	(3) (1) × (2)	
SMSA no. 1	30	60 mill.	1,800	$\dfrac{2,550}{75} = 34$ (weighted CR_4)
SMSA no. 2	50	15 mill.	750	
		75 mill.	2,550	

This procedure ignores the structure of towns and small cities within the division but outside any SMSA. (In the above example, $25 million of the division's sales are derived from non-SMSA areas.) It is assumed, however, that the weighted CR_4, RFMS, and other variables computed in the above manner are reasonable estimates for the entire division. Since the CR_4 and RFMS in small cities tend to be higher than in large cities, this procedure tends to understate the weighted CR_4 and RFMS for a division and to overstate market size.

for several years, on the assumption that short-run aberrations in the data will be offsetting over time. Five-year average profit rates are used in the first three regression models shown in Table 3.5.

Equation 1a is a linear model including six independent variables.* All of the variables have the hypothesized sign and, except for CR_4 and MS, are statistically significant at the 1 percent level. CR_4 is significant at the 5 percent level.

Equation 1b is identical to 1a except that mean store size (SS) is included. As expected, this variable is negatively related to profits (5 percent level of significance) and strengthens the t-value for CR_4. Market size becomes significant at the 10 percent level with the addition of mean store size to the model.

---

*Preliminary investigations revealed that both the SMSA and divisional samples were heteroskedastic. When ordered by firm growth, the variance of the regression residuals became progressively larger as firm growth decreased. This phenomenon is intuitively plausible because it implies that poorly managed firms have not only lower expected rates of profits but also greater variation in the rate of profit for a given market structure.

Heteroskedasticity does not require us to alter our theoretical predictions of the relationship between market structure and performance. It does, however, have serious implications for testing these hypotheses. If ordinary least-square estimation techniques are used, one obtains unbiased estimates of the model's coefficients, but the t-ratios that measure the reliability of these estimates are biased in an unknown direction. A test may assert that a variable is insignificant when in fact it is significant, and vice versa. Both unbiased coefficient estimates and t-ratios in this report were obtained by using a generalized least-squares estimation technique. To construct the generalized weighting matrix, it was assumed that the residual variance was proportional to the natural logarithm of firm growth for each of the annual regressions. For the SMSA average regressions, heteroskedasticity was corrected assuming that the squared residuals were exponentially related to firm growth.

Data transformed by the weighted matrix were analyzed with an ordinary least-squares computer program. While this procedure results in unbiased t-ratios, the resulting R^2 values cannot be interpreted in the same way as R^2 values resulting from ordinary least-squares analysis of untransformed data (as the proportion of the variation in the dependent variable that is explained by the independent variables.)

TABLE 3.5

Multiple-Regression Equations Explaining SMSA Profit-Sales Ratios for Six Companies in 49 SMSAs, 1970-74

Independent Variables[a]

Dependent Variable, Profit-Sales Ratio (P/S)	Intercept	Relative Firm Market Shared (RFMS)	4-Firm Concentration Ratio (CR_4)	Curvilinear Concentration (CCR_4)[b]	Mean Store Size (SS)	Entry (E)	Firm Growth (FG)	Log Firm Growth (LNFG)	Market Growth (MG)	Market Growth Squared (MG^2)	Market Size (MS)	Market Size Squared (MS^2)	A&P Impact (API)	R^2 [c]	F-Value
1a. 1970-74 average	-3.535	.064 (5.806)**	.018 (1.371)†			-.044 (-5.834)**	.045 (6.770)**		.033 (3.102)**		.149 (.851)			.817	40.79**
1b. 1970-74 average	-3.116	.063 (5.808)**	.026 (1.846)*		-1.005 (-1.650)†	-.042 (-5.559)**	.045 (6.965)**		.032 (3.046)**		.272 (1.448)†			.824	36.73**
1c. 1970-74 average	-.215	.063 (5.808)**		3.661 (2.691)**	-.906 (-1.694)*	-.032 (-4.795)**		1.614 (7.568)**		.045 (3.328)**	-1.790 (-3.000)**	.580 (3.460)**		.870	46.14**
1d. 1970-74 average	-.446	.065 (6.532)**		3.119 (2.323)**	-.284 (-.480)	-.034 (-5.455)**		1.832 (7.548)**		.044 (3.494)**	-1.720 (-2.971)**	.547 (3.364)**	.544 (2.010)*	.889	48.82**
2. 1970	-2.679	.076 (6.830)**		7.747 (2.651)**	-1.364 (-1.074)	-.071 (-4.162)**		.599 (1.415)†		.049 (1.440)†	-3.874 (-3.343)**	1.116 (3.334)**	-1.311 (-1.970)*	.689	13.29**
3. 1971	-1.842	.079 (4.045)**		4.935 (2.188)*	-1.247 (-1.298)	-.037 (-3.752)**		1.169		.058 (2.753)**	-2.207 (-2.335)**	.656 (2.457)**	.498 (1.097)	.773	20.72**
4. 1972	.578	.068 (5.058)**		1.708 (.932)	-.294 (-.381)	-.031 (-4.046)**		2.138 (7.267)**		.062 (3.649)**	-1.612 (-2.106)*	.544 (2.514)**	.661 (1.810)*	.812	26.35**
5. 1973	1.841	.057 (5.364)**		.530 (.310)	-.274 (-.364)	-.015 (-1.642)†		2.213 (8.580)**		.046 (2.557)**	-1.747 (-2.476)**	.572 (2.849)**	.952 (2.615)**	.771	20.50**
6. 1974	2.041	.042 (3.879)**		-.201 (-.130)	.604 (.929)	-.022 (-3.317)**		2.351 (9.466)**		.019 (1.296)†	-.584 (-.905)	.188 (1.029)	1.436 (4.668)**	.861	37.69**

Notes: One-tailed t-tests were used in all cases. Figures in parentheses are t-values. There are 71 observations from these 49 SMSAs, since in several instances more than one of the firms operated in an SMSA. One observation was deleted from the 1970 sample because of a prolonged labor dispute. One observation was deleted from each of the SMSA samples because of the questionable calculation of CR_4 by the Census Bureau.

[a]P/S, RFMS, CR_4, and FG are expressed as percentages. LNFG is the natural logarithm of FG expressed in decimals. MG is expressed in percentages; MG^2 is the percentage of market growth squared and divided by 100. MS is expressed in billions of dollars. SS is expressed in million dollar sales per store. E is expressed in percentage.

[b]$CCR_4 = (CR_4 + \alpha)^3 / 1 - 3(CR_4 + \alpha) + 3(CR_4 + \alpha)^2$. This function of CR_4 has positive slope and is symmetric about an inflection point. The inflection point of the curve occurs at the concentration ratio that satisfies the equation $CR_4 = 0.5 - \alpha$. For all equations in this table $\alpha = 0.20$, so the inflection point of the curve is $CR_4 = 0.30$.

[c]Because of computation procedures, R^2 values are not comparable with those in Table 4.3. For care needed in interpretation, see footnote on p. 81.

**Significance level = 1 percent.
*Significance level = 5 percent.
†Significance level = 10 percent.
Source: Compiled by the authors.

Equation 1c adds the A&P impact variable (API) to the model and includes nonlinear functional forms for CR_4, FG, MG, and MS. RFMS and the curvilinear forms of FG, MG, and MS have a stronger relationship to profits in this model than in the first two equations. The nonlinear form of CR_4 becomes significant at the 1 percent level. Setting the shift parameter (a) at .2 minimized the standard error of the regression. Within the sample range the concentration-profits curve rises rapidly until CR_4 equals 60. Thereafter it continues to rise at a modest rate. No threshold level was detected at low levels of concentration.

Because equation 1c is the most general and robust model, we shall examine briefly the relationship between the other independent variables and the profit-sales ratio.

Mean store size (SS) has the expected negative sign but is not significant in this equation. Although not significant, SS is expected to control partially for the understatement of CR_4 in markets with many small stores and, hence, to clarify the relationship between CR_4 and profits.

The entry variable (E) is significant at the 1 percent level and has the hypothesized negative sign. This confirms the expectation that firms entering an SMSA will experience subnormal profits during the first few years, as they attempt to become established in the market.

Firm growth, a proxy for the caliber of management, is introduced in logarithmic form (LNFG) in this equation. It has the expected positive sign and is highly significant. This finding substantiates the hypothesis that the profit rates of an individual chain are determined by factors unique to it as well as by the structure of the markets in which it operates and the other variables used in the analysis.[*]

Market growth is introduced quadratically (MG^2).[†] It is significant at the 1 percent level and has the hypothesized positive sign. All else remaining the same, profits tended to be highest in those divisions where grocery store sales grew most rapidly between 1967 and 1972. Profits also tended to grow at an increasing rate as the rate of market growth increased.

----

[*] Firm growth significantly improves the explanatory power of the overall model, although its inclusion slightly reduces the significance of other variables, reflecting some collinearity.

[†] For markets with negative growth rates, MG^2 was given a negative sign; thus the resulting curve is not a quadratic "bowl." Most growth rates, however, were positive.

Market size is introduced as a complete quadratic (MS, MS^2) and is significant at the 1 percent level. For SMSAs in which grocery store sales exceeded $1.6 billion, there is a positive relationship between profits and market size. This is consistent with the original hypotheses on scale economies and market misdefinition. Most market sales, however, are less than $1.6 billion (approximate size of San Francisco-Oakland SMSA). For SMSAs smaller than $1.6 billion, market size is negatively related to profits, which is contrary to the hypothesized relationship. A logical explanation is not readily apparent. A possible one is that many of the chains in the sample operate a substantial number of stores in low-income areas of large cities. Other studies have shown that the net profits of chain stores operating in such areas are substantially lower than those in other areas.[23] The fact that many chains are closing stores in central city areas also suggests that these areas may be in disequilibrium. Given these facts, chains may have relatively lower profits in large cities, where the cost-increasing factors associated with central city operations are most common. This could explain why profits and market size are negatively related over a wide range, but become positively related in very large cities, where the effect of market misdefinition is sufficiently great to offset the influence of low profits in central cities.

The A&P impact (API) variable has the expected positive relationship to the profits of competing chains and is significant at the 10 percent level. (A&P was not one of the six chains in this sample.) This is consistent with our hypothesis that A&P has been a weak competitor in recent years and that, on average, firms in competition with A&P have had higher profits.

The model shown in equation 1c is tested for individual years in equations 2-6. The results are generally consistent with those discussed above, although several of the variables behave in a significantly different manner in particular years. The market structure, entry, and firm growth variables always have the expected sign and, except for CR_4, are always significant at the 5 or 1 percent levels. This is a remarkably strong showing for analyses based on data for individual years.

The entry variable (E) behaves as predicted. Although it is negative and statistically significant in all years, the value of the regression coefficient is greatest in 1970 and declines thereafter. Since this variable measures entry that occurred during 1967-70, the results indicate the expected—that a new entrant's profits are lowest during its first years in a new market.

The API variable behaves rather erratically in the SMSA models for individual years. This is partly attributable to collinearity with SS and CCR_4 (see Table B.12). In 1970, A&P's presence in a market tended to depress profits of rival chains. In 1971 and 1972 chains tended to have slightly higher profits in markets where they competed with A&P. In 1973 and 1974 this gap widened, so that by 1974, other things remaining the same, chains made substantially higher profits in markets where A&P was a competitor. This suggests that by 1974, in the aftermath of WEO, A&P exerted less competitive pressure on rival chains' profits than it had in 1970.

The most significant finding of the multiple-regression analysis of SMSA profits is that in equations 1a, 1b, and 1c, the two structural variables, RFMS and CR_4, have the expected positive signs and are statistically significant in all cases. RFMS is statistically significant at the 1 percent level in all equations and CR_4 is statistically significant at the 5 percent level when in linear form and at the 1 percent level when in nonlinear form. This indicates that, when all other things remain the same, the higher a firm's RFMS and the higher the level of CR_4 in an SMSA, the greater the firm's profits.

Division Profit Analysis

Profit and sales data on a division basis were provided by 12 chains for 96 divisions. The same basic variables and functional forms were used in the divisional analysis as in the SMSA analysis summarized in Table 3.5. Two variables, mean store size (SS) and entry (E), that were included in the SMSA analysis were not included in the divisional models.* One additional variable, A&P company (APC), was included in the divisional analysis because A&P was one of the 12 chains in this sample.

In the statistical significance and signs of the independent variables, the divisional regression results presented in Table 3.6 are very similar to the SMSA profit analysis. Equation 1a is a linear model including six independent variables. All of the variables have the hypothesized sign and, except for CR_4 and MS, are statistically significant at the 1 percent level. The F-test for the entire model is significant at the 1 percent level.

The A&P impact variable (API) is included in equation 1b. Although it has a modest positive influence on profits, as hypothesized,

---

*This was done to simplify the model. Divisional variables were developed by aggregating data from different SMSAs within a division. E is particularly difficult to measure in this case, since a chain may be operating in some SMSAs in a division at the same time it is entering another SMSA.

TABLE 3.6

Multiple-Regression Equations Explaining Division Profit-Sales Ratios for 12 Companies, 96 Divisions, 1970-74

Dependent Variable, Profit-Sales Ratio (P/S)	Intercept	Relative Firm Market Share (RFMS)	4-Firm Concentration Ratio (CR_4)	Curvilinear 4-Firm Concentration Ratio (CCR_4)[b]	Firm Growth (FG)	Log Firm Growth (LNFG)	Market Growth (MG)	Market Growth Squared (MG^2)	Market Size (MS)	Market Size Squared (MS^2)	A&P Company (APC)	A&P Impact (API)	R^2[c]	F-Value
1a. 1970-74 average	-3.103	0.074 (8.012)**	0.011 (0.829)		0.045 (7.948)**		0.040 (4.283)**		-0.136 (0.874)		-0.792 (2.734)**		.849	71.61**
1b. 1970-74 average	-3.432	0.076 (8.204)**	0.008 (0.639)		0.046 (8.096)**		0.044 (4.595)**		-0.116 (0.753)		-0.883 (3.007)**	0.417 (1.556)†	.854	64.52**
1c. 1970-74 average	-8.232	0.063 (7.540)**		3.473 (2.600)**		1.543 (8.524)**		0.065 (4.708)**	-1.770 (3.238)**	0.501 (3.085)**	-1.115 (3.852)**	0.348 (1.494)†	.894	81.19**
2. 1970	-6.439	0.069 (5.776)**		3.246 (1.693)*		1.118 (4.227)**		0.080 (3.733)**	-2.367 (3.114)**	0.731 (3.217)**	-0.867 (2.338)*	0.593 (1.663)*	.805	39.86**
3. 1971	-8.108	0.063 (5.430)**		5.374 (2.879)**		1.139 (4.463)**		0.068 (3.357)**	-2.449 (3.286)**	0.674 (3.026)**	-1.191 (3.184)**	0.470 (1.387)†	.810	41.33**
4. 1972	-10.834	0.072 (5.938)**		5.369 (2.750)**		1.665 (6.287)**		0.083 (4.056)**	-1.895 (2.397)*	0.542 (2.304)*	-2.433 (5.923)**	-0.080 (0.231)	.808	40.70**
5. 1973	-7.371	0.054 (5.474)**		0.315 (0.206)		1.886 (8.610)**		0.078 (5.213)**	-1.001 (1.462)†	0.317 (1.587)†	-0.678 (1.708)*	0.467 (1.827)*	.859	58.69**
6. 1974	-6.221	0.057 (5.204)**		1.173 (0.666)		1.682 (6.942)**		0.037 (1.875)*	-1.021 (1.460)†	0.224 (1.072)	-0.407 (1.182)	0.257 (0.792)	.813	42.02**

Independent Variables[a]

Notes: One-tailed t-tests were used in all cases. Figures in parentheses are t-values.

[a] P/S, RFMS, CR_4, and FG are expressed as percentages. LNFG is the natural logarithm of FG expressed in decimals. MG is expressed in percentages; MG^2 is the percentage of market growth squared and divided by 100. MG is expressed in billions of dollars. SS is expressed in million dollar sales per store. E is expressed in percentage.

[b] $CCR_4 = (CR_4 + \alpha)^3/1 - 3 (CR_4 + \alpha) + 3(CR_4 + \alpha)^2$. This function of CR_4 has positive slope and is symmetric about an inflection point. The inflection point of the curve occurs at the concentration ratio that satisfies the equation $CR_4 = 0.5 - \alpha$. For all equations in this table $\alpha = 0.20$, so the inflection point of the curve is $CR_4 = 0.30$.

[c] Because of computation procedures, R^2 values are not comparable with those in Table 4.3. For care needed in interpretation, see footnote on p. 81.

**Significance level = 1 percent.

*Significance level = 5 percent.

†Significance level = 10 percent.

Source: Compiled by the authors.

86

it is not statistically significant and has no appreciable effect on other variables.

Equation 1c is identical to 1a except that nonlinear functional forms are fitted to CR_4, FG, MG, and MS. All variables are statistically significant at the 1 percent level except API, which is significant at the 10 percent level.

Because equation 1c is the most general and robust model, we shall examine briefly the relationship between the other independent variables and the profit-sales ratio. Firm growth is introduced in logarithmic form (LNFG); it has the expected positive sign and is highly significant. Market growth is introduced quadratically (MG^2); it is significant at the 1 percent level. Market size is introduced as a complete quadratic (MS, MS^2). For divisions in which average SMSA grocery store sales exceeded $1.7 billion, there is a positive relationship between profits and market size. As indicated previously, however, most markets have sales less than $1.7 billion.

The A&P company (APC) variable was included in the analysis to test the hypothesis that, other things remaining the same, A&P has a significantly poorer profit performance than other chains. It also permits identification of the impact of A&P's WEO program on its own profitability, as opposed to its impact on the profits of direct competitors of A&P. APC had the hypothesized negative sign and is statistically significant. [*]

The A&P impact (API) variable is marginally significant at the 10 percent level. This is consistent with our hypothesis that, on average, firms in competition with A&P have had higher profits in recent years.

The model shown in equation 1c is tested for individual years in equations 2-6. The results are generally consistent with those discussed above, although several of the variables behave in a significantly different manner in particular years.

WEO significantly depressed A&P's profits relative to those of its competitors. Although the coefficient of APC is negative in all years, it attains its lowest value in 1972, when the average A&P division profits were 2.32 percentage points lower than the profits of its average competitor.

---

[*]The coefficient on APC measures the average difference of A&P divisions from those of its competitors, not from all other firms in the sample. To obtain the latter, one must take the sum of the coefficients on the APC and API variables. Based upon equation 1c, for example, A&P's average division profit-sales ratio is 1.09 percentage points lower than those of its competitors and .74 percentage points (-1.090 + .347) less than those of companies with which it does not compete.

The A&P impact variable (API) generally performs as hypothesized. In 1970 and 1971 chains competing with A&P had significantly higher profits than those that did not. In 1972, however, they had lower profits, but the relationship was not statistically significant. In 1973 and 1974 chains competing with A&P again enjoyed higher profits, but the relationship was statistically significant only in 1973.

The most significant finding of the divisional profit multiple-regression analysis is that in equations 1a-1c, the two structural variables, RFMS and CR_4, have the expected positive signs. RFMS is statistically significant at the 1 percent level in all equations, and CR_4 is statistically significant at the 1 percent level when in a nonlinear form. This indicates that, when all other things remain the same, the higher a firm's RFMS and the higher the level of average CR_4 in the SMSA, within a division, the greater its divisional profits.

Divisional Profit Analysis: Controlling for A&P by Excluding A&P Divisions

There is little question that during 1970-74, A&P pursued unique sales and profit strategies. Under WEO its avowed purpose was to expand sales in order to recoup eroded market share. A&P apparently hoped its strategy of deep price cuts would regain its lost position. Insofar as this strategy resulted in a uniformly lower rate of profit for each A&P division, independent of market structure, the APC variable is an effective means of control. However, if A&P's offensive tactics were not independent of market structure, then the coefficients in Table 3.6 are biased. One way to control for this possibility is to drop the A&P observations from the sample. This was done in the equations displayed in Table 3.7. The complete model for the five-year average (equation 1c) is very similar to its counterpart, equation 1c, Table 3.6, which includes A&P observations and the binary control variable, APC. These results imply that APC is an effective control for A&P's unique strategies and that the long-run coefficients of Table 3.6 are unbiased.

Equation 1d provides an alternative means of isolating the impact of the WEO program and price controls by omitting 1972 and 1973 profit data. When profits are averaged for the three most "normal" years—1970, 1971, and 1974—the overall results are very similar to the five-year average results of equation 1c. The intercept value for the three-year model is larger, reflecting the higher profit levels during 1970, 1971, and 1974 than during 1972 and 1973. A&P is also found to have had a stronger positive influence on the profits of its competitors during the three "normal" years than during the entire five-year period. This is as expected.

TABLE 3.7

Multiple-Regression Equations Explaining Division Profit-Sales Ratios for 11 Companies, 68 Divisions, 1970-74

Dependent Variable, Profit-Sales Ratio (P/S)	Intercept	Relative Firm Market Share (RFMS)	4-Firm Concentration Ratio (CR₄)	Curvilinear 4-Firm Concentration Ratio (CCR₄)[a]	Firm Growth (FG)	Log Firm Growth (LNFG)	Market Growth (MG)	Market Growth Squared (MG²)	Market Size (MS)	Market Size Squared (MS²)	A&P Impact (API)	R²[b]	F-Value
1a. 1970-74 average	-2.706	0.067 (6.748)**	0.009 (0.705)		0.046 (8.072)**		0.034 (3.379)**		-0.192 (1.077)			.883	77.58**
1b. 1970-74 average	-8.194	0.054 (6.358)**		4.293 (3.187)**		1.491 (8.723)**		0.055 (4.047)**	-1.855 (3.214)**	0.511 (2.972)**		.925	108.13**
1c. 1970-74 average	-8.207	0.055 (6.499)**		3.934 (2.874)**		1.515 (8.867)**		0.060 (4.318)**	-1.898 (3.296)**	0.527 (3.070)**	0.296 (1.326)†	.929	97.48**
1d. 1970-71, 74 average	-6.930	0.052 (5.755)**		3.848 (2.644)**		1.316 (7.246)**		0.051 (3.314)**	-2.112 (3.498)**	0.567 (3.137)**	0.367 (1.508)†	.922	88.93**
2. 1970	-5.075	0.060 (5.146)**		2.195 (1.187)		1.108 (4.759)**		0.068 (3.242)**	-2.293 (2.999)**	0.686 (2.994)**	0.532 (1.647)†	.869	49.83**
3. 1971	-7.605	0.053 (4.739)**		5.310 (2.967)**		1.146 (5.118)**		0.051 (2.640)**	-2.385 (3.222)**	0.640 (2.884)**	0.360 (1.184)	.879	54.69**
4. 1972	-9.808	0.070 (6.691)**		4.039 (2.399)**		1.728 (8.223)**		0.072 (4.018)**	-1.739 (2.492)**	0.509 (2.434)**	-0.052 (0.184)	.872	51.05**
5. 1973	-8.059	0.048 (5.404)**		1.550 (1.117)		1.830 (9.907)**		0.082 (6.172)**	-1.208 (1.915)*	0.371 (2.010)*	0.456 (2.079)*	.923	89.60**
6. 1974	-7.173	0.045 (4.299)**		3.275 (1.979)*		1.637 (7.895)**		0.033 (1.826)†	-1.793 (2.262)*	0.404 (1.969)*	0.171 (0.603)	.892	61.99**

Notes: These are the same chains as those in equations in Table 3.6, except that A&P is not included. One-tailed t-tests were used in all cases. Figures in parentheses are t-values.

[a] $CCR_4 = (CR_4 + \alpha)^3/1 - 3(CR_4 + \alpha) + 3(CR_4 + \alpha)^2$. This function of CR_4 has positive slope and is symmetric about an inflection point. The inflection point of the curve occurs at the concentration ratio that satisfies the equation $CR_4 = 0.5 - \alpha$. For all equations in this table $\alpha = 0.20$, so the inflection point of the curve is $CR_4 = 0.30$.

[b] Because of computation procedures, R^2 values are not comparable with those in Table 4.3. For care needed in interpretation, see footnote on p. 81.

**Significance level = 1 percent.
*Significance level = 5 percent.
†Significance level = 10 percent.
Source: Compiled by the authors.

The annual equations demonstrate patterns similar to those in Table 3.6 for the coefficients of all variables except CCR_4. In Table 3.6, CCR_4 loses statistical significance in 1973 and 1974. When A&P divisions are excluded (Table 3.7), CCR_4 remains statistically significant in 1974 and approaches significance in 1973.

Table B.13 presents similar regression results for 28 A&P divisions and confirms what the above results suggest. During 1973 and 1974, four firm concentration has a negative and insignificant influence on the profits of 28 A&P divisions. The regression equations for these two years are not significant and explain only 27 to 30 percent of the variation in division profits. Regression equations for the three years 1970 to 1972 are highly significant and explain over 50 percent of the variation in A&P's profits. A marked change in A&P behavior obviously occurred during the last two years of the five year period studied.

Table B.14 summarizes the regression analysis of the profit-sales ratios of 50 divisions from 11 companies which competed directly with A&P. The results are generally similar to those in Tables 3.6 and 3.7.

The Structure-Profit Relationship

The results of the various analyses displayed in Tables 3.5-3.7 are generally the same. Most significantly, they confirm the prediction of industrial organization theory that a firm's profits are influenced by the competitive environment in which it operates. The nature of this relationship is illustrated in Table 3.8. This table displays the estimated relationship between pretax profit rates (measured as a percent of sales) and two structural variables, the relative firm market share (RFMS) of a chain in a market and the four leading retailers' share (CR_4) of that market. The estimated relationship is based on equation 1d of Table 3.7. This equation was selected because it reflected more "normal" conditions than those including 1972 and 1973, years when price controls and WEO depressed profits to abnormal levels.[*] Nonetheless, even for the years used in Table 3.8, average profits of chains were low compared with those of the 1960s.

The estimates in the table measure the extent to which divi-

_____

[*]The relationships shown in Table 3.8 would be essentially the same, however, if equations for 1970-74 had been used. The only significant difference is the slightly lower profits, resulting from the inclusion of 1972 and 1973. Using equation 1c, Table 3.6, the estimated profit rate for a chain with an RFMS of 25 operating in a market with a CR_4 of 40 would be 0.34 percentage points lower than the comparable figure shown in Table 3.8.

TABLE 3.8

Estimated Profit-Sales Ratios for Various Levels of Market
Concentration and Relative Firm Market Share
(average profits for 1970, 1971, and 1974)

Relative Firm Market Share (RFMS)	Four-Firm Concentration (CR_4)			
	40	50	60	70
	Pretax Profits as Percent of Sales			
10	.36	.96	1.18	1.23
25	1.14	1.74	1.96	2.01
40	1.92	2.52	2.74	2.79
55	2.70	3.30	3.52	3.57

Notes: All other independent variables, except MS^2 and API,
are introduced at their means. MS^2 was set equal to the mean of market size squared $(MS)^2$. The binary variable, API, was introduced at 1.
Source: Estimated using equation 1d, Table 3.7.

sional pretax profit rates of a chain vary, depending on its average
relative firm market share (RFMS) and the average four-firm concentration (CR_4) in the markets of the division. For example, if a
chain had an RFMS of 10 and operated in a market with a CR_4 of 40,
it would have an estimated profit rate of .36 percent of sales. On
the other hand, a chain with a RFMS of 55 in a market with a CR_4
of 70 would have enjoyed a profit rate of 3.57 percent of sales. The
effect of other combinations of RFMS and CR_4 is illustrated in the
table.

This analysis indicates that chains holding dominant market
positions in highly concentrated metropolitan areas enjoyed substantial profits even though profits were unusually low during this period.
The profits shown in Table 3.8 are expressed as a percentage of
sales before taxes. The relevant measure in evaluating profits of
firms in one industry relative to those in another is profits expressed
as a percentage of stockholders' investment. Pretax profits of 3.52
percent of sales (the highest shown in Table 3.8) translate to after-
tax profits of over 20 percent of stockholders' investment. This was
far above the average profits of all chains during 1970–74, and well
above the average of all but the most concentrated American industries.

NOTES

1. Joe S. Bain, Industrial Organization (New York: Wiley, 1968); F. M. Scherer, Industrial Market Structure and Economic Performance (Chicago: Rand McNally, 1971).

2. See, for example, Leonard Weiss, "Quantitative Studies of Industrial Organization," in M. D. Intriligator, ed., Frontiers of Quantitative Economics (Amsterdam: North Holland, 1970).

3. This point has been illustrated by comparing the results when employing grouped and ungrouped firm data used in George Stigler, "A Theory of Oligopoly," Journal of Political Economy 72 (February 1964): 44-61. Stigler correlated average profit rates of the leading firms in 17 industries with the level of four-firm concentration of these industries. This explained 28 percent of the variance in industry profit rates. However, when each of the firms used to compute his average profit rates is treated as a separate observation, only 4 percent of the explained variance in profits was explained by differences in market concentration. Reported in Federal Trade Commission, The Influence of Market Structure on the Profit Performance of Food Manufacturing Companies (Washington, D.C.: U.S. Government Printing Office, 1969), pp. 5-6.

4. "Convenience Stores," Progressive Grocer, vol. 4 (Summer 1976) as reported in Weekly Digest (Fair Lawn, N.J.: American Institute of Food Distribution, Sept. 18, 1976): 7.

5. "44th Annual Report of the Grocery Industry," Progressive Grocer 56, no. 4 (April 1977).

6. National Commission on Food Marketing, Organization and Competition in Food Retailing (Washington, D.C.: U.S. Government Printing Office, 1966), p. 149.

7. Ibid., pp. 181-83. These findings must be interpreted cautiously, however. High sales per square foot are easier to achieve when a firm has a strong market position and is able to expand sales faster than store capacity. Thus, increased market power may result in higher store utilization and its associated cost advantages.

8. Ibid., pp. 358-69.

9. "42nd Annual Report of the Grocery Industry," Progressive Grocer (April 1975): 59. Store numbers for the 17 chains are from company annual reports.

10. Chain and total food store sales are from Bureau of the Census, 1974 Annual Retail Trade Report (Washington, D.C.: U.S. Government Printing Office, December 1975), p. 3. These percent figures are slightly overstated because 5-10 percent of total company sales are not food sales.

11. "Banking Against A&P: Loans to Help Struggling Supermarket Chains," Time, December 11, 1972, p. 100.

12. Ibid.

13. Bain, Industrial Organization.

14. Estimates of 1972 firm market shares were based upon either company data supplied to the Joint Economic Committee or data from 1974 Grocery Distribution Guide (Wellesley Hills, Mass.: Metro Market Studies, 1974). Market share estimates based on company data were derived by computing the company's 1972 SMSA sales as a percentage of the 1972 Census Bureau total grocery store sales in each SMSA. In those SMSAs where no company data were available, firm market shares were estimated by multiplying the firm's market share (as reported in the 1974 Grocery Distribution Guide) by the ratio of the 1972 Census Bureau four-firm concentration ratio to the four-firm concentration ratio calculated from the 1974 Grocery Distribution Guide. The price analysis models used both 1972 and 1974 estimates of firm market shares. For estimation procedure, see Appendix B.

15. National Commission on Food Marketing, Technical Study no. 7, op. cit., p. 362.

16. Ibid., pp. 362-63.

17. Joe S. Bain, Barriers to New Competition (Cambridge, Mass.: Harvard University Press, 1956).

18. For other studies using this variable, see FTC, Economic Report on the Influence of Market Structure on Profit Performance of Food Manufacturing Companies (Washington, D.C.: U.S. Government Printing Office, 1969), pp. 10-11; B. Imel, M. Behr, and P. H. Helmberger, Market Structure and Performance (Lexington, Mass.: Lexington Books, 1972); John M. Connor and Willard F. Mueller, Market Power and Profitability of Multinational Corporations in Brazil and Mexico, report to the Subcommittee on Multinational Corporations of the Committee on Foreign Relations, U.S. Senate (Washington, D.C.: U.S. Government Printing Office, August 1976).

19. Bain, Industrial Organization, p. 204.

20. National Commission on Food Marketing, Technical Report no. 7, op. cit., pp. 155-57.

21. The variable was calculated with data for 1974 from Bureau of Labor Statistics, Retail Clerks International, and Amalgamated Meat Cutters and Butcher Workmen of North America. Meat cutter, grocery clerk, and checker wage rates were weighted by the percent that each category of labor represented of total labor expense in food retailing.

22. Joe S. Bain, "The Comparative Stability Market Structure," in Joe S. Bain, Essays on Price Theory and Industrial Organization (Boston: Little, Brown and Co., 1972). Insofar as this assumption

is not met, it tends to bias our results toward zero—that is, it makes our statistical findings appear weaker than they actually are.

23. Donald R. Marion, <u>Food Retailing in Low-Income Areas— An Economic Analysis</u>, Cooperative Extension Service Publication no. 100 (Amherst, Mass.: University of Massachusetts, June 1974), p. 44.

4

MARKET STRUCTURE-PRICE
PERFORMANCE RELATIONSHIPS

The preceding analysis of chain profits indicated that high market shares and concentrated markets tend to be associated with high levels of profit. These results suggest that high profits are due, at least in part, to higher prices. In this chapter the relationship between prices and market structure variables will be examined directly.

The Joint Economic Committee requested each of the 17 chains to supply any price comparison checks that had been conducted during October 1974. There was considerable variation in the quality and quantity of the data supplied in response to this request.

Three large chains—D, K, and H—provided quite complete grocery price data for 35 SMSAs in which one or more operated.[*] From these data 39 observations of the weighted average cost to consumers of a "grocery basket" composed of 94 comparable grocery products was calculated.[†] It also was possible to compute a more extensive "market basket" of 110 comparable frozen foods, dairy

---

[*]For purposes of this study, products included within the grocery product category were all products normally sold in a grocery store, excluding meat, produce, dairy products, frozen foods, and health and beauty aids. For a more detailed description of the product classes included in the grocery product group see Table B.2 and B.3.

[†]Of the 39 observations, 25 were for firm H, 10 were for firm K, and 4 were for firm D. Three distinct but similar grocery baskets were constructed for the three companies. Each grocery basket contained the same 94 grocery products; however, the frequency with which private-label prices were used in the calculations varied. For the firm H grocery baskets, 46 private labels were included, whereas 57 and 45 private-label prices were used in the firm K and firm D grocery baskets, respectively.

products, and grocery products for 22 SMSAs.* Because of the more limited number of "market basket" observations, the "grocery basket" observations were used in the market structure-price relationship analysis.† First, however, we will briefly review the pricing patterns found in the 22 SMSAs for which more complete "market baskets" were calculated.

PRICE PATTERN OF TWO LARGE CHAINS

The cost of a market basket of comparable products varied considerably from city to city for the two chains supplying such data. Tables 4.1 and 4.2 summarize the average costs to consumers for various product groups and for the combined groups. Information was available for three product groups for firm K and four for firm H. The average cost of the market basket of items in firm K stores ranged from $122.84 in city A to $141.14 in city B. The cost of the market basket in city A was 94 percent of the average for the seven cities studied; the cost in city B was 108 percent of this average.

The cost of a comparable market basket in firm H stores ranged from $124.40 in city D to $139.77 in city E, a difference of 12 percent. Although the variation from low to high cities was less for firm H, this company had an average market basket cost in 15 markets that was 1.7 percent higher than that of firm K in seven markets. The average cost of the grocery basket for each company differed by less than 1.0 percent.‡

---

*Two distinct but very similar market baskets were constructed for the two companies. The firm K market basket contained 110 products with 63 products price-checked with respect to both national brands and private labels, bringing the total number of items to 173. The firm H market basket included the same 110 products plus 17 health and beauty aids. For firm H, 56 products were price-checked for both national and private brands, bringing the total number of items to 183. Data were not available to estimate "market basket" average prices for firm D (see Table B.1).

†The terms "grocery basket cost" and "average grocery prices" are synonymous, in that each refers to the average retail price a consumer paid for the 94 products included in the grocery basket. They are used interchangeably throughout the remaining text.

‡The grocery basket for firm K included 57 private-label products, compared with 46 for firm H, suggesting a greater emphasis on lower-priced private labels in the firm K basket. However,

TABLE 4.1

Firm K: Major Group and Market Basket Totals Weighted by National-Brand/Private-Label and Expenditure Weights, Seven SMSAs, October 1974

SMSA	Frozen Food		Dairy		Grocery		Market Basket*	
	Wtd. $	Rank	Wtd. $	Rank	Wtd. $	Rank	Wtd. $	Rank
City B	$15.72	1	$25.00	2	$100.42	1	$141.14	1
City F	14.96	3	25.17	1	97.15	2	137.28	2
City G	15.31	2	23.94	3	95.33	3	134.58	3
City H	14.92	4	23.26	4	91.35	4	129.53	4
City I	14.18	5	21.31	7	91.01	5	126.50	5
City J	14.16	6	22.07	6	88.17	6	124.40	6
City A	13.82	7	22.75	5	86.27	7	122.84	7
Mean	$14.72		$23.36		$92.81		$130.90	
High market as percent of mean	107		108		108		108	
Low market as percent of mean	94		91		93		94	

* Weighted cost of frozen food, dairy, and grocery groups.

Source: Company data provided to the Joint Economic Committee.

TABLE 4.2

Firm H: Major Group and Market Basket Totals Weighted by National-Brand/Private-Label and Expenditure Weights, 15 SMSAs, October 1974

SMSA	Frozen Food		Dairy		Grocery		Market Basket*		Health and Beauty Aids		Market Basket with Health and Beauty Aids	
	Wtd. $	Rank	Wtd. $	Rank	Wtd. $	Rank	Wtd. $	Rank	Wtd. $	Rank	Wtd. $	Rank
City E	$15.80	2	$26.90	2	$97.07	1	$139.77	1	$17.50	2	$157.27	1
City K	15.21	11	23.31	3	95.46	2	133.98	6	16.69	3	150.67	5
City L	15.34	9	25.13	9	94.95	3	135.42	4	—		—	
City M	15.85	1	25.80	4	94.57	4	136.22	3	15.68	9	151.90	3
City N	15.68	3	27.71	1	94.23	5	137.62	2	17.58	1	155.20	2
City C	14.49	14	25.46	7	93.85	6	134.80	7	15.97	8	149.77	7
City O	15.63	4	25.59	6	93.64	7	134.86	5	16.65	4	151.51	4
City P	15.47	6	25.42	8	92.66	8	133.55	9	16.27	6	149.82	8
City Q	15.51	5	25.63	5	92.53	9	133.67	8	16.57	5	150.24	6
City R	14.74	13	24.57	11	92.28	10	131.59	10	15.21	11	146.80	9
City S	15.42	7	23.18	14	92.28	10	130.88	12	14.11	13	144.99	12
City T	14.49	14	24.87	10	92.20	12	131.56	11	—		—	
City U	15.42	7	22.37	15	92.20	12	129.99	14	16.15	7	146.14	10
City V	15.25	10	24.24	12	90.63	14	130.12	13	15.13	12	145.25	11
City D	15.13	12	23.30	13	85.97	15	124.40	15	15.38	10	139.78	13
Mean	$15.30		$24.90		$92.97		$133.16		$16.07		$149.18	
High market as percent of mean	104		111		104		105		109		105	
Low market as percent of mean	95		90		92		93		88		94	

*Weighted cost of frozen food, dairy, and grocery groups.

Source: Company data provided to the Joint Economic Committee.

STRUCTURE-PRICE RELATIONSHIPS
FOR THREE LARGE CHAINS

Economic theory predicts that prices charged by firms depend
in part on the competitive environment in which they operate. Numerous short-run factors, however, may influence the prices of a particular food chain in a particular city in a particular month. As
explained earlier, a useful statistical procedure to reduce such
random price variability is to average observations for longer periods
of time. In the preceding structure-profit analysis it was possible to
use annual and five-year average profit data. This was not possible
in the analysis of price data. Therefore, an analysis relying on
prices in a single month may be expected to yield weaker statistical
relationships than if it had been possible to use average prices for
a longer time period.

Multiple-regression analysis was used to examine the relationships between market structure variables and "grocery basket" costs
while controlling for other market characteristics. In addition to the
cost observations for two firms in 21 SMSAs listed in Tables 4.1 and
4.2, another 15 observations in which only the "grocery basket" cost
could be calculated were included in the analysis.* (See Table B.4.)

---

because of differences in the private-label items included in the two
baskets, private-label products received 14.2 percent of the grocery
basket weights for firm K and 13.6 percent of the weights for firm H.
This difference is estimated to bias the grocery basket costs for
firm K downward by 0.06 percent.

When only the national brands for the 94 products in the grocery
basket were used, the average cost was $94.39 in firm K stores and
$93.77 in firm H stores.

*Three SMSAs for which the cost of the grocery basket was
calculated were dropped from the sample. In the cases of city G
(Table 4.2) and city X, the data available to estimate RFMS and CR_4
for 1972 and 1974 were judged highly unreliable. City Y was dropped
because of reservations about the accuracy of the market structure
data and because it was an extreme outlier in the regression analysis
(standardized residual of -2.76). When city Y was included as an
observation in equation 1b, Table 4.3, the results were as follows:

$$NPC = 89.48 + 7.172 \, RFMS + 18.774 \, CR_4 - .007 \, SS - .440 \, MR - .071 \, MG$$
$$(2.679)^{**} \quad (5.161)^{**} \quad (-3.328) (-4.161)^{**}(-3.177)^{**}$$

$$\bar{R}^2 = .60$$
$$F\text{-ratio} = 11.74^{**}$$

The models and independent variables used in the analysis of pricing performance are similar to those used in examining profits.* The basic model employed was

$$C = B_0 + B_1 RFMS = B_2 CR_4 + B_3 SS + B_4 MR + B_5 MG + B_6 MS + B_7 WR + \epsilon$$

Hypothesis:
$$B_1 > 0 \qquad B_2 > 0 \quad B_3 < 0 \quad B_4 < 0 \quad B_5 \neq 0 \quad B_6 \neq 0 \quad B_7 > 0$$

where

C = the weighted cost of a grocery basket consisting of either national-brand and private-label items (NPC) or national-brand items only (NC)

$RFMS$ = relative firm market share in 1974—a curvilinear form of this variable (CRFMS) was also employed in some models

CR_4 = grocery store four-firm concentration ratio in 1974—a curvilinear form of this variable (CCR_4) was used in several models

SS = 1972 mean store size in each SMSA, measured in dollars of sales per grocery store

MR = market rivalry, measured as the absolute change between 1972 and 1974 in the combined market share of the four leading firms of 1974†

MG = percentage growth in SMSA grocery sales between 1967 and 1974

MS = 1974 SMSA size (dollar grocery store sales)

Without the city Y observation, model 1b had somewhat lower regression coefficients on RFMS and CR_4 and the overall significance of the model was increased (see Table 4.3). Analysis of the residuals suggested that the city Y observation probably resulted in the partial regression coefficients for RFMS and CR_4 being overstated.

*Price-structure models that included firm growth (FG) as an independent variable were specified. While firm growth was found to be highly significant in the profit models, price and firm growth were not found to be significantly related. The entry variable (E) was not specified in a price model because of inapplicability. Market rivalry (MR), which was highly significant in the price models, was not found to be statistically significant when incorporated into a profit model.

†There were two possible ways of calculating the market rivalry values used in the regression analysis. Mathematically, these were the following:

WR = weighted average of 1974 union wage rates for meat cutters, grocery clerks, and checkers in each SMSA

ϵ = disturbance term.

Although most of the analysis used this model, an alternative model employed supermarket structural variables in lieu of grocery store CR_4 and RFMS. Since, as indicated earlier, the supermarket submarket is the more relevant market within which to examine supermarket chain competition, measures of concentration and relative firm market share within the supermarket submarket are expected to be the preferred indicators of chain market power. However, measures of supermarket CR_4 and RFMS were available for 1972 only, whereas the grocery store structural variables were also available for 1974, the same year as the price data. Table 4.3 summarizes the regression analysis, using 1974 grocery store structural

$$(1) \qquad MR_1 = \left| \sum_{i=1}^{4} x_{ij} - \sum x_{ij-2} \right|$$

$$(2) \qquad MR_2 = \sum_{i=1}^{4} \left| x_{ij} - x_{ij-2} \right|$$

where

x_{ij} = the market share for firm i in year j

i = 1, 2, 4, ranked according to greatest market share in 1974

j = 1974, 1973, ...

Equation (1) was used in calculating market rivalry for purposes of this study. This method yields the aggregate absolute net change from 1972 to 1974 in the combined market shares of the four leading firms in 1974. As used in the regression analysis, MR carries no sign. An increase in the market shares of the four leading firms is assumed to reflect a degree of rivalry in the market similar to that for a decline in market shares.

Equation (2), while similar, sums the absolute changes in market share of each of the four leading firms of 1974 from 1972 through 1974. While this may be a superior measure of market rivalry, it requires a level of precision for estimates of individual firm market shares beyond the scope of the available data.

TABLE 4.3

Multiple-Regression Equations Explaining Cost of a Grocery Basket of Three Chains in 36 SMSAs, 1974

Equation Number/ Dependent Variable[a]	Intercept	Relative Firm Market Share (RFMS)	Curvilinear Relative Firm Market Share (CRFMS)[b]	Four-Firm Concentration (CR4)	Curvilinear Four-Firm Concentration (CCR4)[b]	Mean Store Size (SS)	Market Rivalry (MR)	Market Growth (MG)	Market Size (MS)	Union Wage Rate (WR)	R^2	F-Value
1a. NPC	91.05	10.284 (3.475)**		11.957 (2.796)**		-.007 (-3.141)**		-.062 (-2.405)*			.38	6.30**
1b. NPC	90.67	6.582 (2.882)**		15.645 (4.864)**		-.006 (-3.148)**	-.475 (-5.247)**	-.078 (4.067)**			.66	14.87**
1c. NPC	90.67	6.449 (2.714)**		15.259 (4.249)**		-.005 (-1.931)*	-.485 (-4.875)**	-.078 (-3.975)**	-.158 (-.259)		.65	12.02**
1d. NPC	89.93	5.025 (2.130)*		11.121 (3.694)**			-.562 (-5.917)**	-.066 (-3.400)**	-1.019 (-2.333)*		.62	12.53**
1e. NPC	87.00	6.259 (2.752)**		16.074 (4.644)**		-.005 (-1.781)*	-.518 (-4.724)**	-.082 (-4.110)**	-.214 (-.356)	.591 (.572)	.69	11.89**
1f. NPC	77.36	9.539 (3.318)**		14.976 (3.267)**		-.012 (-3.780)**		-.056 (-2.191)*	1.017 (1.418)	2.663 (2.142)*	.46	5.76**
1g. NPC	90.17	6.575 (2.837)**			7.904 (4.436)**	-.005 (-1.828)*	-.486 (-4.360)**	-.076 (-3.798)**	-.309 (-.510)	1.174 (1.109)	.68	11.27**
1h. NPC	91.66		3.287 (3.019)**		7.597 (4.315)**	-.005 (-1.854)*	-.486 (-4.444)**	-.076 (-3.849)**	-.280 (-.468)	1.034 (.988)	.69	11.73**
2e. NC	86.70	6.441 (2.873)**		15.517 (4.549)**		-.004 (-1.341)†	-.553 (-5.124)†	-.074 (-3.720)**	-.006 (-.011)	.670 (.658)	.71	12.61**
2h. NC	91.31		3.399 (3.213)**		7.408 (4.331)**	-.004 (-1.479)†	-.522 (-4.913)**	-.067 (-3.525)**	-.053 (-.092)	1.092 (1.075)	.71	12.93**

Notes: Figures in parentheses are t-values. The statistical significance of the regression coefficients for RFMS, CRFMS, CR4, SS, MR, and WR was tested by means of a one-tailed t-test; MG and MS were tested by means of a two-tailed t-test. The adjusted coefficients of multiple determination were tested by means of F-ratio.

[a]The dependent variable (NPC) in equations 1a-1h is the cost of a grocery basket of national-brand and private-label products. The dependent variable (NC) in equations 2e and 2h is the cost of a grocery basket of only national-brand products. Equations 1a-1d have 36 observations, equations 1e-1h have 35 observations (one observation was omitted for lack of union wage data).

[b]CRFMS and CCR4 = $(x + \sigma)^3 / (1 - 3(x + \sigma) + 3(x + \sigma)^2)$, where x equals RFMS or CR4. Values for each variable were expressed in decimals between 0 and 1. The function of CRFMS and CCR4 has a positive slope and is symmetric about an inflection point. The inflection point occurs at the point that satisfies the equation I = .5 - σ, where I equals the inflection point. For CRFMS, the inflection point for each of the above equations was .35 (that is, σ = .15). For CCR4, the inflection point for each of the above equations was .63 (that is, σ = -.13).

**Significance level = 1 percent.
*Significance level = 5 percent.
†Significance level = 10 percent.
Source: Compiled by the authors.

variables.* (Table 4.4 compares the regression results using 1972 grocery store structural variables with the results realized using 1972 supermarket structural variables.)

---

*Separate regression models were fitted, using estimates of RFMS and CR_4 for 1972 and 1974. The method used for estimating 1974 structural values was similar to that employed in estimating the 1972 observations. For a more detailed explanation see Appendix B. The equations using the 1972 market structure variables appear in Table B.9. The results are essentially the same as those reported in Table 4.3.

As discussed in Appendix B, 23 of the 36 firm market shares for 1972 were based upon "hard" data provided by the firms; the remaining 13 market shares were estimated using the 1974 edition of the Grocery Distribution Guide, Metro Market Studies. Regression equations were estimated using only the 23 observations for which "hard" data were available. The results for equation 1d, Table B.9, werc as follows:

$NPC =$

$$89.68 + 4.636\,RFMS + 18.216\,CR_4 - .001\,SS - .134\,MG - 1.357\,MS - .520\,MR$$
$$(2.039)^* \qquad (4.110)^{**} \quad (-0.576)\ (-4.553)^{**}(-1.807)+\ (-4.210)^{**}$$

$$\bar{R}^2 = .73$$
$$F\text{-ratio} = 10.95^{**}$$

The structure-price relationships found were similar using either the 23 "hard" observations or all 36 observations. For an additional discussion of the method employed in estimating firm market shares see Appendix B.

Three additional independent variables were considered in the regression analysis. The first, firm market share (FMS) was used as an alternative to relative firm market share (RFMS) as a measure of firm power. Relative firm market share is believed to be superior because of the collinearity between FMS and CR_4. An equation replacing RFMS with FMS resulted in a statistically significant model. Although the R^2 was slightly lower, all the variables were statistically significant at the 5 percent level or higher.

The second and third independent variables were binary variables specified and tested to determine if company differences accounted for some of the variation in the dependent variable. These variables were found not to be statistically significant.

In the regression results presented in Table 4.3, two measures of the cost of grocery items were employed as dependent variables: NPC, the cost of a grocery basket composed of both national-brand and private-label items (equations 1a-1h); and NC, the cost of a grocery basket composed only of national-brand items (equations 2e and 2h).

Additional independent variables are progressively included in the model as one moves from equation 1a to 1e. The addition of the market rivalry variable in equation 1b nearly doubles the explanatory power of the model and substantially increases the significance of CR_4 and MG in explaining price variations across SMSAs.

Equations 1g, 1h, and 2h include curvilinear forms of CR_4 and/or RFMS. Comparing models 1g and 1e, including CCR_4 rather than CR_4 has very little effect on results. Unlike the profit models, the inclusion of CCR_4 does not strengthen the explanatory power of market concentration.

Equations 1h and 2h include the curvilinear forms of both four-firm concentration (CCR_4) and relative firm market share (CRFMS). Overall, these are similar to the best linear models (1e and 2e). In comparing the e and h models, the main difference is the tradeoff in significance of relative firm market share and four-firm concentration. Neither model is superior on statistical grounds. However, the h models are more consistent with theoretical expectations.

Figure 4.1 indicates the relationship between grocery prices and four-firm concentration, on the basis of equation 1h. Although the number of observations at extreme levels of concentration was limited (which may explain why linear models performed as well as curvilinear models did), Figure 4.1 suggests that prices level off at CR_4 levels below 40 and at very high levels of concentration (CR_4 of 90 or above). This is consistent with theoretical expectations.

Except for MS and WR, the independent variables shown in Table 4.3 are statistically significant and have the hypothesized signs in all equations. Of particular importance is the consistent positive and significant relationship of the market structure variables (RFMS and CR_4) to grocery prices. These results indicate that RFMS and CR_4 exercise an independent positive influence on grocery prices.

Mean store size (SS) has the expected negative relationship to prices. This variable was included in the analysis because large chains compete primarily with other supermarkets rather than convenience or small mom-and-pop stores. The CR_4 values used in the analysis are computed with universe figures that include small stores

---

*Receipt of Census Bureau-tabulated SMSA supermarket sales and supermarket concentration ratios (SCR_4) allowed a test of whether a

FIGURE 4.1

Empirical Relationship between Grocery Prices
and SMSA Grocery Store Concentration

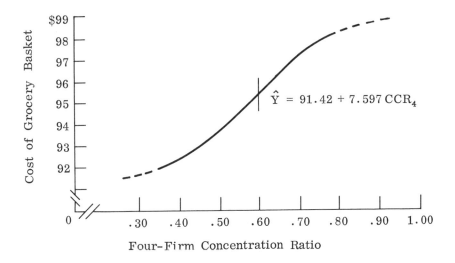

Source: Table 4.3, equation 1h.

as well as supermarkets. SS provides a partial correction of CR_4 as
a proxy for supermarket concentration. The negative relationship
between SS and prices reinforces the positive relationship between
CR_4 and prices.

---

linear combination CR_4 and SS provided a better indicator of SMSA
supermarket concentration than CR_4 alone did. Using a sample of
251 observations, SCR_4 was regressed on CR_4 and SS with the
following result:

$$SCR_4 = 20.751 + 1.223\,CR_4 - 25.19\,SS$$
$$(44.297)^{**} \quad (-18.553)^{**}$$

$$\bar{R}^2 = .89$$
$$F\text{-Value} = 99.74^{**}$$

The results indicate that both CR_4 and SS are significantly related

MR has the predicted negative sign and is highly significant in all equations in which it was included. This means that when other variables are held constant, prices are lowest in markets where firm rivalry is most intense, as measured by changes in the market share of the four leading firms of 1974. The inclusion of this variable nearly doubles the t-values for CR_4 and MG, and substantially alters the coefficients on RFMS and CR_4. When market rivalry is dropped from the full equation (equation 1f), the remaining six independent variables are strongly affected.[*]

MG is negatively related to prices in all equations. That is, other variables held constant, chains tended to have lower prices in rapidly growing markets than in slowly growing markets. Since the profit equations found a statistically significant positive relationship between market growth and firm profits, the price and profit analyses appear to be in conflict. However, if operating expenses per dollar of sales decline significantly in growing markets, chains may pass on at least part of this savings through lower prices, in order to maintain or enhance their market share, and still realize higher profits per dollar of sales.

MS generally was not significantly related to grocery prices. Because of the collinearity between SS and MS ($r = .60$), the relationship of these variables to grocery prices is muted when both of them are included in the model. When SS is excluded in equation 1d, MS has a significant negative relationship to grocery prices. However, on theoretical and statistical grounds, both variables should be included in the model.[†]

WR is included in the last six equations in Table 4.3. Although WR has the hypothesized positive relationship to grocery prices, it

---

to supermarket concentration. Their inclusion provides a better estimate of SCR_4 than CR_4 did alone.

[*]Examination of equations 1e and 1f suggests a fairly high degree of collinearity among the independent variables included in the model. The presence of collinearity does not, however, result in biased parameter estimates, nor does it invalidate any of the statistical tests of hypotheses. More important, exclusion of relevant explanatory variables may result in biased parameter estimates. Since we favor unbiasedness and possible inefficient variance estimates, equations 1e and 1h are preferred. See Jan Kmenta, Elements of Econometrics (New York: Macmillan, 1971), pp. 380-99.

[†]The MS and SS are strongly affected by one observation, Los Angeles. When Los Angeles is omitted from the sample, equation 1e in Table 4.3 produces the following results:

is statistically significant only in equation 1f, which excludes MR.
Given the importance of labor costs in the total operating expenses
of food retailers, the lack of significance of WR is an important and
somewhat surprising finding. WR is collinear with SS. Both are
larger in the West and smaller in the South. However, even when
SS was omitted from the model (results not shown), WR was not significantly related to grocery prices.

Equations 2e and 2h include the same independent variables as
equations 1e and 1h, but use as the dependent variable a grocery
basket consisting solely of national-brand products (NC). Use of a
national-brand grocery basket does not change the results significantly. These results indicate that the inclusion of private-label
products in the grocery basket had little effect on the statistical
findings, and did not introduce a bias into the results.

Most of the models explain about two-thirds of the variation in
grocery basket costs in the sample SMSAs. Given the nature of the
task undertaken and the data available, the regression results should
be viewed with considerable confidence.

RESULTS USING SUPERMARKET STRUCTURAL DATA

We have argued that the supermarket submarket is the relevant
product market within which to examine the competitive performance
of the large grocery chains. In this section, regression results using
1972 supermarket structural variables will be compared with results

---

$$NPC = 90.15 + 5.650 \, RFMS + 13.686 \, CR_4 - .003 \, SS - .541 \, MR$$
$$\underset{(2.586)^{**}}{} \quad \underset{(3.907)^{**}}{} \quad \underset{(-1.276)}{} \quad \underset{(-5.159)^{**}}{}$$

$$- .080 \, MG + .802 \, MS + .009 \, WR$$
$$\underset{(-4.173)^{**}}{} \quad \underset{(1.043)}{} \quad \underset{(.009)}{}$$

$$\bar{R}^2 = .70$$
$$F\text{-value} = 12.11^{**}$$

We had no valid grounds for omitting Los Angeles from the sample.
Indeed, since it is one of the few SMSAs with CR_4 less than 40 percent and is the largest SMSA in the sample, it adds to the range of
competititve situations included in the sample. Since the regression
coefficients on the structural variables are lower when Los Angeles
is omitted, the use of this equation for computing monopoly overcharge would lead to lower estimates.

using 1972 grocery store structural variables. The basic model employed in this analysis had the same basis as that in the 1974 analysis presented in Table 4.3, except that WR was omitted to simplify the comparison.

Table 4.4 presents three comparable equations using the two measures of market structure. The equations using supermarket RFMS and CR_4 have somewhat higher t-values on the structural variables and explain a higher proportion of the variation in prices. The t-values on the other independent variables also are generally higher.

Since SS was included in models 1b and 1c to adjust for CR_4 being an imperfect proxy for SCR_4, this variable was expected to be insignificant when included in the supermarket equations. The results of equation 2b are consistent with this expectation. Although significant in equation 1b, SS becomes insignificant in equation 2b.

Although the differences in the equations using grocery store and supermarket structural variables are relatively minor, the results support the contention that supermarket structural measures are better indicators of the competitive environment faced by large supermarket chains than are grocery store structural measures. However, because grocery store structural measures were also available for 1974, the same year as the price data, and were also employed in the profit analysis, the remainder of our analysis will use grocery store structural measures. *

LIMITATIONS OF REGRESSION RESULTS

We emphasize that the estimates and interpretations of the preceding regression analyses are necessarily influenced by the nature and quality of the data used in making them. One possible source of error is that the price comparison data were available for only one month. We have no reason to believe this biases the results upward or downward. It may lower the level of statistical significance of the analysis because short-term random factors cannot be reduced by the averaging process possible when information is available for longer periods. Therefore, the reported results may well understate the level of statistical significance of our findings.

---

*Supermarket four-firm concentration (SCR_4) was received from a special Census Bureau tabulation after completion of the report for the Joint Economic Committee. Because SCR_4 was available for fewer SMSAs than CR_4 was, and because of the considerable time required to develop these measures for the profit models, a comparison of the results was made only for the price model.

TABLE 4.4

Comparison of Market Structure-Grocery Price Regressions Using Grocery Store and Supermarket Structural Measures, 36 SMSAS, 1972

Equation Number Dependent Variable	Intercept	Grocery Store Relative Firm Market Share (RFMS) / Supermarket Relative Firm Market Share (SRFMS)	Grocery Store Four-Firm Concentration (CR$_4$) / Supermarket Four-Firm Concentration (SCR$_4$)	Mean Store Size (SS)	Market Rivalry (MR)	Market Growth (MG)	Market Size (MS)	R^2	F-Value
1a. NPC	89.28	4.038 (1.692)†	12.932 (3.393)**		-0.433 (-4.612)**	-0.088 (-2.808)**		.55	11.57**
1b. NPC	90.45	5.627 (2.417)*	16.662 (4.275)**	-0.004 (-2.351)*	-0.351 (-3.725)**	-0.108 (-3.542)**		.60	11.72**
1c. NPC	89.71	5.032 (2.178)*	15.954 (3.881)**	-0.002 (-0.592)	-0.441 (-4.127)**	-0.114 (-3.791)**	-0.998 (-1.262)	.63	10.66**
2a. NPC	87.37	4.458 (2.029)*	13.321 (4.173)**		-0.394 (-4.236)**	-0.120 (-3.703)**		.62	14.07**
2b. NPC	88.16	5.114 (2.156)*	13.407 (4.167)**	-0.001 (-0.768)	-0.370 (-3.758)**	-0.123 (-3.734)**		.61	11.21**
2c. NPC	88.74	4.977 (2.332)*	12.299 (3.937)**		-0.420 (-4.634)**	-0.130 (-4.088)**	-1.031 (-1.798)†	.65	12.80**

Notes: Figures in parentheses are t-values. The statistical significance of the regression coefficients for RFMS, CR$_4$, SRFMS, SCR$_4$, SS, and MR was tested by means of a one-tailed t-test; MG and MS were tested by means of a two-tailed t-test. The adjusted coefficients of multiple determination were tested by means of F-ratio. The dependent variable (NPC) is the cost of a grocery basket of national-brand and private-label products.

**Significance level = 1 percent.
*Significance level = 5 percent.
†Significance level = 10 percent.
Source: Compiled by the authors.

109

Another possible source of error is that the regression analysis was based solely on a basket of grocery products. However, prices for items in this product grouping were closely correlated with prices for a basket that also included dairy products, frozen food, and health and beauty aids. Prices for meat and produce items were not included in the larger market basket because of the lack of comparable data. Although we acknowledge the importance of meat and produce prices, quality and service differences in these departments present serious problems in comparing prices—both for consumers and for researchers.

A third possible source of error is that the items checked were considered by the sample chains to be the most price-sensitive or "competitive," and therefore were not representative of nonchecked items. However, since the grocery products included in our grocery basket are directly comparable from one store to another, we expect that these are the products on which retailers have the least pricing discretion. There is no a priori reason for believing that if a firm could elevate prices for the checked items in noncompetitive markets, it could not raise other prices as well. If anything, the bias in our product sample would be expected to understate the price differences between monopolistic and competitive markets.

Finally, the results are based upon the pricing behavior of only three chains in 32 different SMSAs. The firms and metropolitan areas included in the analysis were selected because of data availability, not because of their representativeness. However, we also have no reason to suspect that either the firms or the markets are atypical. Within the ranks of the 17 large chains in this study, the three firms included in our price analysis represent a reasonable cross section in terms of profitability, growth, and average firm market share. Table 4.5 compares the distribution of market shares of the three firms in the price analysis with the distribution of market shares for all 17 chains; the two distributions are very similar.

The 32 SMSAs in the price analysis had a weighted mean CR_4 of 48.8 for 1972; this compares with 49.6 for the 263 SMSAs included in the 1972 census. * The number of markets (32) is also sufficient to perform valid statistical tests of price differences. All in all, while caution is warranted in interpreting the results, we have no grounds for believing that our results are atypical. †

---

*The unweighted mean CR_4 for the 32 sample SMSAs in 1972 was 49.1, compared with 53.3 for all 263 SMSAs, indicating a somewhat larger portion of small SMSAs with high CR_4s in the latter group.

†Unfortunately, there have been no comparable studies of food retail prices. Previous pricing studies generally have been less

TABLE 4.5

Distribution of Market Shares for Three Firms in Price Analysis and
All Chains in Study

Percent Market Share	All Chains		Three Sample Firms	
	No. of SMSAs	Percent	No. of SMSAs	Percent
0-4.9	102	24.3	37	27.4
5-9.9	123	29.4	29	21.5
10-14.9	91	21.7	21	15.5
15-19.9	53	12.6	21	15.5
20-24.9	25	6.0	14	10.4
25 and over	25	6.0	13	9.6
Total	412	100.0	135	99.9

Source: Company data provided to the Joint Economic Committee.

RELEVANCE OF COST AND INCOME VARIABLES TO
PRICE MODEL

The absence in our models of variables measuring certain retail
costs and consumer demand may cause some economists to conclude
that our model is misspecified. Although we were unable to explore
fully the effects of various cost differences because of inadequate data,

---

comprehensive and often have employed questionable methodology.
Studies by H. Mori and W. Gorman, the National Commission on
Food Marketing, and B. Mallen are critiqued in the JEC hearing
record on our study, Joint Economic Committee, Hearings on Prices
and Profits of Leading Retail Food Chains, 1970-74, March 30 and
April 5, 1977 (Washington, D.C.: U.S. Government Printing Office,
1977), pp. 94-96. For an analysis of studies using Bureau of Labor
Statistics food price data, see F. Geithman and B. Marion, "A
Critique of the Use of BLS Data for Market Structure-Price Analysis,"
American Journal of Agricultural Economics 60 (November 1978):
701-05.

there are important reasons for expecting they would contribute little to our results.

Differences in retail costs would logically be expected to affect retail prices. Cost of goods sold, labor costs, transportation costs, and occupancy expense are some of the important retail costs that may vary across metropolitan areas. Differences in retailers' cost of merchandise in different cities may exist for locally produced goods (such as, milk, bread, ice cream, some fresh produce), or result from transportation cost differences for regionally and nationally produced goods. No locally produced items were included in our grocery basket. A crude proxy for transportation costs—the distance of each SMSA from Manhattan, Kansas, the geographic center of agricultural production in the United States—was tested in the price models; the variable was not statistically significant and had little effect on the regression results.

Because labor costs constitute nearly 60 percent of the operating expenses of food retailers, a positive relationship to prices was hypothesized. Two variables were used to measure labor costs—union wage rates (Table 4.3) and the payroll cost of leading firms as a percent of their sales in each SMSA. Payroll data were provided by a special Census Bureau tabulation of food retailing. The two variables were highly correlated, as expected ($r = .71$). When included in the price models, neither variable was statistically significant. They also had little effect on the other variables in the models.

Although we have not exhuasted the possible influence of operating costs, the evidence to date suggests that differences in nondiscretionary costs do not account for the price differences found. If operating costs were expected to be related to CR_4 or RFMS, our regression results would be more subject to challenge. However, there is no a priori basis for expecting wage rates, transportation costs, occupancy expense, or cost of merchandise to be related to market concentration or the market position of chains. These costs would be expected to be influenced by size of city and geographic region. However, size of city was found to be negatively related to prices. If costs are higher in larger cities, a positive relationship would be expected.

Possible regional differences in prices were examined by adding regional dummy variables to the models. Some apparent regional differences (southern SMSAs high in price and western SMSAs low relative to the rest of the country) proved not to be significant when SS was included in the models.

Thus, our analysis to this point indicates no significant relationship between grocery prices and the cost of important inputs to food retailing. We were not able to examine discretionary costs, such as advertising, or intentional development of excess capacity to deter entry; nor have we considered the efficiency with which resources

were used. These factors may result in higher retail costs in noncompetitive markets, but they are discretionary costs under the control
of retail managers. For this reason it is important to distinguish these
cost-influencing factors from wage rates, cost of merchandise, and
other items over which retailers have limited control.

Because measures of income are often included in commodity
demand models, the absence of a consumer-income variable may concern some economists. Could differences in consumer income in different metropolitan areas account for some of the difference in grocery prices?

Across SMSAs, differences in consumer income may influence
the total quantity of food consumed, but are most likely to affect the
mix of products purchased. Wealthy individuals purchase a higher percentage of expensive meat cuts and other goods. However, the wholesale prices of nearly all products sold through grocery stores are
established in regional or national markets—not in local markets. For
the grocery products included in our grocery basket, wholesale prices
are determined largely in national markets. Thus, consumer income
in different SMSAs is expected to have no influence on the wholesale
price of Maxwell House coffee or Del Monte peaches. Since the cost
of grocery products to retailers in an SMSA is not affected by the income of consumers in that SMSA, there is no a priori reason to expect that income will affect retail prices, given similar competitive
conditions.

A study by newspaper food editors of food prices in 19 cities
provides some support for the market basket indexes used in our analysis. Although the sample of products and SMSAs and the analytical
procedures used by the food editors were more limited than ours, the
results are of interest. Only five SMSAs were the same in both studies.
However, the relative prices in those five cities were remarkably
similar in the two studies, with one exception. Expressed as a percent of Phoenix, the lowest-price city in both studies, the prices were
as shown below.

City	JEC Oct. 1974	Food Editors June 1977	Difference
Phoenix	100. 0	100. 0	
Dallas	107. 4	107. 3	0. 1
St. Louis	108. 8	107. 9	0. 9
Denver	105. 5	109. 3	3. 8
Washington, D. C.	116. 4	116. 8	0. 4

Of the five cities included in both studies, Washington and Phoenix had the highest and lowest prices in both cases, differing by about

16 percent in 1974 and 1977. The relative prices for Dallas and St. Louis also were very close in the two studies. The only substantive change in relative prices occurred in Denver, where prices were 3.8 percent higher (relative to Phoenix) in June 1977 than in October 1974. This is particularly interesting because Denver was a large outlier in our analysis. On the basis of the high level of concentration and relative dominance of the leading firms in Denver, our statistical analysis predicted higher prices in Denver than actually existed in October 1974. The prices found by the food editors in June 1977 were much more in line with our predicted prices for Denver, suggesting that our 1974 prices may have been temporarily depressed by short-term price rivalry in the market. Had we used a price for Denver comparable with that found in June 1977, our regression results would have been even stronger. This finding supports our contention that any errors in our analysis that are due to prices being temporarily out of line during October 1974 would weaken the relationships found. (See Appendix C for the full report on the food editors' study.)

ESTIMATED STRUCTURE-PRICE RELATIONSHIPS

Despite the qualifications made above, the findings of the regression analysis lend considerable support to the structure-profit relationships identified in Chapter 3. The structure-price relationships strongly suggest that the higher observed profits are due, at least in part, to the higher prices that chains are able to charge in less competitively structured markets.

Table 3.8 presented the profits estimated by the regression model for various combinations of RFMS and CR_4 when all other variables are held constant. Table 4.6 is a similar table, with the costs of grocery baskets predicted by equation 1h, Table 4.3. The figures in parentheses represent the percentage change in grocery basket cost from the RFMS of 10 percent and CR_4 of 40 percent.

These estimates indicate that firm grocery store prices rise significantly as CR_4 increases. A chain with an RFMS of 10 operating in a market with a CR_4 of 70 would have prices an estimated 5.4 percent higher than a chain with a RFMS of 10 in a market with a CR_4 of 40. Similarly, a chain's prices rise as its RFMS rises. The chain with a RFMS of 55 in a market with a CR_4 of 40 would have estimated prices 3.2 percent higher than a chain in the same market with a RFMS of 10.

Prices would be highest, of course, for the chain that had a high RFMS and operated in a market with a very high CR_4. The chain with a RFMS of 55 in a market with a CR_4 of 70 would have estimated prices 8.6 percent higher than the chain with a RFMS of 10 in a market with a CR_4 of 40.

TABLE 4.6

Estimated Costs of Grocery Baskets for Different Combinations of
Relative Market Share and Four-Firm Concentration, October 1974

Relative Firm Market Share	Four-Firm Concentration			
	40	50	60	70
	Cost and Percentage Change			
10	$90.97	$91.88	$93.72	$95.91
	(0%)	(1.0%)	(3.0%)	(5.4%)
25	91.60	92.51	94.35	96.54
	(0.7%)	(1.7%)	(3.7%)	(6.1%)
40	92.97	93.88	95.72	97.91
	(2.2%)	(3.2%)	(5.2%)	(7.6%)
55	93.90	94.81	96.65	98.84
	(3.2%)	(4.2%)	(6.2%)	(8.6%)

Notes: The cost of a grocery basket at various levels of RFMS
and CR_4 was estimated using equation 1h, Table 4.3, when all other
variables were introduced at their mean values. Percentage changes
were calculated from the base of $90.97 and are shown in parentheses
under the estimated grocery basket costs.
Source: Compiled by the authors.

The wide differences in estimated prices suggest that profits
also would vary substantially among markets. The relationship between prices and profits is discussed in Chapter 5.

PRICING OF NATIONAL-BRAND AND PRIVATE-LABEL
PRODUCTS

The higher grocery prices in more concentrated markets revealed by the preceding analysis may be due to higher prices on national-brand grocery products, private-label products, or both. In
this section the pricing patterns on national-brand and private-label
products will be examined to compare the pricing strategies employed
by the three chains across markets and to determine how national-
brand/private-label pricing has changed over time.

The National Commission on Food Marketing stimulated interest in the pricing of comparable national (or advertised) brands and private-label (or store-brand) products. On the basis of a sample of ten products, the commission reported that, on average, advertised brands were priced 21. 5 percent higher than private-label items. [1]

In the present study it was possible to compare the national-brand and private-label prices on a large number of products (46 products for firm H, 57 for firm K, and 45 for firm D). * Prices were compared by calculating the costs of three grocery baskets. First, the cost of the grocery products was calculated on the assumption that only national-brand items were purchased. The second calculation assumed that only private-label items were purchased. Finally, the "effective" cost was calculated with national-brand/private-label weights. †

The resulting costs of grocery baskets showed that for firm K the prices for private-label items were, on the average, 86. 7 percent of the prices for national-brand items. For firm H private-label prices averaged 92. 4 percent of national-brand prices. For firm D private-label prices averaged 88. 9 percent of national-brand prices (see Tables B. 4, B. 5, and B. 6). The simple average of private-label/national-brand ratios in the three companies was 89. 3 percent. Expressed differently, national-brand prices, on average, were about 12. 0 percent higher than private-label prices (the change in base results in a higher percentage spread). ‡

Differences in the prices of national and private brands also were computed for the same ten products examined by the National Commission on Food Marketing. National-brand prices averaged 9. 9 percent higher than private-label prices for the ten products—less than half the price spread found in the mid-1960s. A study conducted at Cornell University found a less severe decline in national-brand/private-label price differences. For ten products (nine were the same ones used in National Commission on Food Marketing [NCFM] study), national brands averaged 13. 0 percent higher in price than private-label products. [2]

----

*National-brand and private-label items were matched. That is, for firm H, 46 national-brand grocery items were priced along with 46 comparable private-label items; for firm K, 57 national-brand items were matched with 57 private-label items.

†National-brand/private-label weights were simply estimates of the proportion of each product sold as national brands and the proportion sold as private brands.

‡Firm K, firm H, and firm D national-brand/private-label average price ratios were 115. 3, 108. 2, and 112. 5, respectively. The calculated simple average was 112. 0 percent.

The spread between national-brand and private-label prices across markets is shown in Figures 4.2 and 4.3. Markets are ordered from left to right, according to the cost of the national-brand grocery basket. In going from low-cost to high-cost markets, national-brand prices increased at a more rapid rate than private-label prices; both the absolute and the percentage price spread between national and private brands tended to widen.

To determine whether market structure factors influenced the price relationship of national-brand and private-label products, multiple regression was employed. The cost of the private-label grocery basket was calculated as a proportion of the national-brand grocery basket cost. The resulting ratio was the dependent variable in the regression analysis. Thirty-six private-label/national-brand price ratios were used in the regression analysis, covering three firms and thirty-two markets.

There has been little theoretical or empirical analysis of the manner in which market structure influences the relative price levels of national and private brands. Therefore, no specific relationships were hypothesized between variables. A stepwise regression routine was used in the analysis, with the independent variables included in the selection process being the same as those used for the price-structure analysis. In addition, two binary variables were included to take into account differences in relative pricing strategies among firms. The regression model using 1974 estimates of structural values and yielding the lowest standard error of estimate is shown below.

$$PL/NB = .93417 - \underset{(-2.678)^*}{.04487\,RFMS} - \underset{(-1.280)}{.00017\,MG} + \underset{(1.245)}{.00418\,MS}$$

$$- \underset{(-10.553)^{**}}{.05554\,\text{firm K}} - \underset{(-5.568)^{**}}{.03945\,\text{firm D}}$$

$$\bar{R}^2 = .81$$
$$\text{F-ratio} = 30.32^{**}$$

The regression results were highly significant statistically. Relative firm market share, market growth, and the two firm binaries were negatively related to the private-label/national-brand ratio. Relative market share and the two firm binaries were significant at the 5 percent and 1 percent level, respectively, whereas market growth was not statistically significant. Market size was positively related to the private-label/national-brand ratio; however, the regression coefficient was not significant.

The results indicate that firm K and firm D employed strategies significantly different from those of firm H in the relative pricing of

FIGURE 4. 2

Firm K Cost of Grocery Items: National Brand, Private Label, "Effective" Cost

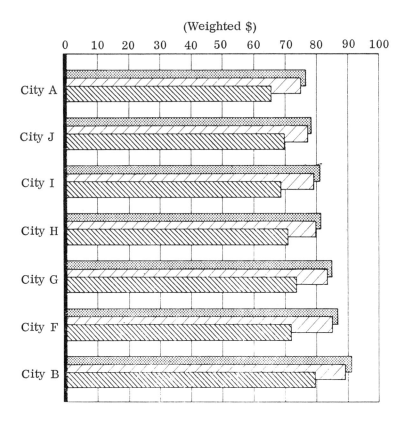

Cost of National-Brand Grocery Items
"Effective" Market Cost of Grocery Items
Cost of Private-Label Grocery Items

Source: Company data provided to the Joint Economic Committee.

FIGURE 4.3

Firm H Cost of Grocery Items: National Brand, Private Label,
"Effective" Cost

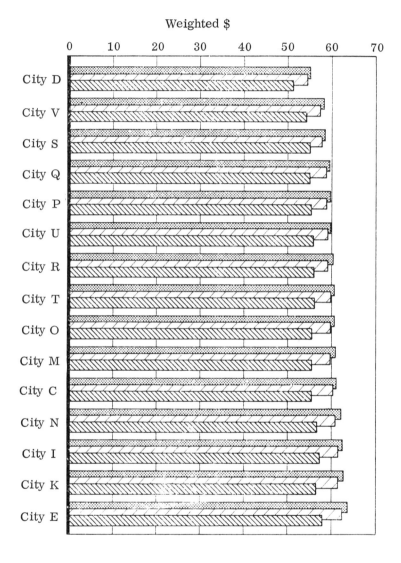

Weighted $

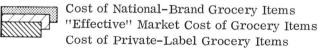
Cost of National-Brand Grocery Items
"Effective" Market Cost of Grocery Items
Cost of Private-Label Grocery Items

Source: Company data provided to the Joint Economic Committee.

national-brand and private-label products, with firm H having a much narrower price spread, on average. The results also reveal that, other things the same, as RFMS increased, the price spread between private-label and national-brand products increased. That is, as a firm's market power increased, it tended to increase both national-brand and private-label prices, but the former more rapidly than the latter.

PRICE PATTERNS IN FOUR CITIES

The general relationships between the level of prices and various market structure and control variables were examined by the regression analysis in this chapter. A substantial percentage of the price variation in the sample cities and firms was explained by the regression models. The reader may better comprehend these results by examining the actual structural characteristics and price patterns in four of the sample cities.

This discussion of individual markets necessarily differs from the preceding regression analysis, where the emphasis was on explaining price variations across markets through the use of control variables such as average store size, market growth, and market rivalry. In the discussion that follows, price patterns within as well as across cities will be examined and related to the two critical market structure variables—CR4 and RFMS. What follows, then, is not an attempt to explain all the forces found to influence prices but, rather, four illustrations of the impact of CR4 and RFMS.

A few comments are warranted concerning the price patterns within a particular market. The regression analysis examined prices across markets; the strong positive relationship found between RFMS and the grocery prices of the three chains was consistent with the theory that dominant firms have pricing discretion in addition to that resulting from the level of market concentration.

In examining the prices of different firms within the same market, an additional factor must be considered. Retail firms attempt to differentiate themselves by providing some unique combination of products, service, location, facilities, and prices. For a particular chain, its "product-service mix" is generally similar from one city to another. Hence, in analyzing a particular firm's price across markets, this factor can be ignored. However, for different firms in the same market, one cannot assume that product-service mixes are similar;

rather, it is expected that a variety of mixes with different costs and different consumer appeals will exist. *

The combined influence of RFMS and product-service mixes is illustrated in Figure 4.4. Firms X, Y, and Z are each assumed to

FIGURE 4.4

Price Patterns of Three Firms with Different Product-Service Mixes and Relative Firm Market Shares

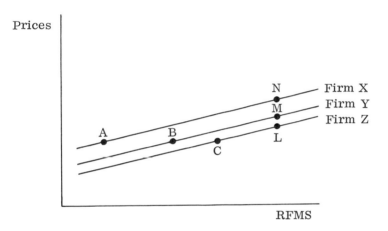

Source: Compiled by the authors.

---

*Possible differences in the product-service mixes of various firms must also be considered in examining the structure-price relationship for several firms operating in multiple markets. Such differences could lead to spurious results, particularly if the analysis includes a large number of firms, each of which operates in a small number of markets. In the present study only three firms were included in the structure-price analysis, with an average of 12 observations per firm.

To test for company differences in prices attributable to factors other than those specified in the models, (such as, company differences in product-service mix), firm binary variables were specified and included in the regression analysis. These variables were not statistically significant.

operate across several markets. For each firm a positive relationship between prices and RFMS is assumed across different markets.
The three firms are also assumed to have different product-service
mixes, as reflected in the different levels of their price lines.

Given this assumed situation, the prices of the three firms
would be N, M, and L in a market where all three had the same RFMS.
In another situation (A, B, and C), their prices would be equal but
each firm would have a different RFMS. Finally, consider the combination A, B, L, in which the highest-priced firm would be firm Z because of a dominant market share. Thus, in those markets where
RFMS and different product-service mixes both influence prices, myr-
iad price combinations are possible. While we would expect to observe
a general positive relationship between RFMS and prices within individual markets if a large number of markets are examined, such a
relationship may not exist in any particular market.

Prices in City B, A Highly Concentrated Eastern City

City B is one of the most concentrated food retail markets of all
SMSAs with population exceeding 500,000. The four largest chains controlled almost 76 percent of sales in 1974 (Table 4.7);* the combined
market share of the two dominant firms in 1974 was estimated at 62.3
percent.

The average four-firm concentration in 1974 for all sample
SMSAs was 51.0 percent, or 24.5 percentage points below the concentration level in City B. The two dominant firms each held over 30 percent of the market, which gave them relative market shares of just
over 40 percent, considerably greater than the sample average of 24.0
percent. The third- and fourth-largest firms each had about equal relative market shares considerably below the leading two firms and the
sample mean.

Given the high level of concentration and the dominance of two
firms, our regression results suggest that average grocery prices in
city B would be well above the average prices in other cities. Also,
given the pattern of market shares, specifically the dominant positions
of firm E and firm K, we would expect these chains' prices to be higher
than the prices of those holding small market shares.

---

*The market share data shown in Tables 4.7-4.10 are estimates
derived from market shares reported in Grocery Distribution Guide.
These data are quite close to the data used in the regression analysis,
which are not reported to avoid disclosure. The four-firm concentration ratios shown in these tables were used in the regression analysis.

TABLE 4.7

Average Cost Indexes for Four Types of Food Baskets, Five Firms, City B, October 1974.

Company	1974 Market Share[a]	Grocery Basket	Market Basket[b]	Meat Basket	Market and Meat Basket
E	31.8	102.4	102.2	103.4	102.5
K	30.5	102.3	102.0	100.0	101.5
A	6.8	100.0	100.2	100.5	100.3
F	6.4	99.7	99.3	102.8	100.2
I	1.4	95.5	96.3	93.3	95.5

Note: See Appendix B. Indexes were derived by expressing the estimated market basket costs as a percent of the mean values.

[a]The market shares are the average market share for each firm from the 1975 and 1976 issues of Grocery Distribution Guide, Metro Market Studies, Inc., adjusted proportionally to equal the 1974 concentration ratio. The latter was estimated from the 1972 Census Bureau concentration ratio, hard data, and Metro Market. Studies data, see Appendix B.

[b]Contained frozen foods, dairy products and grocery products.

Sources: Metro Market Studies, Inc., Grocery Distribution Guide (1974, 1975, 1976); company data provided to the Joint Economic Committee.

The facts are consistent with these expectations. The range in prices for the five chains was 6 to 10 percent, with firm E consistently the highest and Firm I the lowest. The two dominant chains, firm E and firm K, had essentially identical prices for a grocery basket and for a broader market basket that included grocery, dairy, and frozen food products. With the addition of the meat basket, firm E clearly had the highest overall prices (1. 0 percent greater than firm K). Firm A and firm F, the third- and fourth-ranked firms in the market, had similar prices but were about 2 percent lower than the market leader. Prices of firm I, which operated discount stores, were well below all other chains.

The observed data for city B conform quite well with the theoretical expectations. Chains with relatively high market shares are expected to charge higher prices than those with lesser market positions. But, in addition, the costs of the grocery basket for firms E and K in city B were higher than any observation in our study, and were 7. 8 percent greater than the sample mean. Although firm F, the fourth-ranked firm, had average grocery prices in city B that were 2. 6 percent lower than those of firm K, its prices were still 5. 2 percent above the sample average. Thus, not only did those chains with dominant market positions enjoy relatively higher prices than their small rivals, but the high level of market concentration raised the overall level of prices in the city. The weighted average grocery basket price for the five firms examined was 7. 2 percent greater than the sample mean.

The high and nearly identical market basket costs of the two dominant firms suggest that little, if any, price competition existed between them. A comparison of the actual prices used in tabulating the market basket indexes showed that these firms had identical prices on 66 percent of the items. Furthermore, an analysis conducted by the staff of the Joint Economic Committee revealed that of the 460 price changes made by firm K during October 1974, 364 (75. 2 percent) resulted in identical prices for the two firms. These findings support the expectation that little price rivalry occurs in highly concentrated markets, particularly among the dominant firms. The absence of keen rivalry in the market conduct of competitors explains why highly concentrated markets tend to have higher prices and profits than less concentrated ones do.

Prices in City C, a Midwestern City

City C is an example of a moderately concentrated market. In 1974 the top four firms made about 47. 7 percent of grocery store sales in the SMSA (3. 3 percent below the sample mean). The leading firm

(firm T) had a market share of 15. 8, followed closely by firm H with 14. 1 percent and firm J with 10. 9 percent. This pattern was in marked contrast with city B, where the top two firms alone did over 60 percent of the business and each was over four times larger than the third- and fourth-largest firms.

The differences in the city C and city B market structures suggest that prices have significantly different competitive settings in the two cities. City C has neither the concentration nor the dominant firm characteristics of city B. Given the more competitive market structure in city C, we would expect the prices of the leading firm and the average market price to be much closer to the sample average than those in city B.

The actual costs of market baskets in city C are summarized in Table 4. 8. No systematic relationship existed between firm prices and market share. The third-largest firm had the highest average cost of grocery and/or market baskets. Firm H had the lowest average market basket costs, 2. 6 percent lower than firm T. Firm T, a local chain with the leading market share, had prices that were higher than those of firm H but lower than those of firm J and firm A. Moreover, the average level of prices in city C did not differ much from the sample mean. Firm H's grocery prices were only 0. 7 percent greater than the average grocery basket price found across all sample cities. The weighted grocery basket price computed for all five firms for which data were available averaged only 1. 8 percent above the sample mean. Thus, both the level and the distribution of prices in city C were generally consistent with its market structure.

Prices in City F, A Western City

Food retailing in city F was moderately concentrated in 1974, with the top four firms making about 49. 3 percent of sales. Firm K held a dominant market share of 26 percent, and a relative market share of 53 percent. Firm B, the second largest firm, had only 9 percent of the market share (see Table 4. 9).

While the moderate level of concentration would not lead to an expectation of above-average prices, firm K's dominant market position would be expected to result in its charging significantly higher prices than its competitors, thereby raising the average price level of the market. Thus, we would expect average grocery prices in city F to exceed the average price across all markets.

These expectations are generally supported by the observed prices. Firm K's grocery basket price in city F was 4. 5 percent above the sample mean, although it was 3. 3 percent below its prices in city B. The relative grocery basket price for the four firms for which data

TABLE 4.8

Average Cost Indexes for Four Types of Food Baskets, Five Firms, City C, October 1974

Company	1974 Market Share[a]	Grocery Basket	Market Basket[b]	Meat Basket	Market and Meat Basket
T	15.8	99.6	99.6	99.7	99.7
H	14.1	98.9	98.7	96.1	98.2
J	10.9	101.4	101.3	102.5	101.7
A	6.9	100.9	100.5	101.1	100.7
S	2.4	99.1	99.3	100.3	99.6

Note: See Appendix B. Indexes were derived by expressing the estimated market basket costs as a percent of the mean values.

[a]The market shares are the average market share for each firm from the 1975 and 1976 issues of Grocery Distribution Guide, Metro Market Studies, Inc., adjusted proportionally to equal the 1974 concentration ratio. The latter was estimated from the 1972 Census Bureau concentration ratio, hard data, and Metro Market. Studies data, see Appendix B.

[b]Included grocery and dairy products, frozen foods, and health and beauty aids for all firms except Thriftimart, in which case health and beauty aids were not included.

Sources: Metro Market Studies, Inc., Grocery Distribution Guide (1974, 1975, 1976); company data provided to the Joint Economic Committee.

TABLE 4.9

Average Cost Indexes for Four Types of Food Baskets, Four Firms, City F, October 1974

Company	1974 Market Share[a]	Grocery Basket	Market Basket[b]	Meat Basket	Market and Meat Basket
K	25.9	100.9	101.4	99.9	101.1
B	9.0	100.8	100.5	101.2	100.7
U	8.0	–	–	–	–
I	6.3	98.6	98.3	98.7	98.4
V	5.1	99.7	99.8	100.2	99.9

Note: See Appendix B. Indexes were derived by expressing the estimated market basket costs as a percent of the mean values.

[a]The market shares are the average market share for each firm from the 1975 and 1976 issues of Grocery Distribution Guide, Metro Market Studies, Inc., adjusted proportionally to equal the 1974 concentration ratio. The latter was estimated from the 1972 Census Bureau concentration ratio, hard data, and Metro Market. Studies data, see Appendix B.

[b]This market basket contained frozen foods, dairy products, and grocery products.

Sources: Metro Market Studies, Inc., Grocery Distribution Guide (1974, 1975, 1976); company data provided to the Joint Economic Committee.

were available was 3.8 percent higher than the sample average. The relative price pattern conforms to the expected ranking of chain prices, but the distinctions are not so great as expected solely on the basis of the relative market share variable in the regression model. Firm K's market basket prices were 0.9 percent above second-place firm B's and averaged above 2 percent above the fourth- and fifth-largest firms.

Although city F is much less concentrated than city B, both markets are clearly dominated by one or two companies. In a general sense the results were quite similar. In both markets the dominant firm(s) charged the highest prices and contributed to above-average prices for the market.

Prices in City Z, A Southern City

City Z was a relatively concentrated market in 1974, with a four-firm concentration ratio of 61.3. Major chains were the leading four firms in the city, with firm N holding the leading position. Firm A and firm W followed and held identical market shares. Firm H was a distant fourth, with a market share of 6.2 percent and a relative market share of 9.8 percent. This was 14.0 percentage points lower than the sample average. Given the high level of concentration and distribution of market shares, we would expect higher-than-average grocery prices, with the leading firm having the highest prices.

The average cost of a grocery basket in city Z, based on the grocery basket index and market shares shown in Table 4.10, was 3.1 percent greater than the sample mean. This is consistent with the expectation that average prices are higher in markets with relatively high levels of market concentration.

On the basis of the relative dominant position of firm N in the market, we would expect it to be the highest-priced chain. In fact, however, second-place firm A's prices were highest, 1.5 percent above those of firm N. Firm N's prices were higher than those of the other leading chains. Comparison of firm H's cost of a grocery basket in city Z with the average cost of a grocery basket across all markets in the sample shows that firm H's prices were 1.1 percent higher than the mean.

The general level of prices in city Z was consistent with expectations. Except for firm A, the ranking of chain prices was also as expected.

In these four markets the positive influence of CR_4 and RFMS on prices is generally apparent, particularly where one or more firms dominate a market. Where market shares are relatively equally distributed and concentration is moderate, as in city C, both the average

TABLE 4.10

Average Cost Indexes for Three Types of Food Baskets,
Four Firms, City Z, October 1974

Company	1974 Market Share[a]	Grocery Basket	Market Basket[b]
N	24.5	100.7	100.7
A	15.3	102.3	102.8
W	15.3	98.5	98.5
H	6.2	98.4	98.0

Note: See Appendix B. Indexes were derived by expressing the estimated costs as a percent of the mean values.

[a]The market shares are the average market share for each firm from the 1975 and 1976 issues of Grocery Distribution Guide, Metro Market Studies, Inc., adjusted proportionally to equal the 1974 concentration ratio. The latter was estimated from the 1972 Census Bureau concentration ratio, hard data, and Metro Market. Studies data, see Appendix B.

[b]This market basket contained frozen foods, dairy and grocery products, and health and beauty aids.

Sources: Metro Market Studies, Inc., Grocery Distribution Guide (1974, 1975, 1976); company data provided to the Joint Economic Committee.

level and the pattern of prices reflect a more competitive market situation. Thus, although the regression models are not expected to explain the prices in any particular market, the price patterns in these markets illustrate the general relationship between price and the state of competition as measured by our price-structure models.

NOTES

1. National Commission on Food Marketing, Special Studies in Food Marketing, Technical Study no. 10 (Washington, D.C.: U.S. Government Printing Office, June 1966).

2. Cooperative Extension, New York City Programs, Focus on the Food Markets (November 17, 1975).

5

IMPLICATIONS OF PROFIT
AND PRICE REGRESSION RESULTS

The structure-price findings in Chapter 4 lend considerable support to the structure-profit relationships discussed in Chapter 3. The structure-price relationships strongly suggest that the higher observed profits are due, at least in part, to the higher prices that chains are able to charge in less competitively structured markets.

Unfortunately, the data series did not permit a direct comparison of price and profit levels across SMSAs. About half of the SMSAs in the price analysis were included in the profit analysis. It is informative, however, to compare the results indicated by the profit and price models for markets with certain structural characteristics. Table 5.1 combines Tables 3.8 and 4.6 to indicate the relative prices and profits predicted by the regression models for various combinations of RFMS and CR4 when all other variables are held constant.

The table shows an index of estimated grocery prices; when CR4 is 40 and RFMS is 10, the index equals 100. By comparison, in a market situation where RFMS is 55 and CR4 is 70, the index of estimated firm grocery prices is 108.6 (8.6 percent higher). If the operating expenses per dollar of merchandise were similar in these two market situations, the difference in profit-sales ratios would be expected to be similar to the percentage difference in prices. * However, Table 5.1

---

*Analysis of the demand for food indicates that a 10 percent rise in the price of food, all else being the same, will result in a reduction in the quantity of food purchased of about 3.5 percent and an increase in dollar sales of 6.15 percent. However, in comparing two metropolitan areas with considerably different market structures and prices, it is reasonable to assume that market power and higher price levels evolve gradually. If so, then market capacity would be expected to be regulated to conform to the restricted output resulting from higher prices. With similar levels of efficiency, average costs per unit of

130

TABLE 5.1

Estimated Index of Grocery Prices and Pretax Profit-Sales Ratios Associated with Various Levels of Market Concentration and Relative Firm Market Share

| Relative Firm Market Share (RFMS) | Four-Firm Concentration Ratio (CR_4) | | | | | | | |
| | 40 | | 50 | | 60 | | 70 | |
	Index of Grocery Prices[a]	Profits as Percent of Sales[b]	Index of Grocery Prices	Profits as Percent of Sales	Index of Grocery Prices	Profits as Percent of Sales	Index of Grocery Prices	Profits as Percent of Sales
10	100.0	.36	101.0	.96	103.0	1.18	105.4	1.23
25	100.7	1.14	101.7	1.74	103.7	1.96	106.1	2.01
40	102.2	1.92	103.2	2.52	105.2	2.74	107.6	2.79
55	103.2	2.70	104.2	3.30	106.2	3.52	108.6	3.57

[a] The estimated grocery basket cost for each combination of RFMS and CR_4 was calculated using equation 1h, Table 4.3, and holding other independent variables at their respective means. The index was constructed by setting the grocery basket computed for RFMS=10, CR_4=40 equal to 100.0.

[b] Profits as a percent of sales were estimated for each combination of RFMS and CR_4 using equation 1d, Table 3.7, introducing all other variables except API at their means; the binary variable API was introduced with a value of 1. Equation 1d was developed using the average division profit levels for 1970, 1971, and 1974. The grocery price models were based upon 1974 prices.

Source: Compiled by the authors.

indicates expected profit/sales ratios of .36 and 3.57 in these two
situations, an increase of 3.21 percentage points. Thus, it appears
that higher prices are only partially reflected in higher profits. In
the above comparison, higher profits account for about 37 percent of
the difference in prices. This suggests that increases in expenses
absorb the remaining 63 percent. *

Put another way, the results of the price and profit models suggest that increases in profits stem entirely from increases in profits.
Operating expenses, instead of declining as a percent of sales as market share increases, appear to move in the opposite direction. These
results provide no support for the notion that higher-profit divisions
and SMSAs largely reflect lower operating costs. †

---

output would then be similar in different markets, while average revenue per unit of output would vary directly with price levels.

*The values in Table 5.1 are the average prices and profits
that would be expected under various structural conditions, based
upon our regression results. Confidence intervals provide additional
information about the estimated values. The 95 percent confidence
intervals for the price estimates at three levels of concentration,
holding all other variables (including RFMS) at their means, are
shown below.

CR_4	Index of Mean Price	Lower Limit	Upper Limit
40	100.89	99.92	101.86
50	101.90	101.23	102.57
60	103.92	102.99	104.86

The confidence intervals indicate that the estimated average
price in markets with CR_4 of 40 is not significantly different from
the estimated average price in markets with CR_4 of 50. However,
the estimated average prices for CR_4 of 50 and 60 are significantly
different. It follows that a significant difference exists between estimated prices for CR_4 or 40 and 60.

These results are what one would expect, given the values in
Table 5.1. The predicted price differences between CR_4 of 40 and 50
is quite modest. The markets posing particular public policy problems are those in which four-firm concentration approaches or
exceeds 60 percent.

† A study of food retailing in Canada provides modest additional
evidence. Although the methodology used is subject to question, the

Economists have long recognized that market power tends to result not only in excess profits but also in higher costs. Prices in monopoly markets tend to be greater not only because of larger cost-price margins but because of higher costs as well. [1] This expectation is supported by empirical studies that show per-unit costs tend to rise when profits are high. [2] In his article dealing with this phenomenon, called "X-inefficiency," H. Leibenstein said, "We have instances where competitive pressures from other firms or adversity lead to efforts toward cost reduction, and the absence of such pressures tends to cause costs to rise." [3]

Another possible reason that prices between two markets differ by more than the profit-to-sales ratios is the ability of multiple-division chains to allocate costs among divisions in such fashion that high-profit divisions carry a disproportionately high burden of corporate overhead. This, of course, would result in cross-subsidization of low-profit/competitive divisions by high-profit/monopolistic ones. *

For the above reasons, relatively high observed profits are merely the tip of the monopoly-power iceberg. An example from the

---

study found both net operating profits and price levels were positively related to the level of concentration in various metropolitan areas. Using relatively weak statistical tests, no correlation was found between four-firm concentration and operating expenses. Bruce Mallen, "A Preliminary Paper on the Levels, Causes and Effects of Economic Concentration in the Canadian Retail Food Trade: A Study of Supermarket Market Power," Reference Paper no. 6 (Montreal: Concordia University, February 1976).

*Ray A. Goldberg of the Harvard Business School has suggested that rapidly increasing labor and raw material costs during the period studied, excess capacity in the industry, and changes in inventory valuations due to inflation and shifts in inventory methods may have been responsible for the price and profit relationships found, Joint Economic Committee, Hearings on Prices and Profits of Leading Retail Food Chains, 1970-74, March 30 and April 5, 1977 (Washington, D.C.: U.S. Government Printing Office, 1977), pp. 66-67. Labor and raw material costs increased sharply during 1970-74. However, there is no reason to expect nor evidence to suggest that these costs increased more rapidly in concentrated markets than in less concentrated ones. The widespread practice of regional pattern setting in union bargaining with food retailers makes it improbable that wage rate levels or increases are influenced by the level of market concentration. The analysis in Chapter 4 indicated no significant relationship between the level of union wages (by SMSA) in 1974 and

food processing industry illustrates the point. From 1955 through 1964, wholesale bakers and food chains in the state of Washington successfully conspired to fix the price of bread. Prior to the conspiracy and after its termination in 1965, bread prices in Washington were about equal to the U. S. average.[4] During the conspiracy prices were between 15 and 20 percent above the U. S. average, resulting in an overcharge to consumers of about $3.5 million annually. But this large overcharge was not fully reflected in higher profits of the wholesale bakers. Whereas in 1964 wholesale bakers in Seattle enjoyed higher average profits than those located in five other states—3.1 per-

---

grocery price levels. There is also little reason to expect raw material costs to be related to market concentration.

Thus, it seems likely that the higher operating expenses in concentrated markets suggested by our study results were due to factors such as overstoring, advertising and promotion expenditures, employee productivity, and company overhead expenses—expense factors that are largely controllable by management and that tend to become inflated in markets where competition is ineffective.

Rising raw material costs during the period have an inflating effect on stated retail profits where the FIFO method of inventory valuation was used. As a result, three chains included in the profit analysis switched from FIFO to LIFO in 1974 (see note to Table A.5). Since company profits in various divisions or SMSAs were analyzed for each individual year and for the average profits realized over the five-year period, changing inventory valuations would not introduce any apparent bias into the analysis. Had the analysis been conducted using time series rather than cross-sectional data (for instance, an analysis of Winn-Dixie profits in the Jacksonville division across different years), changes in inventory valuation would be a valid concern. This was not the case, however.

Excess capacity in food retailing probably affects retail costs and prices. However, excess capacity helps explain our findings only if it is positively related to market concentration. If excess capacity is uniformly present in all markets or occurs randomly in different markets, it would not account for the higher prices, higher profits, and inferred higher costs in concentrated markets. Although evidence is lacking, we expect excess capacity to be especially common in concentrated markets, where it serves as a barrier to entry and as a depressant—not a stimulus—to competition.

Thus, while we acknowledge the alternative interpretations offered by Professor Goldberg, neither logic nor empirical evidence suggests that they are likely to account for the relationships found.

cent of sales versus 1. 0 percent of sales—this was far short of the differences in prices. [5] Evidently, the absence of price competition among these bakers caused them to divert their competition to non-price forms that resulted in inflating their selling and delivery costs to 9. 7 cents per pound, compared with an average of 6. 7 cents per pound for bakers in other states. [6] This difference of 3 cents was equal to 13 percent of the wholesale price. Thus, the higher noncompetitive prices encouraged bakers to pursue policies that inflated their costs, thereby preventing them from capturing the full benefits of the conspiratorial prices. On the basis of the results of the present study, a similar phenomenon appears to exist in grocery retailing. *

Events in Phoenix, Arizona, illustrate that prices can be reduced under competitive circumstances by much larger amounts than profit margins can. According to Chain Store Age, "In December 1975 grocery department gross margins averaged 15 percent. In December 1976, they were down to 10 percent-12 percent. Two or three years

---

*One possible source of inflated costs is excess store capacity in metropolitan areas. A Canadian study estimated that excess capacity increased grocery store costs by 4 percent. See Report of the Royal Commission on Consumer Problems and Inflation (Regina, Sask.: Queen's Printer, 1968). Dominant firms in concentrated markets may intentionally maintain excess capacity as a barrier to new entrants. Without evidence, this is only conjecture, but worthy of investigation.

The definition of "excess capacity" is critical to any analysis. Bruce Mallen defined optimum capacity as that which would realize the minimum cost rate of store utilization. The utilization rate found to minimize costs was $11.25 per square foot of selling space per week. See Bruce Mallen and M. Haberman, "Economies of Scale: A Determinant of 'Overstoring and Super Storing?'" in Canadian Association of Administrative Sciences Conference Proceedings (Edmonton, Alta.: 1975). This is much higher than the $5.50 per square foot optimum utilization rate found by the National Commission on Food Marketing in the mid 1960s. Both studies found store utilization to be the most important factor affecting store operating expenses; the absolute size of store had a modest influence.

Data in this study allowed a limited analysis of store operating expenses. Detailed expense data were available for 58 stores of one company in seven different SMSAs. The stores had comparable departments (grocery, meat, produce, and bakery) and ranged from 13,000 to 31,000 square feet in size. Multiple-regression analysis of these data indicated the following results:

ago net-to-sales averaged 1 1/4 to 1 1/2 percent. Today it is one-half to four-fifths of 1 percent. "[7] Thus, while grocery gross margins (and therefore average grocery prices) declined by 3-5 percent (and possibly by as much as 7 percent, because margins probably were near 17 percent in earlier years), net profits-sales declined by a much smaller amount. This illustrates that when chains are under keen competitive pressure, they find ways to reduce costs as well as prices.

It should be emphasized that average chain profits during 1970-74 were depressed by a combination of unusual factors. Nonetheless, this analysis indicates that chains holding dominant market positions in highly concentrated metropolitan areas enjoyed substantial profits. The profits shown in Table 5.1 are expressed as a percentage of sales before taxes. The relevant measure in evaluating profits of firms in one industry relative to those in another is profits expressed as a percentage of stockholders' investment. Pretax profits of 3.57 percent of sales (the highest shown in the table) translate to after tax profits of over 20 percent of stockholders' investment. This was far above the average profits of all chains during 1970-74, and well above the average of all but the most concentrated American industries.

$$SOE/CGS =$$

$$.33 - .000\,SS^2 - 1.422\,SU + .004\,SU^2 + .021\,M_1 + .030\,M_2 + .075\,M_3$$
$$(-0.85) \quad (-3.05) \quad (2.09) \quad (3.73) \quad (4.58) \quad (7.73)$$

$$\bar{R}^2 = .68$$

where

SOE/CGS = store operating expenses minus district and corporate allocated overhead expenses as percent of cost of goods sold

SS = store size in thousand square feet

SU = store utilization measured as cost of goods sold per thousand square feet

M_1 = binary variable for Seattle SMSA

M_2 = binary variable for Portland SMSA

M_3 = binary variable for northern California SMSAs (San Francisco, San Jose, and Sacramento)

Costs of goods sold was used to avoid the influences of price differences in different markets. However, a similar model was developed using sales instead of cost of goods sold. The results were

ESTIMATED MONOPOLY OVERCHARGE

The preceding analyses have provided strong evidence that both CR_4 and RFMS have a positive influence on the levels of profits and prices. A relevant public policy question is how much more consumers pay for retail grocery products because some markets are not competitively structured.

Overcharges in noncompetitive industries can be estimated in various ways. Profits in excess of "competitive" profits is one measure, but carries the implicit assumption that costs are the same in competitive and noncompetitive markets. If there are reasons to expect higher discretionary costs in noncompetitive markets due to X-inefficiency and emphasis on nonprice competition, then excess profits may provide a poor indication of monopoly overcharge. In addition, the excess profit approach is valid only during relatively normal profit periods. If profits are temporarily depressed, as was true in food retailing during most of the period studied, a measure of excess profits is misleading.

A second alternative, where data permit, is to estimate overcharges from the differences in prices in competitive versus noncompetitive markets. Price differences include both profit and cost differences. To the extent that the differences in prices attributable to

---

essentially the same. When converted to the same base, the minimum points on the two curves were similar—$4.66 and $4.80 in sales per square foot per week. Unfortunately, very few stores in the sample had utilization rates above $4.25 per square foot (two standard deviations from the mean utilization rate). Thus, although these results tend to support the National Commission results, the lower right-hand portion of these cost curves (sales per square foot above $4.00) was not adequately defined with the available data.

Since the defined minimum-cost points are beyond nearly all observations, there is little assurance that these are true minima. The results do indicate, however, that the cost curves have leveled off and are relatively flat near the minimum-cost point. For example, a 20 percent reduction in store utilization from the defined minima increased operating expenses from 21.0 to 21.6 percent of cost of goods sold.

Average store wage rate was included as an independent variable in some models, with overall results similar to the above. Significant collinearity was found between store size, wage rate, and the SMSA binaries. With a limited sample, the interrelated effects were difficult to isolate.

the competitive environment are due to differences in profits and discretionary costs, this measure is an appropriate measure of the overcharge paid by consumers. To the extent that there are nondiscretionary cost differences reflected in these price differences, the measure may either overstate or understate consumer overcharges.

The price-difference approach is less dependent on the normality of business conditions than the excess profit approach is. There is no a priori basis for expecting that prices in competitive markets relative to prices in monopolistic markets will change during depressed profit periods vis-à-vis normal profit periods.

In this study monopoly overcharge is estimated from the differences in grocery prices that were attributable to the competitive structure of markets. Our measure is therefore a measure of excess prices—not of excess profits.

Before we can estimate monopoly overcharges, we must define what constitutes a competitively structured market. We shall assume that a market is competitively structured where the top four firms make 40 percent of all grocery store sales and each of these firms holds 10 percent of the market—that is, where CR_4 is 40 and RFMS is 25. The CR_4 level was selected because the empirical analyses show that both profits and prices are continuing to rise in the range around CR_4 40. As Figure 4.1 indicates, prices tend to level off at CR_4 levels below 40. Thus, empirical findings suggest that competitive prices (where prices are equal to minimum long-run average costs, including a return for capital invested and risk) occur when CR_4 is 40 or less. We selected an RFMS of 25 as the appropriate one because in such market settings, the four largest firms have equal market shares and, therefore, comparable positions of market power.

Employing these assumptions, estimates were made of the percent overcharge in each of the 31 sample markets. Using equation 1h, Table 4.3, the grocery prices for each of the four leading firms in the 31 sample SMSAs were estimated, using appropriate SMSA values for each variable specified. For all firms with estimated prices above a competitive level, the overcharges were then summed. The total monopoly overcharge across the 31 sample markets, expressed as a percent of the total sales of the leading four firms, was 1.51 percent, or $151 million in 1974.

Using the above estimate of the percentage of monopoly overcharge, national monopoly overcharges were calculated. Since the above monopoly overcharge estimates apply only to the leading four firms in each SMSA, the sales total across all 263 SMSAs was multiplied by the weighted national mean four-firm concentration of 49.6 percent. The resulting estimate of the total sales of the four largest firms in all SMSAs ($41.4 billion) was then multiplied by 1.51 percent, yielding an estimate of national monopoly overcharges of $625 million in 1974. *

These results indicate that in many markets, consumers are paying the leading food retailers extremely large dollar overcharges because of the retailers' market power. Although this is not a precise estimate, it probably errs on the low side. First, it includes only sales of the top four firms. There is reason to believe that in highly concentrated markets, the entire price level, not just that of the four largest firms, tends to be higher. Second, these estimates include only sales in SMSAs. About 27 percent of grocery store sales are made by retailers outside SMSAs. Since market concentration generally is higher in small communities than in SMSAs, there may be substantial monopoly overcharges in areas outside SMSAs.

The preceding discussion deals solely with aggregate monopoly overcharges. Actual overcharges vary considerably among cities. In cities where a strong dominant firm does not exist and where four-firm concentration does not greatly exceed 40, estimated monopoly overcharges are negligible. Examples of such cities are city J (Table 4.1), which had no estimated monopoly overcharge, and city C (Tables 4.2 and 4.8), which had estimated overcharges by the top four firms of $2.0 million in 1974 (0.4 percent of sales). On the other hand, in cities with very high market concentration and one or more dominant firms, the overcharges are likely to be substantial. The leading example of such a city is city B (Tables 4.1 and 4.7), which has the second-highest concentration of any large city and has two dominant firms. We estimate 1974 monopoly overcharges of $82 million (6.8 percent of sales) for the top four chains in city B.

Unfortunately, data limitations make it impossible to make precise estimates of monopoly overcharges nationwide. The firms and the SMSAs included in the price analysis were not preselected to be representative of all firms and all SMSAs; rather, their selection, as noted earlier, was based solely on the availability of adequate data. At the same time, however, we have no reason to suspect that the firms and markets included in the analysis are atypical. Thus, while there are limitations in the data used in the analysis, there is no basis for concluding that our results are biased significantly in a particular direction.

The magnitude of our monopoly overcharge estimates may strike some as unrealistic. When grocery chains had average profits after

---

*If CR_4 of 50 and RFMS of 25 are used as the competitive norm, the overcharge estimate drops to $422 million or 1.0 percent of the sales of the four largest firms in all SMSAs .

taxes of less than 1 percent of sales in 1970-74, how can one contend that there were monopoly overcharges of 1, 2, or 5 percent? Have we selected a competitive norm so severe that it would "bankrupt the industry"? First, we reemphasize that our estimates are of price overcharges, not of excess profits, and are pretax. A 1 percent drop in prices, all else remaining the same, would reduce posttax profits by about 0.6 percent.

Second, the period included in the profit analysis was atypical for the grocery retailing industry by nearly any standard. During more normal periods the profit-sales figures included in the analysis would likely have been at least 50 percent higher (Table A.3). Even the profit figures on which the estimates in Table 5.1 are based (1970, 1971, and 1974) are significantly lower than the long-term average in food retailing.

Estimated profits of 1.03 percent of sales for the structural combination selected as the competitive norm (Table 5.1) translate to about 6.2 percent of owners' equity after taxes. While this is a low profit rate, it is not inordinately low for 1974, when 24 chains with sales exceeding $500 million had average net profits on equity of 9.2 percent and 24 publicly owned chains with sales under $500 million had average net profits on equity of only 4.7 percent. Profit rates before and after this period confirm that profits were abnormally and temporarily depressed.

It is also important to remember that many of the competitors of large chains operate in only one market. The fact that independent supermarkets and small chains are able to survive in markets with low levels of concentration indicates that price levels are not at the "bankrupting" level for well-run firms.

Finally, the results of the analyses suggest that averages may be seriously misleading. If both expenses and profits are inflated in markets where considerable monopoly power exists—as the data suggest—then profit levels provide only a partial indication of possible monopoly overcharges. The inflated costs that frequently accompany monopolistic situations must also be included in any estimate of overcharges.

Perhaps part of the explanation is the practice of cross-subsidization across markets, where a firm "robs Peter to pay Paul." Undoubtedly, some of this does occur among large multimarket food chains, whose unprofitable divisions are subsidized by profitable ones. The result is to lower the average profits of chains that "carry" divisions that could not survive if forced to rely solely on their own resources. Although we believe that it provides only a partial explanation, cross-subsidization by itself is not an untarnished virtue. Where it involves charging different prices to customers in different markets, it penalizes some customers and subsidizes others. In addition, since only multimarket or multi-industry firms can engage in cross-subsidization, single-market grocery retailers may be placed at a serious competitive disadvantage if large chains choose to charge loss-producing prices in a particular market while reaping profits in other markets. Moreover, even if a chain does not charge higher prices in an unprofitable division, welfare losses result if the inefficient division remains in business for protracted periods despite its higher costs and resulting losses. In this case, society would be better served if the retail services were provided by more efficient firms.

NOTES

1. F. M. Scherer, Industrial Market Structure and Economic Performance (Chicago: Rand McNally, 1971, pp. 405-09.

2. R. M. Cyert and J. G. March, A Behavioral Theory of the Firm (Englewood Cliffs, N. J. : Prentice-Hall, 1963, p. 37.

3. H. Leibenstein, "Allocative Efficiency vs. 'Inefficiency,'" American Economic Review 56 (June 1966): 309-10.

4. Federal Trade Commission, Economic Report on the Baking Industry (Washington, D. C. : U. S. Government Printing Office, November 1967), pp. 66-71.

5. Ibid. , p. 110.

6. Ibid. , pp. 110-14.

7. "Phoenix, First Crack in the Sunbelt," Chain Store Age (February 1977): 31.

6

PUBLIC POLICY ALTERNATIVES

Grocery store sales in many metropolitan areas are quite highly concentrated and have become increasingly so since the 1950s. This has important public policy implications because our analysis provides strong evidence that consumers pay substantially more in highly concentrated markets dominated by one or two firms than they do in less concentrated markets without a dominant firm.

We emphasize, however, that whereas our study strongly suggests that there is a market concentration problem in food retailing, many markets are still quite competitively structured. Moreover, many independents and small chains, as well as large chains in many of their markets, do not have significant market power. We emphasize this point lest our findings be misinterpreted as implying that all retailers have market power. The chief problem for public policy is the troublesome fact that the number of highly concentrated markets (where four firms make over 60 percent of sales) has increased substantially—from 5 percent of the total in 1954 to 25 percent in 1972—and is continuing to increase.

Our analysis of change in concentration strongly suggests that large chains enjoy conglomerate power that has been used to increase their individual market shares and that when they enter new markets, either by acquisition or de novo, they trigger retaliatory response by established large chains, which increases concentration still further. These findings support the hypothesis that market concentration will continue to rise, especially in markets occupied by many large chains and in markets that large chains enter either by internal growth or by merger.

This raises the question of what can be done to preserve competition where it still exists and to increase competition in markets that are very concentrated. We shall discuss five ways to help maintain or increase competition in grocery retailing. Four of the options involve fostering an environment where "natural" economic forces will erode concentration, prevent its emergence, or intensify competition without changing the levels of concentration in the short run. The fifth approach involves direct actions to reduce excessive market concentration.

REDUCING ENTRY BARRIERS

Concentration can be reduced—absent direct public actions—only if new firms enter the market or if smaller firms already in the market expand at the expense of the market leaders. As shown earlier, the economics of food retailing create significant entry barriers for new competitors. Most of these barriers are not in violation of present antitrust laws and cannot easily be reduced. There are some barriers, however, that can be lowered.

An important barrier to new entrants, as well as an impediment to the expansion of independent retailers and small chains, is the difficulty in gaining access to preferred store sites. Leading chains in a market are generally the preferred tenants in shopping centers. In some cases restrictive lease arrangements limit competition in a center. These practices act to further strengthen the market power of leading retailers in a market. The antitrust agencies should continue to investigate this problem and act aggressively in striking down discriminatory and restrictive site arrangements.

Entry barriers can also be magnified if firms already in the market engage in selective price cutting aimed at the stores of the new entrant. This occurred in Washington, D. C., in 1967, when Stop Rite (Foodarama), an aggressive discounter headquartered in New Jersey, attempted to enter the market. The stores of two leading chains "located near the stores of the new entrant cut their prices substantially below those charged in the rest of the metropolitan area. In doing so, these stores operated on abnormally low margins and—for those stores for which data were available—sustained substantial losses."[1] This strategy of discouraging entry succeeded, and Shop Rite ultimately withdrew from the market. Such selective price cutting seriously raises entry barriers to would-be entrants, thereby protecting established firms from potential competition.

The American antitrust agencies have not challenged this practice in food retailing since the A&P case.[2] However, the Canadian government has prohibited such predatory behavior. In 1973 the attorney general of Canada initiated an antitrust action under the Canadian Combines Act, challenging Canada Safeway Ltd. for alleged "actions directed toward its competitors which limited the expansion of its competitors and created barriers to entry of other competitors to the market."[3] One provision of a consent order in the case is that for a period of six years

> The Defendant shall not knowingly charge a price for any
> grocery item in any one or more of its stores in Calgary
> for the purpose of meeting or undercutting the price of a
> competitor, unless the price so charged by the Defendant
> is applied uniformly and simultaneously by it, for the iden-
> tical grocery item in all of its Calgary grocery stores. [4]

The order also recognized that entry barriers and a new entrant's costs can be raised by massive advertising. One provision of the decree therefore stated: "A further prohibition prohibits Safeway for five (5) years from engaging in market saturating advertising policies. "[5]

Selective price cutting and massive advertising that discourages entry also probably violate the Robinson-Patman Act and/or the Federal Trade Commission Act, and perhaps even the Sherman Act. If so, the antitrust agencies should challenge such practices in addition to stating their views on such behavior. If these practices cannot be challenged under existing laws, Congress should consider strengthening them.

MERGER POLICY

In the 1960s the Federal Trade Commission (FTC) entered agreements with six food chains prohibiting future grocery store mergers for ten years without prior FTC approval. * In the only fully litigated case, the commission found that National Tea's 26 acquisitions of grocery retailers, with combined sales of $251 million, violated Section 7 of the Clayton Act. [6] The commission found that National Tea was the leading factor in a merger movement that "portends a drastic restructuring of the national food markets as a whole and of the individual markets in which these acquisitions occurred. "[7] The anticompetitive effects of these mergers, in the FTC's review, stemmed in part from the overall merger movement in which many leading chains were participating: "As these largest chains pursue their parallel policies of geographic expansion, they inevitably meet each other in a number of cities. The result is frequently a market completely dominated by three or four chains. "[8] In markets dominated by a few

---

*Consent orders involved Grand Union (1965 and 1968), National Tea (1966), Winn-Dixie (1966), Consolidated Foods (1968), H. C. Bohack (1968). An affidavit of voluntary compliance was entered with Lucky Stores in 1968.

large chains, the record in National Tea showed, "hard" price competition was likely to give way to "soft" competition. [9] In addition, the FTC found that National Tea achieved substantial power because it operated across hundreds of markets, in some of which it held commanding positions, and that it could use, and sometimes did use, such power to entrench and expand the market position of retailers that it acquired. [10] In its subsequently issued merger guidelines in food distribution, the commission emphasized the power National Tea enjoyed by reason of its multimarket operations: "The record in [National Tea] illustrated that the large multimarket character of firms of this size may give substantial advantages over smaller firms, and that some of these advantages are entirely unrelated to economic efficiency." [11]

The FTC also found that National Tea's merger actions had eliminated many viable potential competitors, thereby depriving consumers of the benefits of potential competition: "As we understand the merger law, a firm already on the periphery of a particular geographic market, with the known capacity and inclination to expand into that market, is even then reckoned as a definite competitive force in that market." [12] These various findings, in the commission's view, made it imperative that it call a halt to National Tea's merger-achieved expansion.

Following this decision, in January 1967, the FTC issued its food distribution merger guidelines, which said that any but very small acquisitions by large chains (defined as chains with annual sales exceeding $500 million) would be carefully scrutinized. The guidelines applied to both horizontal mergers (those between direct competitors) and market extension mergers (those between chains that operated in different metropolitan areas).

These various actions sent a clear signal to large chains that the commission would probably challenge any substantial market extension mergers by large chains as well as horizontal mergers that violated the standards established by the Supreme Court decision in the Von's Grocery Co. case. [13] For a decade these actions had the effect of virtually stopping acquisitions by large chains. Not all mergers were prevented, nor was this the FTC's intent. Although total acquisitions of food retailers rose in subsequent years, practically all (85 percent) acquisitions were made by retailers smaller than the top 20, by wholesale distributors, or by nongrocery chain conglomerate firms. Thus, a salutary effect of the FTC actions was to channel mergers away from the industry leaders, thereby slowing the trend toward growing local and national concentration in food retailing.

By the mid-1970s the FTC was at a public policy crossroads. As its consent orders with leading chains began expiring, the industry waited for signals indicating the direction of future policy. The FTC was given ample opportunity to act during 1975 and 1976, when five substantial mergers occurred.

In 1975, Lucky Stores requested premerger clearance of its proposed acquisition of Arden-Mayfair's grocery stores in Seattle and Tacoma. This horizontal merger, which involved sales of $40 million, increased Lucky's market share in both cities. The FTC approved Lucky's request, and the merger was consummated.

In 1976, shortly after its ten-year consent decree restricting acquisitions expired, Winn-Dixie expanded into the Southwest by acquiring Kimbell Stores, headquartered in Texas. This market extension merger was the largest acquisition in Winn-Dixie's history. [14] Kimbell operated 135 food stores and a wholesale division serving 1,500 independents in the Southwest. Its total sales exceeded $500 million in 1975. [15]

Allied Supermarkets' purchase in 1976 of Great Scott Supermarkets reportedly tripled Allied's share of the Detroit market—from 8 percent to over 20 percent, making Allied the market leader. [16] The top four chains held 50 percent of the Detroit market in 1972. Allied, the acquiring chain, reportedly had financial difficulties prior to the merger.

A&P purchased 62 National Tea stores in Chicago in 1976. This merger increased A&P's market share from about 4 percent to 11 percent, making it the second- or third-largest chain in the market.

In early 1976 two regional North Carolina chains—Food Town and Lowe's Food Stores—announced their intention to merg. In 1975 Food Town had sales of $130 million and Lowe's had sales of $76 million. The two chains were actual competitors in several markets and potential competitors in others. The only merger challenged during 1975-76 was that of Food Town-Lowe's. Following this challenge the FTC won a temporary restraining order by the Court of Appeals, after which the chains abandoned the merger.

The failure of the FTC to challenge other mergers, especially the horizontal merger involving Lucky and Mayfair and the market extension merger involving Winn-Dixie and Kimbell, evidently has led some large chains to infer that the FTC has abandoned the policy adopted in the 1960s. As Supermarket News put it, the "FTC looked the other way when Winn-Dixie swallowed Kimbell, Inc." [17] Since then other chains have announced that they intend to resume making acquisitions. Lucky announced that it would do so when its FTC consent agreement terminated in late 1977. * Likewise, in April 1978 the president

---

*The president of Lucky was quoted as saying that the FTC's failure to challenge recent acquisitions "gives us the idea that the FTC will look more kindly on acquisitions." Supermarket News, November 22, 1976, p. 1. He reportedly stated that Lucky would accel-

of Grand Union, which is owned by the British conglomerate Cavenham Ltd. , stated that the firm would resume making acquisitions when its consent decree terminated in June 1978. He said the company was in a strong "cash position" and was especially interested in acquiring retailers "adjacent to or where we now do business. "[18]

Grand Union proved true to its word. Barely a week after its consent agreement with the FTC expired in June 1978, Grand Union announced a tender offer to acquire Colonial Stores, a $1. 1 billion chain operating in seven mid-Atlantic and southeastern states. Grand Union's operations straddle those of Colonial. On its face the merger violates the potential competition standards established by the FTC in several cases during the 1960s. [19] Although the FTC did not seek to enjoin the merger, Grand Union agreed to "hold separate" the Colonial operations until November 1978.

On the basis of our analysis in Chapter 2 of the impact of market extension mergers by large food chains, the abandonment of the FTC's past policy toward such mergers will result in further centralization of food retailing in local and national markets. Prior to initiation of a strict policy toward market extension mergers in the mid-1960s, the top 20 chains acquired 55 chains with combined sales of $2. 1 billion. These mergers were largely responsible for these chains' increased share of grocery store sales between 1948 and 1964. [20] Our analysis strongly suggests that when a large grocery chain or large nonfood firm makes a market extension merger, an increase in concentration in the market involved can be expected. Thus, there is persuasive evidence that competition in food retailing will be injured if the FTC abandons the policy toward market extension mergers adopted in the 1960s. Additionally, our analysis warrants extending this policy to acquisitions of food retailers by large, powerful firms not engaged in food retailing, and challenging several large mergers of this type that have occurred, such as Cavenham, Ltd. 's acquisition of Grand Union in 1974 and Brown & Williamson's acquisition of Kohl's in 1972 (Table A. 8).

Since the 1965 Supreme Court decision in Von's,* both antitrust agencies have pursued a relatively strict line on horizontal mergers.

---

erate acquisitions shortly after its consent agreement expired in late 1977. Ibid.

*In addition to the FTC's Food Town-Lowe's case, the Department of Justice in 1974 challenged the acquisition by Albertson's (Boise, Idaho) of Mountain States Wholesale Co. (also of Boise). This case was settled with a consent decree requiring Albertson's to divest Mountain States and to refrain for five years from acquiring any grocery wholesalers in Idaho or eastern Oregon without prior approval.

However, during 1975-76 they permitted three substantial horizontal mergers by large companies (Lucky, Allied, and A&P). Each of these acquisitions was made by one of the nation's largest food chains and resulted in greater combined market shares than those in the Von's-Shopping Bag case.* In addition, four-firm concentration was much higher in each of these cities than in Los Angeles at the time of the Von's-Shopping Bag merger, which the Supreme Court found to be illegal.

The FTC's approval in 1975 of Lucky's acquisition of Arden-Mayfair's Seattle and Tacoma operations warrants special scrutiny. The failure to challenge this acquisition is particularly significant because Lucky had previously signed an "assurance of voluntary compliance" (AVC no. 895) in connection with another matter that required Lucky to secure FTC approval prior to acquiring food stores. By permitting the merger the commission gave explicit approval of a merger of this type, thereby providing precedent for the large horizontal mergers made by Allied and A&P in 1976.

The salient facts are these. With sales of $2.9 billion, Lucky was the fourth-largest U.S. food retailer in 1974, and with sales of $649 million Arden-Mayfair was the twentieth-largest. Lucky and Arden-Mayfair each operated stores with annual sales of about $33 million in the Seattle metropolitan area.[21] This resulted in a combined share of about 10 percent.† The combined shares in the Tacoma market appeared to be somewhat higher.‡

On the basis of its analysis of the probable competitive effects, the commission staff recommended that the proposed acquisition not be approved. But, according to the FTC chairman, Louis Engman, "The Commission, after careful consideration approved the acquisition, with Commissioner Hanford dissenting."[22] He stated that important in the decision was "the distinct possibility that Lucky and Arden-Mayfair would leave the Seattle and Tacoma markets if the acquisition was not permitted." Arden-Mayfair, whose Seattle-Tacoma

------

*In Von's the merging retailers had a combined market share of only 9 percent of the Los Angeles market. In 1968 the FTC disapproved a proposed merger where the acquiring company's market share was 18 percent and the proposed acquired retailer operated three supermarkets with about 1.5 percent of the market. Federal Trade Commission, Advisory Opinion Digest, no. 344 (1968).

†This is an estimate. Metro Markets estimates the shares of Lucky and Arden-Mayfair as 6.1 percent and 4.7 percent, respectively.

‡Metro Markets estimates respective shares as 12.8 percent and 2.6 percent.

operation allegedly had suffered a loss in the first quarter of 1975, told the commission it was withdrawing from these markets. Lucky informed the commission that it also would leave the market "because of the below-normal profits unless it could strengthen its operation by the proposed acquisition."[23] Engman further stated that "departure of Lucky and Arden-Mayfair would likely result in Safeway becoming more entrenched. Therefore, although the acquisition would combine the operations of two competitors, disapproval of the proposal could have a very substantial adverse effect on the state of competition in the relevant markets."[24]

The FTC's justification for its action was questionable at best. The merger made Lucky the second-largest chain in both Seattle and Tacoma; in each market the top four firms made 49 percent of sales. Although the merger may well have improved Lucky's profit and growth prospects, this is not a sufficient public policy ground for approving the merger. It is incorrect to infer that what is good for Lucky is good for competition. Insofar as the merger strengthened Lucky's position vis-à-vis Safeway, it presumably also strengthened its position vis-à-vis smaller retailers. Indeed, by permitting the merger the commission may have fostered the emergence of two dominant firms instead of one, as well as contributing to an increase in four-firm concentration. Our economic analysis indicates that under these circumstances, consumers in these markets are likely to pay higher prices.

Many independent retailers in the Seattle and Tacoma markets expressed fears that FTC approval would have adverse competitive effects. F. N. McCowan, executive director of the Washington State Food Dealers Association, which represents about 1,000 retail grocers in the state of Washington, told the FTC that after the merger "the market would be controlled by three chains (Safeway, Lucky, and Albertson's)."[25]

Morrie Olson, owner of a number of small stores in Seattle, urged the commission to withhold its approval because

> The monopoly resulting from this transaction would intensify the growth and dominance of these three chains in the Seattle area, as well as enabling them to expand this dominant control into the outlying communities of western Washington.[26]

Richard C. Rhodes, owner-operator of three supermarkets, observed the irony that Lucky and Mayfair "got their start" in the market by acquiring successful small businesses, but were now asking to merge with one another rather than giving small businessmen a chance to buy Mayfair's stores. He wrote:

It is interesting that Lucky and Mayfair got their start in this market through acquisition of successful small companies who couldn't turn down the lucrative offers made by these two chains.

The independent retailer's position is not being jeopardized because of his skill or ability to compete price-wise or management-wise, but because of the lack of opportunity for growth. If the opportunity to purchase the Mayfair stores were presented to the independent grocers, I doubt that Mayfair would have difficulty in disposing of their stores—providing the price was fair. [27]

Since neither Lucky nor Mayfair was a failing firm, they could not rely on the "failing company" doctrine. And while Mayfair-Arden evidently was intent on leaving these markets, Lucky merely threatened to do so (unless the commission permitted the merger) because it was earning "below normal profits."

In rejecting its staff view that the merger not be permitted, the FTC traded off lower market concentration and the probable increased competitive viability of several small chains (that would have purchased the Mayfair-Arden stores) for increased four-firm concentration and the hope that increasing Lucky's market share would increase competition. This was a dubious trade-off. It was based on the assumption that competition is more likely to be enhanced by a merger leading to a market dominated by two or three chains than by several smaller acquisitions that would lessen concentration and strengthen the competitive position of a number of smaller chains. Not only did the commission's decision have an adverse effect on the Seattle and Tacoma markets, but it set an unfortunate precedent for other mergers, specifically the two large horizontal mergers permitted by the FTC in 1976 (Allied and A&P).

An FTC official, Owen J. Johnson, Jr., director of the Bureau of Competition at the time, testified that the commission did not challenge the horizontal mergers involving Allied-Great Scott and A&P-National Tea because "the circumstances warranted a 'failing company' defense." [28] This is an unusual application of the "failing company defense" because it was not the companies that were failing, but the divisions involved in the merger. The application of this defense was especially perverse in the case of the Allied-Great Scott merger: Not only was the alleged failing company a division rather than a company, but the unprofitable division involved was that of the acquiring—not the acquired—company. Thus, an allegedly unprofitable, inefficient division of a large chain was permitted to solve its problems by making an anticompetitive acquisition of a profitable company.

In sum, the antitrust agencies have not been enforcing the merger policies announced and pursued quite successfully in the 1960s. With respect to horizontal mergers, they should enforce the law as strictly as enunciated by the Supreme Court in its Von's decision. With respect to market extension mergers, they should not abandon the policy expressed in the National Tea decision[29] and the FTC's 1967 food distribution merger guidelines. The latter states:

> . . . whereas mergers by retail firms with annual sales in excess of $500 million may contribute to further concentration of buying power, in addition to any adverse effect that they may have at the retail selling level, it is unlikely that the prohibition of mergers by such companies would have an adverse effect on efficiency. Moreover, insofar as economies of scale require fairly large scale operations, the goal of promoting efficiency might be better achieved by channeling mergers away from the largest firms to those whose efficiency would be enhanced by further growth. [30]

Section 7 of the Clayton Act cannot be used to challenge de novo entry by a conglomerate even though such entry may result in increased concentration. However, the inability of the antitrust laws to challenge some anticompetitive practices does not legitimize anticompetitive practices that can be challenged. Additionally, a strict policy prohibiting large conglomerate retailers from entry by merger may have salutary effects, because many chains that are stopped from entering by merger may remain potential competitors. A strict merger policy prohibiting market extension mergers by large conglomerates (similar to the policy FTC pursued in the 1960s) may result in fewer large chains expanding into new geographic markets. But because oligopolistic firms within a market realize that de novo entry by a conglomerate very likely will severely erode their profits in the short run, and conceivably their long-run market shares and profits as well, the established oligopolists have an incentive to set prices at levels that will discourage entry. [31]

Apart from the probable salutary effects of a merger policy preventing significant market extension mergers by large conglomerates (grocery chains and large corporations not previously involved in food retailing), the finding that even conglomerate de novo entry tends to increase concentration warrants the attention of antitrust agencies. The appropriate regulatory action is not easy to define. It should be recalled, however, that our analysis of the effects of de novo entry was restricted to such entry into markets with relatively low and moderate concentrations. Although it did not demonstrate the effects of de novo entry in highly concentrated markets, economic analysis suggests that entry into highly concentrated markets with one or more dominant firms may have a beneficial effect on competition and can probably be achieved only by conglomerates with the ability to subsidize their operations in the entered market. In highly concentrated markets the chances that conglomerate entry will stimulate competition seem greater than the probability that competition will be depressed.

In relatively unconcentrated markets, the competitive impacts of conglomerate de novo entry are less clear. If such entry triggers a competitive battle among the chains in the markets, which may be particularly likely when the new entrant is viewed as a powerful competitor, concentration may be increased substantially, to the long-run detriment of competition.

Although the appropriate remedy is not clear, the lack of interest displayed in the past by the antitrust agencies in conglomerate de novo entry is inappropriate. We recommend that the FTC develop a monitoring program for conglomerate de novo entry that carefully scrutinizes the post-entry conduct of all powerful participants to determine the consequences in different market environments. If our entry-reducing recommendations described above are adopted, the concentration-increasing effects of conglomerate entry de novo or via toehold mergers may be substantially reduced or eliminated. With the elimination of restrictive leasing arrangements, selective price cutting, and saturation advertising, entry might occur without triggering the price and nonprice warfare waged most effectively by conglomerates, to the detriment of small chains.

IMPROVING CONSUMER INFORMATION

The results of this study indicate that a firm's prices in different metropolitan areas are positively related to its market share and the level of market concentration. This suggests that price differences within markets persist, at least in part, because consumers are unable to accurately evaluate the price levels of the competing sellers. *

---

*Since, in a market economy, "sovereign" consumers are relied upon to direct the allocation of resources, either misinformed or uninformed consumers can lead to faulty market signals. Consumers may be "sovereign" in a technical sense (their decisions still determine the allocation of resources among alternative uses) but are unable to exercise this power knowledgeably for their own best interest.

The complexity of the retail grocery market requires consumers to possess substantial amounts of information in order to evaluate alternative sellers. Individual consumers can seldom afford the time required to become adequately informed when the average supermarket stocks 8,000 items, changes prices relatively often, and offers a variety of weekly specials to attract customers. A significant gap between the information needed and available to consumers is therefore likely.

Few empirical studies have examined the adequacy or influence of market information. Two Canadian studies examined the effects of increased retail food price information. They teach important lessons for U. S. consumers as well.

A study in Ottawa-Hull in 1974 collected prices weekly on 65 food items in 26 supermarkets over a 28-week period. [32] Prices were collected but not published for 17 weeks, after which they were collected and published in daily newspapers for the following five weeks. Thereafter prices were monitored for six weeks but not published.

The impact of this information program on the level and dispersion of store prices in the market was substantial. Immediately prior to the publication of information, there was a 15 percent difference in the weighted market basket price at the highest- and lowest-priced stores. An 8 percent difference existed between the average prices of the highest- and lowest-priced corporate or voluntary chains.

During the information publication period, price dispersion across stores dropped to 5-8 percent, suggesting that previous price differences did not accurately reflect consumer valuation of the differences in the goods and services offered. The difference in the average prices of different chains declined to 3-5 percent.

Average prices for the entire market declined about 7.0 percent during the period when price information was published, as high-priced stores rapidly dropped prices to become competitive. During the six-week post-information period, in which prices were monitored but not published, average prices increased 8.8 percent. Because the study took place during a period of inflationary food prices, prices in other Canadian markets increased throughout the study period. Thus, even with the post-information increase of almost 9 percent, Ottawa-Hull prices at the end of the study were lower relative to other markets than before the comparative price information program.

Pre-test and post-test surveys of Ottawa consumers indicated some significant shifts in patronage from higher- to lower-priced firms. The largest chains in the market generally benefited from this shift; four-firm concentration increased from 74 percent during the pre-test period to 81 percent during the post-test period. Although the evidence suggests that the market became more competitive during the publishing of price information, the resultant increase in market concentration could lead to a deterioration in long-run competitive performance.

A post-test survey indicated consumers would be willing, on average, to pay 34 cents per week for the price comparison information. With approximately 120,000 families in the Ottawa-Hull area, the perceived value of the information was about $40,000 per week. The cost of the program, including consumer questionnaires, was approximately $875 per week.

Although the results of the Ottawa study were impressive, information was published for too short a period to ascertain the long-run effects. The price reductions may have been a short-run response that would not, and perhaps could not, be sustained over a longer time period. In the long run a price information program might also be used as an instrument for the collusion of leading companies, particularly in highly concentrated markets.

A follow-up study by the same researcher was conducted in Regina and Saskatoon during 1976. Prices were published weekly over a six-month period. Results indicate similar, though less dramatic, results. [33] The dispersion of prices across stores and firms was reduced; average prices in both markets also declined. When prices in Regina and Saskatoon were compared with prices in other Canadian cities prior to and during the information period, the information program was estimated to have led to a 1-2 percent decline in prices over the six-month period. Although the reduction in prices that occurred at the outset of the information program was less than in Ottawa, a substantial portion of this price decrease was maintained throughout the six-month publication period. Both markets are highly concentrated. However, there was no noticeable change in concentration as a result of the information program.

No comparable studies have been conducted in the United States. In a few cases consumer organizations or newspapers have published comparative prices on a sample of items. The accuracy, duration, and effects of these efforts have not, to our knowledge, been assessed.

The effect of comparative price information programs on market concentration is an important long-run concern. The results of the present study indicate that a firm's prices are positively related to its position in the market. In markets where this is true (such as city B in the report), comparative price information would be expected to cause some shift in patronage to the lower-market-share and lower-price firms (thereby reducing concentration) and/or a rapid realignment of prices in the market. In the long run, shifts in consumer patronage would depend upon the cost levels of competing sellers (and, hence, their ability to compete on a price basis) and the importance to consumers of differences in the nonprice offers of competing firms. Although large chains appear to enjoy some cost advantages, independent supermarkets and small chains may have lower wage rates and superior store-level operations.

The ability of large chains to subsidize across markets could result in their using comparative price information programs to restructure markets. This makes it particularly important to develop price monitoring programs in a number of metropolitan areas (whether or not the information is published in all cases), so that cross-subsidizing behavior can be detected.

An important long-run salutary effect of a comparative price information program is the erosion of entry barriers. The advertising advantages of large, established firms would be substantially reduced by a credible and readily available source of price information. Established firms would find themselves in less secure positions, and would be expected to reduce prices to a level that discourages new entrants. Thus, whether entry is actually increased or not, the reduction in entry barriers would be expected to have beneficial results.

The potential impact of increased information on consumer and seller behavior is sufficient to warrant additional exploration and analysis by government agencies. The Bureau of Labor Statistics, Department of Agriculture, and Federal Trade Commission are likely the most logical federal agencies to explore the feasibility of such a program. Appropriate state agencies might also be encouraged to support such programs. Various publication procedures should be tested, including continuous publishing every week, periodic publishing for four-six weeks but with continuous price monitoring, and continuous price monitoring with monthly publishing of the previous four weeks of data. The number of metropolitan areas involved in the program should gradually be expanded to allow analysis of the impact of comparative price information in different market environments. If data were available for 30-50 markets with a variety of structural characteristics, efforts to collude in any particular market would be quickly detectable. Such a body of data would also allow periodic analyses of the factors affecting both price levels and price changes in different markets.

The cost of such an effort would be reasonable, considering the potential benefits. The Canadian studies employed professional price takers at $15 per store per week for a market basket of 65 items. Using this rate, if 20 stores were price-checked in 30 markets every week of the year, the total annual collection cost would be approximately $450,000. If the Bureau of Labor Statistics were to collect the data, the complementarity with its present price collection efforts should result in an incremental cost that is lower than this estimate. The costs of analyzing and publishing the data must also be considered, but are not likely to exceed the cost of price collection.

Some may argue that such comparative price information programs constitute public invasion of business privacy. However, we believe public comparison of privately displayed prices is a legitimate function of the public sector, not unlike the many market news programs for farm products sponsored by the Department of Agriculture and many states. Since informed consumers are a sine qua non of a viable market system, programs to improve consumer information should be an essential part of an overall policy to promote competition.

CONSUMER COOPERATIVES

Consumer cooperatives play a small role in food retailing in the United States compared with some other nations. For example, consumer cooperatives make only about 0.5 percent of U.S. grocery store sales, compared with about 17 percent in Great Britain and 27 percent in Sweden. [34] They also are very important in some Canadian cities.

Although various factors may explain the historically low profile of consumer cooperatives in the United States, perhaps one reason is that food retailing here has generally been more competitive than in other nations. In any event, given the increasing concentration in food retailing and the resulting noncompetitive prices and profits in some markets, consumer cooperatives should be included among the alternative public policy options dealing with excessive market power in food retailing.

One of the few empirical studies of the subject found that chain prices were generally lower in markets where they competed with a consumer cooperative than in comparable markets without a cooperative. The average price difference for the 27 paired markets studied was approximately 1 percent and was statistically significant. [35] Although the price difference was modest, the results support the hypothesis that consumer cooperatives are a beneficial influence on competition.

Many cooperatives in this study apparently had little or no impact on competition. Some, however, did result in sizable savings to their customers—on the order of 3-6 percent. This suggests that consumers can expect to realize meaningful savings only if cooperatives are well-run and of sufficient size to achieve all or most economies of scale.

The potential benefits of successful consumer cooperatives are illustrated by the Calgary Cooperative Association, reportedly the largest consumer cooperative in North America. [36] In 1976, its eighteenth year of operation, the Canadian cooperative's 114,000 members included two-thirds of the population of Calgary. [37] It had total sales of $92.5 million in 1976, $67 million of which came from its eight supermarkets.

Not only were its supermarket gross margins below 17 percent, but it paid its members a patronage rebate of 3.2 percent of sales. Its effective gross margin of less than 14 percent was well below the average gross margins of large chains in the United States.

The Calgary Cooperative example is especially relevant because of the competitive environment in which it operates. The top four chains in the market (including the cooperative) had over 80 percent of market sales in 1976. Although Safeway is the market leader, with nearly 50 percent of sales, by 1976, Calgary Cooperative had expanded its share to approximately 30 percent.

Our analysis shows that a dominant chain in a comparably concentrated U.S. market would enjoy prices about 9 percent above a more competitively structured market where the top four firms each had 10 percent of sales. This indicates the magnitude of savings that consumers could realize from efficient consumer cooperatives in highly concentrated markets.

Several steps can be taken to promote the creation of efficient consumer cooperatives in the United States, where to date they generally have had lackluster records. Two of the above recommendations—lowering entry barriers and improved consumer information—would improve the environment for the development of cooperatives. But additional steps are needed. Consumer organizations should give high priority to aiding the development of consumer cooperatives, especially in highly concentrated markets where the stakes are high. The legislation creating a bank for consumer cooperatives should prove helpful in providing the capital necessary for creating new cooperatives and in aiding existing consumer cooperatives to become more efficient competitors. Aggressive efforts should be made to ensure that funds provided by this program are used to establish viable cooperatives in food retailing.

INDUSTRY RESTRUCTURING

The options mentioned above may not be sufficient to erode concentration or eliminate its adverse effects in markets that have become highly concentrated, especially where one or two firms dominate a market. In these cases, which fortunately are still relatively few, more direct action may be required to reduce market power or its effects.

One alternative is to permit such power to exist but to control its use through government regulation. We reject this as an unrealistic alternative. Setting "appropriate" prices in food retailing would be a regulatory nightmare.*

A second alternative is industry restructuring. This requires a case-by-case approach. In excessively concentrated markets, however defined, there are two main options.

The more drastic approach requires leading firms to divest part of their business in a particular market. An alternative approach would place restraints on the growth of the dominant chain (or chains) in a market until such time as its (or their) market share is reduced to some target level.

The Canadian consent decree mentioned earlier limited Safeway's expansion for three and one-half years in the cities of Calgary and Edmonton. It provided that Safeway "will not significantly increase the total square footage occupied by its stores and will be restricted to opening only one (1) new store in each of the two cities."[38]

Many public policy officials and courts are reluctant to restore competition through industry restructuring. This often reflects a fear that such actions will drastically disrupt business affairs, eliminate jobs, injure stockholders, and perhaps even harm consumers.

While not unmindful that difficult problems may arise in the course of publicly ordered restructuring, in our judgment such fears are greatly exaggerated. Experience has shown that businessmen are adept at restructuring strategies that result in high concentration. Such actions likely inflict greater costs on injured competitors and consumers than those inflicting them would experience if forced to divest themselves of some properties or to be limited for a time in their expansion.

The public policy issue is clear: Where excessive market power cannot be adequately redressed by other means, is there sufficient concern about the costs to consumers and competitors to take the steps necessary to reduce such power?

NOTES

1. Federal Trade Commission, Food Chain Selling Practices in the District of Columbia and San Francisco (Washington, D. C.: U. S. Government Printing Office, July 1969), p. 4. See also Federal Trade Commission, Discount Food Pricing in Washington, D. C. (Washington, D. C.: U. S. Government Printing Office, March 1971), p. 11.

---

*The price controls in effect during 1971-74 did not deal with the monopoly problem in food retailing or in other industries. They

2. U. S. v. Great Atlantic & Pacific Tea Co., 67 Fed. Supp. 626 (1946).

3. Statement by the judge in summarizing the prohibitions contained in a consent order in Regina v. Canada Safeway Limited, October 5, 1973, as reported in Antitrust Bulletin 19, no. 1, New York, N. Y., Federal Legal Practices (Spring 1974): 61.

4. Ibid., p. 63.

5. Ibid.

6. National Tea, FTC Docket no. 7453, Final Decision and Order (Washington, D. C.: U. S. Government Printing Office, 1966).

7. Ibid., p. 5.

8. Ibid., p. 7.

9. Ibid., p. 8.

10. Ibid., p. 14.

11. FTC, Enforcement Policy with Respect to Mergers in Food Distribution (Washington, D. C., Federal Trade Commission, January 3, 1967), p. 6.

12. National Tea, FTC Docket no. 7453, "Findings of Fact," (1966) p. 72.

13. U. S. v. Von's Grocery Co., 384 U. S. 270 (1966).

14. Supermarket News, January 3, 1977, p. 16.

15. Ibid., May 19, 1976, p. 36.

16. Ibid., May 24, 1976, p. 12.

17. Ibid.

18. "GU Eyes Acquisition Trail as End of FTC Pact Nears," Supermarket News, April 3, 1978, p. 22.

19. Especially Beatrice Foods, FTC Docket no. 6653 (1965); National Tea, FTC Docket no. 7453 (1966).

20. FTC, Structure and Competitive Behavior of Food Retailing (Washington, D. C.: U. S. Government Printing Office, January 1966), pp. 164-67.

21. Letter from Lewis A. Engman, chairman of the FTC, to Congressman Edward Mezvinsky, December 30, 1975.

22. Ibid.

23. Ibid.

24. Ibid. Emphasis added.

25. Letter from F. N. McCowan to FTC, May 21, 1975. The FTC requested public comment on the proposed merger. Four grocery

---

limited price increases of all retailers, whether in competitive or highly concentrated markets. As shown in our report, profits of food retailers were positively associated with the level of concentration and firm dominance during the price control years, as well as before.

retailers, a food wholesaler, and the executive director of a retail grocery association opposed the merger. (The retailers operated from two to ten stores each.) Two Mayfair stockholders wrote in favor of the merger.

26. Letter from Morrie Olson to FTC, May 15, 1975.

27. Letter from Richard C. Rhodes to FTC, May 19, 1975.

28. Testimony of Owen M. Johnson, Joint Economic Committee, Hearings on Prices and Profits of Leading Retail Food Chains, 1970–74, March 30 and April 5, 1977 (Washington, D. C. : U. S. Government Printing Office, 1977), p. 142.

29. National Tea, FTC Docket no. 7453 (March 4, 1966).

30. FTC, Enforcement Policy with Respect to Mergers in the Food Distribution Industries.

31. Joe S. Bain, Barriers to New Competition (Cambridge, Mass. : Harvard University Press, 1956).

32. D. Grant Devine, "An Examination of the Effects of Publishing Comparative Price Information on Price Dispersion and Consumer Satisfaction" (PhD diss. , Ohio State University, 1976).

33. D. Grant Devine, "A Review of the Experimental Effects of Increased Price Information on the Performance of Canadian Retail Food Stores in the 1970s," Canadian Journal of Agricultural Economics, 26 (November 1978).

34. Loys L. Mather, "Consumer Cooperatives in the Grocery Retailing Industry" (Ph. D. diss. , University of Wisconsin, 1968).

35. Ibid. , pp. 93–130.

36. Coop Consumer, Greenbelt Consumers Service, Inc. , Savage, Maryland (February 1977): 3.

37. Ibid. ; Calgary Cooperative Association, 20th Annual Report.

38. Regina v. Canada Safeway Limited, "Consent Order," p. 62.

APPENDIX A
SUPPORTING MATERIAL FOR CHAPTER ONE

TABLE A. 1

Percentage of Grocery Store Sales Made by Single-store and Multi-store Operators, 1948-72

Number of Units	1948	1954	1958	1963	1967	1972
Single Store	58. 7	51. 8	47. 0	43. 1	38. 9	32. 2
2-3 stores	3. 6	4. 8	4. 8	5. 0	5. 0	5. 1
4-10 stores	3. 2	4. 0	4. 2	4. 8	4. 8	5. 7
Total independents*	65. 5	60. 6	56. 0	52. 9	48. 7	43. 0
11-100 stores	7. 0	9. 9	11. 7	12. 6	15. 3	17. 4
100 or more stores	27. 4	29. 4	32. 3	34. 5	36. 1	39. 6
Total chains*	34. 4	39. 3	44. 0	47. 1	51. 4	57. 0

Note: Details may not total due to rounding.

*Independents include single-unit operations as well as multiunit operations of fewer than 11 stores. No distinction is made between affiliated and unaffiliated independents.

Chains are defined as multiunit operations with 11 or more stores under the same management.

Sources: U. S. Bureau of the Census, Census of Retail Trade, 1972, Subject Reports, Establishment and Firm Size RC 72-S-1 (Washington, D. C. : U. S. Government Printing Office, 1975); Census of Retail Trade, 1967, Subject Reports, U. S. Summary (Washington, D. C. : U. S. Government Printing Office, 1970); Census of Retail Trade, 1963, Subject Reports, U. S. Summary (Washington, D. C. : U. S. Government Printing Office, 1966); Census of Retail Trade, 1958, Subject Reports, U. S. Summary (Washington, D. C. : U. S. Government Printing Office, 1960).

TABLE A. 2

Typical Gross Profit Margins and Operating Expense Ratios, Supermarkets, 1965–77
(percent of sales; median figures)

Item	1965	1966	1967	1968	1969	1970	1971	1972	1973	1974	1975	1976	1977
Store door margin	18.4	18.1	18.0	18.3	18.1	18.3	18.1	18.0	17.4	17.9	18.6	18.6	18.5
Expenses													
Store labor	8.3	8.5	8.8	8.8	9.1	9.2	9.1	9.6	9.6	9.5	9.5	9.8	10.0
Advertising and promotion[a]	1.1	1.1	1.2	1.1	1.0	1.0	1.0	1.0	.9	.9	1.0	1.0	1.1
Store supply	.9	.9	.8	.8	.9	.9	.8	.8	.8	.9	.9	.9	.9
Rent and real estate	1.5	1.4	1.4	1.4	1.4	1.4	1.3	1.4	1.4	1.3	1.3	1.3	1.3
Utilities	.7	.7	.7	.6	.7	.6	.6	.7	.7	.8	.9	.9	.9
Equipment depreciation or rental costs	.8	.7	.7	.7	.7	.7	.7	.7	.7	.6	.7	.6	.7
Maintenance and repair	.3	.3	.4	.4	.4	.4	.4	.4	.4	.4	.5	.4	.4
All other expenses	1.2	1.1	1.0	1.2	1.1	1.1	1.1	1.1	1.0	1.0	1.2	1.9	.8
Total operating expenses[b]	16.1	16.3	16.2	16.1	16.3	16.5	16.3	16.7	16.4	16.1	16.9	17.1	17.2
Net operating profit	1.8	1.8	1.8	1.7	1.5	1.7	1.6	1.3	1.3	1.8	1.5	1.3	1.4

Notes: These data were compiled from a sample of both single-store and multiple-store operators. Figures are median figures for varying samples of firms. For this reason, the individual figures do not sum to the total in many cases.

[a]Advertising and promotion expense does not include trading stamp expense. Trading stamp expense was not included among store operating expenses because the incidence of trading stamp usage by grocery chains has waned since the late 1960s. For example, about 28 percent of the firms included in the Figure Exchange reported trading stamp expenses in 1974, whereas 47 percent reported trading stamp expenses in 1965. Thus, for earlier years advertising and promotion expenses are understated relative to the later years.

The expense for the firms handling trading stamps declined from 2.0 percent in 1965 to 1.5 percent in 1974, then increased to about 1.7 percent of sales in 1977.

Note that the median total operating expense category does not exclude trading stamp expenses.

[b]Total operating expense median figures for 1965–71 are based on fourth-quarter data. Total operating expense median figures for 1972–77 are annual figures.

Sources: Super Market Institute, Figure Exchange; Food Marketing Institute, Operations Review.

162

TABLE A.3

Gross Margins, Selected Expenses, and Earnings, Grocery Chain Store Operations, 1965-66/1976-77

Item	1965-66	1966-67	1967-68	1968-69	1969-70	1970-71	1971-72	1972-73	1973-74	1974-75	1975-76	1976-77
Gross margin	22.32	22.23	21.46	21.48	21.31	21.39	21.53	20.93	20.90	21.15	21.22	21.35
Expenses												
Payroll	10.51	10.46	10.51	10.53	10.65	11.09	11.38	11.57	11.59	11.71	11.68	12.03
Supplies	.96	.97	.88	.90	.92	1.01	.94	.93	.97	1.12	1.10	1.07
Utilities	.78	.76	.75	.73	.71	.74	.78	.79	.82	.94	1.05	1.02
Services purchased	1.25	1.34	1.33	1.22	1.35	1.31	1.25	1.35	1.25	1.21	1.31	1.26
Promotional activities	1.48	1.41	1.35	1.49	1.43	1.32	1.20	1.07	.71	.51	.40	.42
Property rentals	1.84	1.78	1.69	1.58	1.52	1.49	1.46	1.42	1.40	1.37	1.32	1.28
Depreciation	.97	.91	.89	.84	.82	.85	.86	.81	.81	.75	.77	.72
Other*	2.83	2.96	2.83	2.90	2.77	2.66	2.72	2.52	2.92	2.91	3.07	3.13
Total expense before interest	20.62	20.59	20.33	20.19	20.18	20.47	20.59	20.74	20.47	20.52	20.70	20.93
Total interest	.76	.74	.74	.70	.69	.73	.69	.65	.60	.64	.60	.55
Total expenses	21.38	21.33	20.97	20.89	20.87	21.20	21.29	21.39	21.08	21.17	21.31	21.48
Net operating profit	.94	.90	.49	.59	.45	.19	.23	-.45	-.18	-.02	-.09	-.13
Net other income	1.45	1.33	1.38	1.44	1.41	1.54	1.32	1.40	1.28	1.28	1.27	1.25
Total net earnings before income tax	2.40	2.23	1.87	2.03	1.86	1.73	1.55	.94	1.10	1.25	1.17	1.12
Total income taxes	1.09	1.04	.88	1.01	.94	.87	.73	.44	.54	.57	.55	.45
Net earnings	1.31	1.19	.99	1.02	.92	.86	.82	.49	.55	.67	.62	.66

Note: Details may not total due to rounding.
*Includes the following expenses: communications, travel, professional services, donations, insurance, taxes and licenses (except income taxes), equipment rental, repairs, and unclassified.

Source: Operating Results of Food Chains (Ithaca, N.Y.: Cornell University, selected years).

163

TABLE A. 4

Net Profits after Income Taxes as Percent of Stockholders' Equity, Leading Food Chains, 1963-76

Company and 1973 Sales Classification	1963	1964	1965	1966	1967	1968	1969	1970	1971	1972	1973	1974[a]	1975	1976
$1 billion and over														
Allied	12.1	11.0	10.5	9.5	7.0	3.4	-10.8	-36.9	3.7	9.9	1.7	-8.5	-35.8	-18.3
Acme	9.1	8.4	6.6	5.8	5.1	6.4	7.1	8.1	6.5	.5	9.0	13.0	13.4	10.1
Food Fair	7.6	8.9	11.6	10.7	9.2	9.7	n.a.	8.1	8.1	-1.0	1.6	6.4	-2.6	2.8
Grand Union	8.5	10.7	11.2	10.4	10.0	10.2	11.2	10.8	8.5	5.4	1.5	6.2	7.3	10.2
A&P	10.3	9.0	8.8	9.2	8.9	7.1	8.0	7.4	2.2	-8.6	2.0	-35.4	1.0	5.0
Jewel	11.1	12.1	12.8	12.2	12.3	13.1	13.0	-1.9	12.2	12.5	13.8	10.6	9.5	11.2
Kroger	9.8	11.9	12.8	11.3	9.6	12.1	12.5	12.0	9.2	5.2	7.6	10.8	8.1	10.6
Lucky	14.0	19.5	22.6	22.6	26.4	26.7	26.8	23.0	22.6	19.7	18.9	20.5	21.1	19.7
Safeway	14.3	14.7	13.9	15.7	12.6	12.8	11.9	13.9	14.7	15.0	13.1	16.5	18.7	11.9
Southland	n.a.	18.6	18.0	18.3	20.4	12.1	13.1	13.2	13.0	10.5	10.9	12.2	12.6	13.2
Stop & Shop	13.3	13.0	9.5	12.6	16.2	12.7	12.6	9.1	5.6	9.6	12.2	14.7	15.6	11.3
Supermarket General	21.3	23.2	24.5	17.6	22.4	19.9	13.4	14.4	16.1	6.4	10.9	3.7	10.1	13.1
Winn-Dixie	21.3	20.9	23.5	20.2	20.2	20.0	18.7	20.3	19.7	19.1	18.8	22.8	18.7	18.8
Weighted average	11.5	11.8	11.9	11.9	11.1	11.0	11.2	11.0	10.1	6.8	9.5	6.9	11.7	11.2
$500 million-$1 billion														
Albertson's	19.1	21.4	22.2	17.9	17.5	15.2	15.5	14.2	15.5	16.5	17.7	19.3	17.3	17.4

164

Arden–Mayfair	7.4	9.0	13.5	10.2	1.0	6.6	5.2	-7.4	5.0	-2.6	-82.6	9.9	-6.4	-18.4
Colonial	10.6	11.6	12.1	13.2	11.8	13.0	11.0	11.9	12.7	10.8	13.7	15.5	14.2	11.6
Dillon	18.0	17.0	17.9	16.7	17.8	15.5	16.0	17.6	19.2	19.3	21.0	22.0	23.7	24.3
First National	7.4	6.6	2.5	-.8	-7.8	1.4	5.6	4.2	-.9	.04	-22.7	9.0	-2.4	-7.0
Fisher	-1.8	-2.5	-.5	10.8	19.9	22.0	17.6	17.5	19.0	16.8	16.8	18.9	16.1	14.8
Giant	10.1	10.3	14.0	11.5	13.8	14.3	15.6	9.8	16.9	12.4	12.3	14.0	15.2	13.4
National Tea	7.2	8.9	8.9	9.2	8.8	6.0	8.0	6.1	7.0	-38.7	-19.8	-3.5	-7.1	-92.0
Pueblo International	20.0	20.4	21.5	21.4	18.2	23.6	19.9	11.1	14.3	-1.6	9.5	4.1	-14.2	-64.8
Weighted average	8.6	9.5	9.8	9.0	7.2	9.7	10.8	8.4	10.3	.8	1.3	12.2	9.5	2.7
22 chains over $500 million: simple average	11.9	12.9	13.6	13.0	12.8	12.9	12.0	8.5	11.5	6.2	4.0	9.2	7.0	-1.9
24 chains under $500 million[b]														
Weighted average	10.1	11.7	11.2	11.5	10.9	11.8	11.1	9.8	8.5	5.8	5.6	7.2	10.4	11.4
Simple average	12.1	14.7	13.8	13.0	12.4	12.4	11.3	10.3	8.4	2.8	4.2	4.7	10.6	10.9
Total weighted average	10.9	11.5	11.5	11.4	10.6	10.9	11.1	10.5	9.9	5.8	8.0	7.7	11.2	10.2
Total simple average	12.0	13.8	13.7	13.0	12.6	12.7	11.6	9.5	9.9	4.4	4.1	6.8	8.8	4.2

Notes: Net profits include extraordinary items. Data for fiscal years ending on or before June 30 are applicable to the prior year.

[a]See notes to Table A.5 for adjustments made due to changes in inventory valuation methods.

[b]Bohack was excluded from the sample in 1974; Penn Fruit and Loblaw, in 1975; and Big Bear, in 1976.

Sources: Federal Trade Commission, Food Chain Profits, report R-6-15-23 (Washington, D.C.: U.S. Government Printing Office), p. 31; Moody's Industrial Manual, New York, N.Y., Moody's Investor Service, Inc., (1977).

TABLE A.5

Net Profits after Income Taxes as Percent of Sales, Leading Food Chains, 1963–76

Company and 1973 Sales Classification	1963	1964	1965	1966	1967	1968	1969	1970	1971	1972	1973	1974	1975	1976
$1 billion and over														
Allied	1.2	1.1	1.0	0.8	0.5	0.2	-0.5	-1.3	0.1	0.4	0.1	0.3	-1.2	-1.5
Acme	1.2	1.1	.9	.7	.6	.7	.8	.8	.7	.05	.8	1.0	1.0	.7
Food Fair	.7	.8	1.0	.9	.8	.8	n.a.	.6	.6	-.1	.1	.4	-.1	.2
Grand Union	1.1	1.3	1.4	1.3	1.2	1.3	1.4	1.3	1.0	.6	.2	.6	.7	1.1
A&P	1.1	1.0	1.0	1.0	1.0	.8	.9	.9	.3	-.8	.2	-2.3	.1	.3
Jewel	1.5	1.6	1.7	1.6	1.4	1.6	1.5	1.5	1.5	1.5	1.6	1.2	1.0	1.2
Kroger	1.1	1.2	1.2	1.1	.9	1.1	1.1	1.1	.9	.5	.7	1.0	.6	.8
Lucky	1.2	1.6	1.7	1.7	1.8	1.4	1.7	1.6	1.7	1.5	1.4	1.5	1.5	1.4
Safeway	1.7	1.8	1.6	1.8	1.5	1.8	1.3	1.4	1.5	1.5	1.3	1.5	1.5	1.0
Southland	n.a.	1.3	1.4	1.3	1.5	1.5	1.5	1.5	1.6	1.7	1.7	1.8	1.9	1.9
Stop & Shop	1.3	1.2	.9	1.1	1.4	1.0	1.0	.7	.4	.6	.8	1.0	1.1	.8
Supermarket General	n.a.	n.a.	1.4	.9	1.2	1.4	1.0	1.0	1.0	.4	.6	.2	.5	.7
Winn–Dixie	2.3	2.5	2.7	2.3	2.3	2.1	1.0	2.1	2.1	2.0	1.9	2.2	1.9	1.8
Weighted average	1.3	1.3	1.3	1.3	1.2	1.1	1.1	1.1	1.0	.6	.9	.6	.9	.9

$500 million–$1 billion

Albertson's	1.5	2.0	1.9	1.4	1.2	1.1	1.2	1.1	1.1	1.1	1.1	1.1	1.2	1.2
Arden–Mayfair	0.7	1.0	1.1	0.8	0.1	0.5	0.4	-0.4	0.3	-0.2	-2.8	0.4	-.3	-.8
Colonial	1.1	1.2	1.3	1.4	1.3	1.5	1.2	1.3	1.4	1.3	1.3	1.5	1.4	1.2
Dillon	1.8	1.6	1.8	1.6	1.7	1.8	1.8	1.7	1.8	1.8	1.7	1.8	2.0	2.1
First National	1.0	.9	.3	-.1	-1.0	.2	.6	.4	-.1	.0	-1.7	0.6	-.2	-.4
Fisher	.2	.3	-.04	.8	1.8	1.6	1.3	1.3	1.4	1.2	1.1	1.1	.9	.9
Giant	1.0	1.1	1.4	1.1	1.3	1.3	1.4	.9	1.5	1.4	1.1	1.2	1.4	1.2
National Tea	.8	.9	1.0	.9	.9	.6	.7	.5	.6	-3.3	-1.6	-.2	-.4	-2.9
Pueblo International	4.2	3.9	4.2	4.3	2.8	1.7	1.6	1.0	1.4	-.1	.8	.3	-.9	-2.9
Weighted average	1.0	1.1	1.1	.9	.7	.9	1.0	.7	.9	.1	.1	.8	.7	.2
24 chains*under $500 million: weighted average	1.1	1.3	1.3	1.3	1.3	1.3	1.2	1.0	1.0	0.6	0.5	0.6	.9	1.0
Total weighted average	1.2	1.3	1.3	1.2	1.1	1.1	1.1	1.0	1.0	.6	.7	.6	.9	.8

	Profit–Sales (LIFO)	Profit–Stockholder Equity (LIFO)
Acme	.7	9.0
Colonial	1.0	11.2
Giant	.9	11.1
Safeway	1.0	11.4
Winn–Dixie	1.9	19.1

Notes: In 1974, Acme, Colonial, Giant, Safeway, and Winn–Dixie switched to the LIFO (last in, first out) accounting method for inventory valuation. The change to this method of accounting effectively reduced 1974 net earnings for those companies and decreased both their profit–sales and profit–stockholder equity ratios. In order to maintain a consistent basis for evaluating all firms over time, the profit–sales and profit–stockholder equity ratios for the affected firms have been restated in FIFO (first in, first out) for 1974 in this table and Table A.4. The profit–sales and profit–stockholder equity ratios for the affected firms under LIFO are as follows:

Net profits includes extraordinary terms. Data for fiscal year ending on or before June 30 are applicable to the prior year.
*See footnote b, Table A.4, for exclusions.

Sources: Federal Trade Commission, Food Chain Profits, report R-6-15-23, Washington, D.C.: U.S. Government Printing Office, p. 40; Moody's Industrial Manual, New York, N.Y., Moody's Investor Service, Inc., (1977).

TABLE A.6

Food Products Manufactured by the 40 Largest Chains, 1963 and 1967

Census Industry Code	Number of Companies Reporting Production			Value of Shipments of the Top 40 Chains Reporting (thousands)		
	1963	1967	Net Change	1963	1967	Percent Change
2011 Meat packing	4	5	1	220,165	271,435	23.3
2013 Prepared meats	9	10	1	46,029	41,063	-10.8
2015 Poultry dressing	3	2	-1	D	D	D
2021 Butter	5	4	-1	9,081	8,775	-3.4
2022 Natural cheese	8	5	-3	8,187	4,537	-44.6
2023 Concentrated milk	9	5	-4	48,576	48,419	-0.3
2024 Ice cream	17	16	-1	86,527	107,527	24.3
2026 Fluid milk	13	13	0	259,449	363,145	40.0
2031 Canned seafoods	2	1	-1	D	D	D
2032 Canned specialties	3	4	1	D	16,499	D
2033 Canned fruits and vegetables	10	10	0	56,177	44,282	-21.2
2034 Dehydrated fruits and vegetables	2	1	-1	D	D	D
2035 Pickles and sauces	10	11	1	25,050	31,764	26.8
2036 Packages seafoods	2	2	0	D	D	D

2037 Frozen fruits and vegetables	12	10	-2	12,412	11,331	-8.7
2041 Flour milling	3	1	-2	D	D	D
2042 Dog and cat food	—	1	1	—	D	—
2045 Flour mixes	1	2	1	D	D	D
2046 Wet corn	1	2	1	D	D	D
2051 Bread products	30	28	-2	419,388	451,452	7.6
2052 Biscuits and crackers	16	20	4	47,625	51,457	8.0
2071 Confectionery products	9	11	2	50,900	54,194	6.3
2072 Chocolate products	1	1	0	D	D	D
2086 Soft drinks	6	7	1	4,197	15,300	264.5
2087 Flavorings	6	7	1	5,753	8,364	45.4
2091 Cottonseed oil	1	—	-1	D	—	—
2092 Soybean oil	1	—	-1	D	—	—
2094 Grease and edible tallow	1	—	-1	D	—	—
2095 Roasted coffee	21	19	-2	155,759	131,368	-15.7
2096 Shortening and cooking oils	2	1	-1	D	D	D
2098 Macaroni and noodles	1	1	0	D	D	D
2099 Miscellaneous	13	20	7	80,866	97,603	20.7
Total				1,609,502	1,822,628	13.2

D = Not shown because of disclosures of individual company data.

Sources: Federal Trade Commission, Economic Report on the Dairy Industry, (Washington, D. C.: U. S. Government Printing Office, March 1973). Data are from Federal Trade Commission, Food Retailing Survey (Washington, D. C.: U. S. Government Printing Office, 1965 and 1969).

TABLE A. 7

Average Four-Firm Concentration Ratios for a Sample of 194 SMSAs, Classified by Magnitude of Definitional Change between 1954 and 1972

Magnitude of Definitional Change in SMSA[a] (percent)	Number of SMSAs	Percent of Sample	Average CR$_4$ (percent)		Percentage Change in Average CR$_4$	Mean Growth[b] (percent)
			1954	1972		
No change	85	43.8	44.8	53.9	20.3	210.5
Less than 10	39	20.1	45.2	52.5	16.2	183.1
10.0–19.9	31	16.0	44.8	48.4	8.0	164.5
20.0–29.9	16	8.2	45.3	48.6	7.3	242.4
Over 30	23	11.9	46.7	50.2	7.5	193.4
Total	194	100.0	45.1	52.1	15.5	199.6

[a]Change in SMSA definitions between 1954 and 1972 were treated as if they had occurred in 1972. The 1972 grocery store sales for the area added to each SMSA between 1954 and 1972 were taken as a percent of the 1972 grocery store sales of the SMSA as defined in 1954. Thus, the magnitude of the definitional change indicates the percentage increase in the size of the SMSA attributable to the change in definition.

[b]Growth is the percentage increase between 1954 and 1972 in the undeflated grocery store sales of the sample SMSAs as they were defined in 1972; thus, comparable geographic areas were used to calculate SMSA growth. Census data limitations precluded the computation of growth estimates for 19 of the 194 SMSAs in the sample. These SMSAs were located principally in New England states.

Source: Bureau of the Census, 1954 Census of Business, Retail Trade (Washington, D.C.: U.S. Government

TABLE A. 8

Acquisitions of Grocery Retailers by Nongrocery Store Firms, 1967–74

Year	Acquiring Firm	Acquired Firm	Acquired Firm's Sales (million dollars)
1967	Gamble–Skogmo, Inc.	Red Owl	488
1967	E. F. MacDonald Co.	Shopping Bag Stores	110
1968	Petrolane, Inc.	Stater Bros.	77
1968	General Host Corp.	Li'l' General Stores	44
1968	Federated Department Stores	Ralph's Grocery Co.	160
1969	Ruddick Corp.	Harris–Teeter	70
1970	Household Finance	Von's Grocery Co.	247
1970	J. C. Penney Co.	Supermkts. Interstate, Inc.	111
1971	Pneumo Dynamics Corp.	P&C Food Markets, Inc.	119
1972	Brown & Williamson Tobacco Co.	Kohl's	205
1974	Cavenham (Overseas Ltd.)	Grand Union Co.	1,400

Sources: Moody's Industrial Manual, Moody's Investor Service, Inc., various issues; Fairchild Publication, Supermarket News, New York, N. Y., Capital Cities Media, Inc., various issues; American Institution of Food Distribution, Weekly Digest, Fair Lawn, N.J., American Institute of Food Distribution, various issues; FTC, merger notification reports supplied to the Joint Economic Committee.

TABLE A. 9

Horizontal Acquisitions during 1967-75 by the Top 20 Food Retailers of 1976, by SMSA

Acquiring Firm's Share of SMSA Sales	Acquired Firm's Share of Grocery Store Sales in SMSA										
	0-1%	1%	2%	3%	4%	5%	6%	7%	8%	9%	10%
Under 1%	0	1	0	0	0	0	0	0	0	0	0
1%	4	1	0	0	0	0	0	0	0	0	0
2%	2	1	0	0	0	0	0	0	0	0	0
3%	3	0	0	0	0	0	0	0	0	0	0
4%	0	1	0	0	0	0	0	0	0	0	0
5%	4	2	0	0	1	0	0	0	0	0	0
6%	0	1	0	0	0	0	0	0	0	0	0
7%	0	0	0	0	0	0	0	0	0	0	0
8%	1	0	0	0	0	0	0	0	0	0	0
9%	1	0	1	0	0	0	0	0	0	0	0
10%	0	0	1	0	0	0	0	0	0	0	0
11-15%	4	0	2	0	0	0	0	0	0	0	0
16-20%	4	0	0	0	0	0	0	0	0	0	1
Over 20%	1	0	0	1	0	1	0	0	0	0	0
Total	24	7	4	1	1	1	0	0	0	0	1

Notes: In cases where a chain acquired a retailer operating in more than one SMSA, the acquired stores are allocated to the appropriate SMSA.

Sources: Data from 1949-66 are from Federal Trade Commission as Reported in Willard F. Mueller, The Celler-Kefauver Act: Sixteen Years of Enforcement, report to the Antitrust Subcommittee of the Committee on the Judiciary, House of Representatives (Washington, D.C.: U.S. Government Printing Office 1, Oct. 16, 1967). Data for 1967-75 from FTC merger notification reports supplied to the Joint Economic Committee; and from secondary sources such as Moody's Industrial Manual, various years, Supermarket News, various issues, and Weekly Digest, various issues. FTC data reported 185 retail acquisitions with combined sales of $4.455 billion. Secondary sources reported 142 retail acquisitions with combined sales of $2.954 billion. Of this latter total, eight acquisitions had combined sales of $1.265 billion. These large acquisitions involved the acquisition of large food retailers by large firms not involved in food retailing. The FTC notification program did not require reporting these mergers.

Large Horizontal Acquisitions during 1967–75 by Grocery Retailers Other than 20 Largest of 1976, by SMSA

Acquiring Firm's Share of SMSA Sales	Acquired Firm's Share of Grocery Store Sales in SMSA								
	0–1%	1%	2%	3%	4%	5%	6%	7%	8%
Under 1%	1	1	0	0	2	0	0	0	0
1%	1	1	0	1	1	0	0	0	0
2%	2	2	1	0	0	0	0	0	0
3%	0	2	0	1	0	0	0	0	0
4%	3	0	0	1	1	0	0	0	0
5%	0	1	0	0	1	0	0	0	0
6%	0	0	1	0	0	0	0	0	0
7%	0	0	0	0	0	0	0	0	0
8%	0	1	0	0	0	1	0	0	0
9%	0	0	1	0	0	0	0	0	0
10%	1	0	0	1	0	0	0	0	0
11–15%	0	1	0	0	1	0	0	0	1
16–20%	0	0	1	0	0	0	0	0	0
Over 20%	1	0	0	0	0	1	0	1	0
Total	9	10	4	4	6	2	0	1	1

Notes: Large mergers are defined as those in which the acquired retailer had sales of $10 million or more. In cases where a chain acquired a retailer operating in more than one SMSA, the acquired stores are allocated to the appropriate SMSAs.

Sources: Data from 1949–66 are from Federal Trade Commission as reported in Willard F. Mueller, The Celler–Kefauver Act: Sixteen Years of Enforcement, report to the Antitrust Subcommittee of the Committee on the Judiciary, House of Representatives, (Washington, D.C.: U.S. Government Printing Office, Oct. 16, 1967). Data for 1967–75 from FTC merger notification reports supplied to the Joint Economic Committee; and from secondary sources such as Moody's Industrial Manual, various years, Supermarket News, various issues, and Weekly Digest, various issues. FTC data reported 185 retail acquisitions with combined sales of $4.455 billion. Secondary sources reported 142 retail acquisitions with combined sales of $2.954 billion. Of this latter total, eight acquisitions had combined sales of $1.265 billion. These large acquisitions involved the acquisition of large food retailers by large firms not involved in food retailing. The FTC notification program did not require reporting these mergers.

APPENDIX B
SUPPORTING MATERIAL FOR
CHAPTERS TWO THROUGH FOUR

CONSTRUCTION OF MARKET BASKET DATA

Data used in the price analysis were drawn from price comparison reports submitted by major retail food chains to the Joint Economic Committee. The surveys on which they were based were not conducted at the request of the Joint Economic Committee, but had been done by the companies for their own purposes prior to the committee data request. The price surveys varied with respect to the number and type of items price-checked, date(s) on which the price checks were conducted, forms on which the price checks were recorded, and the number of price comparison reports submitted by each company.

Only two chains submitted price information on a substantial number of items and for a large number of SMSAs. These price surveys were for the month of October 1974. For these two chains, firms H and K, a "market basket" was developed containing a broad cross section of products on which prices were available from the price comparison reports. Meat and produce items were not included in the market basket because data for these items were incomplete. It was possible to develop the cost of a market basket of dairy, frozen food, and grocery products. For firm H it also was possible to include health and beauty aids.

In several cases difficulties were encountered in drawing prices from the price comparison reports, for the following reasons:

Two or more price surveys were submitted by a company for a particular SMSA during October 1974
Two or more prices for the same item were recorded on the same price check
Prices were not recorded for items in the market basket
Several private-label brands were carried by the companies, raising questions as to which private-label brand was most comparable with the national brand included in the market basket.

With respect to the first two difficulties, prices believed to be in effect on or nearest to October 15, 1974, were chosen. Where the price in effect closest to October 15 could not be ascertained, the company involved was asked to clarify the approximate dates the prices were in effect. The third major difficulty was partially resolved by excluding those SMSA price surveys that covered relatively few items. In those cases where a small percentage of the items contained in the market basket were omitted, an estimate of the prices was made. * If a large percent of any one major group or subgroup of items was omitted, but not a large percent of the total market basket, then that particular group of items was deleted.

Private-label brands chosen were based upon quality as measured by price. For example, brand "A" and brand "B" are two firm K private-label brands of peanut butter. † In the preliminary examination it was found that brand "A" was generally priced higher than brand "B. " Therefore it was assumed that brand "A" peanut butter was of higher quality and brand "A" was chosen as the private-label brand to be included in the market basket. Once the choice of the private-label brands for each company had been made, only those brands were used in tabulating the costs of grocery items. ‡

The products included in the market basket were selected after screening 18 price comparison reports submitted by firm A, firm H,

---

*Estimates of prices were based on other price surveys submitted by a given firm. Generally, these estimates were based on mean prices observed from SMSAs located within the same geographic region. Also, when possible, estimates were based upon the ratio of prices between SMSAs. For example, assume that for two SMSAs located near one another, prices observed for canned peaches were $.20 and $.25 respectively. If the first SMSA had an observed price of $.30 for canned pears and the second SMSA did not price-check that product, the estimated price was calculated as $.20/.25 = .30/x; x = .375,$ or $.38. It was necessary to make estimates for less than 3 percent of the grocery prices used in the analysis.

†Firm K reported in its 1973 annual report that it carries approximately 3,000 items under a private-label brand. Note that the terms "product" and "item" are not synonymous. Products are differentiated by the type of food (such as canned peas), whereas items are differentiated according to brand and package size. Thus, it is possible to be referring to one product when comparing ten items.

‡An additional aid in determining which private-label brands should be compared with national brands came from price surveys. One chain conducting a survey in city B showed its comparisons on computer printout sheets that arrayed products in such a manner as to show competing private-label and national-brand items in a clearly distinguishable manner.

and firm K. Products chosen were those most frequently price-checked. * The general market basket contained 127 distinct products (see Table B. 3). Seventy of the products were price-checked with respect to both national brands and private labels, bringing the total number of items in the general market basket to 197. Table B. 1 indicates the number and type of products included in the firm K and firm H market baskets.

The product group and market basket data were developed by the following weighting procedures. First, different weights were assigned to national brands and private-label brands of particular products on the basis of estimated consumption of each. These estimates relied on data from National Commission on Food Marketing Technical Study no. 10 and from Selling Areas Marketing, Inc. , for the Cincinnati-Dayton-Columbus market area. The weights reflect the proportion of a product's sales realized by national brands and "other" brands (Table B. 3).

Weighting the individual products according to national-brand and private-label weights takes into account the impact of buying a particular brand on the average price of a particular product. These weights do not take into account the relative importance of a particular product in terms of overall food consumption or expenditures on all food consumed. Therefore, the price of each product was weighted by the expenditures on that product relative to the expenditures on all food products. For example, if milk represents 2 percent of the total expenditures for food at home and grapefruit represents 0. 5 percent, the prices of the two products would be weighted by . 02 and . 005.

The expenditure weights used in this study are based on a study by Chain Store Age. As Table B. 2 indicates, several important product categories were not included in the market basket because of lack of data. Meat, produce, and bakery goods were the most important unrepresented categories. Together these account for 36 percent of consumer expenditures in supermarkets. Several product groups in the grocery department also were not represented. These account for an additional 13 percent of consumer expenditures. In large part these were tobacco, alcoholic beverages, and nonfood products.

Thus, the products included in the market basket represent those categories that account for approximately one-half of a supermarket's sales. Within each category several products were generally priced. For example, nine frozen food products were included in the market

---

*Results of the screening process demonstrated that firm A did not price-check the same items across SMSAs with enough frequency to allow for meaningful analysis of the prices it submitted.

basket. Together these accounted for 5.43 out of the 6.10 percent of expenditures that go for frozen foods. In assigning weights it was assumed that the price of a single product (for example, Campbell's tomato soup) was an accurate indicator of the price level for closely related products (for example, canned condensed soups). Products were weighted accordingly. In total, the products included in the market basket account for 37 percent of consumer expenditures in supermarkets and are felt to be representative of product categories accounting for one-half of expenditures.

The price data submitted on meat products were limited in the number of markets covered and in the consistency of products price-checked from one market to another. For three markets, however, the available meat price data allowed the construction of a meat basket. The types and cuts of meat selected were similar to those included in the Consumer Price Index. Quantity weights were developed from the Household Food Consumption Survey, 1965-66. Since the costs of meat baskets were used only for comparison within an SMSA, minor variations in the cuts included for different SMSAs were allowed (for instance, sirloin steak instead of T-bone).

The costs of the various baskets were indexed in these case studies because quantity weights were used in calculating the cost of the meat basket, whereas expenditure weights were used for other products. The meat and market baskets were combined by weighting the index for each basket by the percent of consumer expenditures represented by the basket. Chain Store Age shows that expenditures on nonmeat items account for 77.27 percent of all expenditures in supermarkets. Thus, the market basket index was multiplied by .7727 and the meat basket index by .2273 to produce a combined meat and market basket index.

ESTIMATION OF FIRM MARKET SHARES

Estimation of 1972 and 1974 firm market shares and relative firm market shares relied heavily upon four sources: company-supplied sales data; the 1974, 1975, and 1976 editions of Grocery Distribution Guide, published by Metro Market Studies (hereafter referred to as Metro '74, '75, '76); 1972 Census of Retail Trade; and Sales Management estimates of 1974 supermarket sales by SMSA. *

---

*In addition, two other sources—Market Scope, published by Progressive Grocer, and Grocers' Spotlight, published by Shamie—were used in calculating market shares for cities FF, E, and KK.

The 1972 firm market shares used in the price analysis were primarily estimated by using company-supplied sales data and Census data. Of the 36 observations used in the price analysis, the RFMS estimates for 23 (64 percent) were based on sales data supplied by the companies (hereafter referred to as "hard" market shares). * The remaining 13 observations were estimated using Metro '74 data, Census CR_4s, and the available "hard" market shares for other firms present in the market. † The ratio of the Census CR_4 to the Metro CR_4 for 1972 was used to adjust the market shares of the four leading firms reported in Metro '74. If "hard" market share data for any of the four leading firms were available, the ratio of Census CR_2 or CR_3 to Metro CR_2 or CR_3 was used to adjust Metro's market shares for the leading firms without "hard" data.

Estimates of market share for firms not ranking in the top four were calculated by taking the ratio of $1-CR_4$ (Census) to $1-CR_4$ (Metro) after subtracting available "hard" market shares. Thus, for each market two ratios were calculated, one for adjusting Metro market shares for the leading four firms and one for adjusting the market shares of all other firms. These ratios were also used to adjust the average market shares reported in Metro '75 and '76.

The 1972 "hard" market shares were computed by using company sales by SMSAs when available and Census total grocery store sales by SMSA. "Hard" market shares for 1974 were estimated by using company-supplied sales data and total "supermarket" sales by SMSA for 1974, as reported by Sales Management. Since companies were requested to supply data for the first three quarters of 1974, company sales data for 1974 were generally for the first six to nine months. In estimating "hard" market shares, Sales Management supermarket sales figures were adjusted to be consistent with the proportion of the

---

The methods used in adjusting the reported market shares were the same as those described above.

*We have not used the Census CR_4 of 32. 1 for city R because we believe it to be in error. Based on hard data for three firms and an estimate for one, we estimate the correct CR_4 to be 42. 4.

†Metro estimates of market share do not follow a calendar year. The Metro 1974 estimates of market share were approximately for the period July 1, 1972–June 30, 1973. Because of definitional differences between the 1973 and 1974 Metro editions, Metro 74 was used to estimate 1972 market shares. For the 1974 estimates of market shares, the average of the 1975 and 1976 editions of Metro were used because they collectively applied to the period July 1, 1973–June 30, 1975.

year represented in company sales data. For example, if a firm supplied sales data for selected SMSAs through September 1974, Sales Management sales data were multiplied by 0.75. The estimated market share was assumed to hold for the entire year.*

Market shares estimated from "hard" data or from Metro Market for the leading four firms were summed to arrive at an estimated 1974 CR_4 for each SMSA. The individual firm market shares were used in conjunction with the estimated CR_4s in calculating each firm's relative market share (RFMS).

Market shares shown in Tables 3.5-3.8 were not necessarily used in the regression analysis or in estimating monopoly overcharges. To avoid disclosure of any firm's actual market share, market shares shown in Tables 3.5-3.8 were estimated by following the same procedure used in estimating 1972 market shares, except that "hard" market shares were ignored and the estimated 1974 CR_4s were used. Thus, the individual market shares shown were not necessarily those used in the analyses. However, the CR_4s in these tables were used in the analysis. †

---

*The quality of the 1974 "hard" market share data depended heavily upon the accuracy of Sales Management estimates of total supermarket sales. Definitions of SMSAs and of supermarket sales were also important. The SMSA definitions used by Census and Sales Management were identical for 1972 for those markets used in the price analysis. Sales Management supermarket sales figures were approximately equivalent to the Census total grocery store sales. In order to evaluate the accuracy of Sales Management estimates, the computed 1974 "hard" market shares for each firm were compared with the 1972 "hard" market shares to identify any radical errors. With the exception of city I, the differences in these estimates were small. The Sales Management estimate of 1974 supermarket sales for city I was judged to be understated, and was adjusted by the ratio of the 1972 Census estimate of grocery store sales to the 1972 estimate of supermarket sales reported by Sales Management. Estimates of market shares using the adjusted supermarket sales figure were consistent with private industry estimates.

†There were no firm sales data for estimating "hard" market shares in city N. In this and all other cases where no "hard" data were available, the market shares shown in the tables were the same as those used in the regression analysis and/or the monopoly overcharge estimates.

TABLE B. 1

Number of Products and Items Included in
Firm K and Firm H Market Baskets

Product Categories	Firm K	Firm H
Grocery Basket		
National Brand	94	94
Private label	57	46
Dairy		
National brand	7	7
Private label	3	4
Frozen foods		
National brand	9	9
Private label	3	4
Health and Beauty aids		
National brand	0	17
Private label	0	2
Market Basket		
Total number of products[a]	110[a]	127[a]
Total number of items[b]	173[b]	183[b]

[a]The total number of national-brand items equals the total number of products carried in the market baskets. With the exception of health and beauty aids, the number and type of products included in the market baskets for each firm were identical.

[b]The number of national-brand items plus private-label items equals the total number of items included in the market baskets. In all cases private-label items have national-brand counterparts and hence do not represent additional products.

Source: Compiled from company data provided by Joint Economic Committee.

TABLE B.2

Product Categories Represented and not Represented in Market Basket, and Expenditure Weights Used

Product Category Represented	Expenditures in Supermarkets (percent)	Weight in Market Basket	Product Category Not Represented	Expenditures in Supermarkets (percent)
Frozen foods	6.10	(5.43)	Meat	22.73
Dairy	11.83	(5.36)	Produce	7.33
Grocery			Grocery	
Canned fruits, vegetables, juices, drinks	3.83		Bakery products	6.26
			Dried fruit	0.15
Canned meat and fish, prepared foods, tomato products	2.84		Beer	2.85
			Wine	0.26
Cold and hot cereals	1.55		Liquor	0.54
Pasta, dried vegetable products	1.09		Pickles, olives, relishes	0.55
Coffee, tea, soft drinks	4.93		Candy, gum	1.24
Baking needs	3.73		Nuts	0.36
Syrups, spreads	2.72	(1.77)	Dietetic/low cal.	0.26
Baby products, condensed milk products	0.87		Tobacco	4.62
Pet food	2.07	(0.52)	Housewares	1.13
Household cleaning products	3.34	(1.80)	Soft goods	0.39
Paper and foil products	2.49	(3.34)	Waxes, polishes	0.21
		(1.78)	Misc. household supplies	0.21
Total Grocery	29.46	23.60	Magazines, stationery, school supplies, misc.	0.42
Health and beauty aids	3.09	2.92	Total grocery	19.45
Total represented	50.48	37.31	Total unrepresented	49.51

Source: "Supermarkets," Chain Store Age 51, no. 7 (July 1975).

TABLE B.3

Market Basket of 127 Products and Their Weights Used in the Price Analysis

Product	Nat'l. Brand	Size		Nat'l. Brand Weight	Pvt. Label Weight	Expenditure Weight
Frozen foods						
Strawberries		16	oz.		*	.09
Orange juice	Min. Md.	12	oz.	.20	.80	.76
Grape juice	Welch	12	oz.	.80	.20	.03
Grn. beans, cut	Brdeye	9	oz.	.21	.79	.27
Corn niblets	Grn. Gt.	10	oz.	*		.39
Green peas	Brdeye	10	oz.	.19	.81	.42
French fries		16	oz.		*	.33
Chicken dinner	Swanson	11.5	oz.	*		2.06
Pound cake	Sara Lee	11.25	oz.	*		.96
Dairy						
Butter	Lnd-O-Lks	1	lb.	.40	.60	.69
Velveeta cheese	Kraft	2	lb.	*		1.16
Cream cheese	Phila.	8	oz.	.50	.50	.82
Ice cream		0.5	gal.		*	1.55
Cool Whip	Brdeye	9	oz.	*		.04
Margarine, qtrs.	Bl. Bnet.	1	lb.	.82	.18	.83
Corn oil marg.	Fleischmn.	1	lb.	.82	.18	.27

182

Grocery

Can. frt., vege., juice, drinks

Fruit cocktail	Del Monte	17	oz.	.51	.49	.12
Applesauce	Mott's	16	oz.	.55	.45	.15
Y. c. peach, malv.	Del Monte	16	oz.	.54	.46	.18
Pear halves	Del Monte	16	oz.	.46	.54	.10
Pnaple. chnk., nat. juice	Dole	20	oz.	.51	.49	.12
Pork n beans	Van Camps	16	oz.	.69	.31	.20
Grn. beans, cut	Del Monte	16	oz.	.70	.30	.40
W.k. corn	Del Monte	17	oz.	.70	.30	.26
Grn. peas	Del Monte	17	oz.	.68	.32	.22
Orange juice	Treeswt.	46	oz.	.80	.20	.14
Prune juice	Sunswt.	32	oz.	.80	.30	.38
Tomato juice	Libby	46	oz.	.62	.38	.17
Orange drink	Tang	27	oz.	.80	.20	.05
Frt. drnk., flav.	Hi-C	46	oz.	*		.27
Grape drink	Welchade	46	oz.	.80	.20	.09

Can. meat and fish, prep. food, tomat. products

Tomato sauce	Hunt	15	oz.	.33	.67	.18
Tomato paste	Hunt	6	oz.	.33	.67	.13
Beef stew	Dnty Moore	24	oz.	.99	.01	.11
Spam	Hormel	12	oz.	*		.13
Spaghetti	Frnco. Amer.	15	oz.	*		.18
Chnk. lite tuna	Starkist	6.5	oz.	.69	.31	.69

(continued)

Table B.3, continued

Product	Nat'l. Brand	Size	Nat'l. Brand Weight	Pvt. Label Weight	Expenditure Weight
Tomato soup	Cmpbells.	10.75 oz.	.90	.10	.51
Vienna sausage	Armour	5 oz.	*		.07
Potted meat	Armour	3.5 oz.	*		.01
Deviled ham	Underwood	4.5 oz.	*		.01
Cold and hot cereals					
Corn flakes	Kellogg's	18 oz.	.80	.20	.27
Cheerios	Gen. Mills	15 oz.	*		.27
Rice Krispies	Kellogg's	13 oz.	*		.23
100% nat'l. cereal	Quaker	16 oz.	*		.31
Oats, quick	Quaker	18 oz.	.85	.15	.17
Instant brkfst.	Carnation	6 envl.	.95	.05	.23
Pasta, dried veg. products					
Elbow macaroni	Mueller	16 oz.	*		.18
Spaghetti, thin	Mueller	16 oz.	*		.16
Mcrmi and cheese din.	Kraft	7.25 oz.	*		.09
Hamburger Helper	Betty Crock.	7–8.5 oz.	*		.06
Cheese pizza mix	Cf. Boy–Ar–D	15,8 oz.	*		.02
Instant rice	Minute	14 oz.	.85	.15	.25
Hgry. Jk. inst. pot.	Pillsbury	16 oz.	*		.10
Coffee, tea, soft drinks					

Item	Brand	Qty	Unit			
Coffee, regular	Mxwl. Hse.	2	lb.	.84	.16	1.09
Coffee, instant	Maxl. Hse.	10	oz.	.97	.03	.30
Instant coffee	Sanka	4	oz.	*		.12
Instant tea	Lipton	3	oz.	.97	.03	.12
Tea bags	Lipton	48	oz.	.84	.16	.22
Cola	Shasta	12	oz.	.95	.05	2.80
Baking needs						
Flour	Gold Mdl.	5	lb.	.88	.12	.05
B.m. biscuit mix	Bisquick	40	oz.	.88	.12	.13
B.m. panck. mx.	Aunt Jem.	32	oz.	.88	.12	.10
Corn mufn. mix	Jiffy	8.5	oz.	*		.10
Cake mix	Duncan Hns.	18.5	oz.	.94	.06	.29
Sugar, granul.	Domino	5	lb.	.20	.80	.94
10X powd. sugar	Domino	16	oz.	.20	.80	.05
Oil	Crisco	24	oz.	.76	.24	.40
Corn oil	Mazola	32	oz.	*		.20
Shortening	Crisco	3	lb.	.76	.24	.20
Salt	Morton	26	oz.	*		.05
Semi swt. mrsls.	Nestle's	12	oz.	*		.02
Syrups, spreads						
Peanut butter	Skippy	12	oz.	.80	.20	.29
Grape jelly	Welch	20	oz.	.80	.20	.17
Corn syrup	Karo	16	oz.	*		.01
Maple flv. syrup	Log Cabin	12	oz.	*		.18
Chocolate syrup	Hershey	16	oz.	*		.03

(continued)

Table B. 3, continued

Product	Nat'l. Brand	Size		Nat'l. Brand Weight	Pvt. Label Weight	Expenditure Weight
Jello gelatin	Jello	6	oz.	*		.13
Mayonnaise	Hellmn's.	32	oz.	.90	.10	.29
Miracle Whip	Kraft	16	oz.	.90	.10	.13
French dressing	Kraft	16	oz.	.90	.10	.23
Catsup	Heinz	14	oz.	.88	.12	.14
Spaghetti sauce	Ragu	15	oz.	*		.17
Baby prod., cond. milk prod.						
Baby food	Gerber	4.5	oz.	*		.06
Baby cereal	Gerber	8	oz.	*		.01
Baby juice	Gerber	4.2	oz.	*		.04
Nonfat dry milk	Carnatn.	20	qt.	.70	.30	.19
Evaporated milk	Carnatn.	13	oz.	.70	.30	.13
Nondairy creamer	Coffee Mate	16	oz.	.80	.20	.09
Pet-food						
Dog chow	Purina	25	lb.	.93	.07	.32
Beef chunks	Alpo	14.5	oz.	.93	.07	.60
Dog food, burgers	Ken-L-Rtn.	72	oz.	.97	.03	.24
Cat chow	Purina	4	lb.	*		.17
Cat food, fish flv.	Puss-n-Bts.	15.25	oz.	*		.47
Household cleaning products						

Category	Brand	Size	Unit			
Bleach	Clorox	0.5	gal.	.80	.20	.21
Dry bleach	Clorox II	40	oz.	.97	.03	.08
Cleanser	Comet	14	oz.	.96	.04	.12
Cleaning prod.	Spic-n-Spn.	16	oz.	*		.19
Fabric softener	Downy	64	oz.	.90	.10	.26
Laundry detergent	Tide	84	oz.	.98	.02	1.01
Liquid detergent	Ivory	22	oz.	.98	.02	.33
Dishwasher deterg.	Cascade	35	oz.	.98	.02	.16
Bath soap	Dial	3.5	oz.	.98	.02	.38
Scouring pads	S. O. S.	10	ct.	*		.19
Paper and foil prod.						
Trash can liners	Glad	20	ct.	.75	.25	.34
Aluminum foil	Reynolds	75	sq. ft.	.75	.25	.17
Wax paper	Cutrite	125	ft.	*		.02
Facial tissues	Kleenex	200's		.88	.12	.27
Paper towels	Bounty	Jumbo		.94	.06	.48
Toilet tissue	Lady Scott	2's-500		*		.50
Health and Beauty Aids						
Shampoo, concentr.	Prell	5	oz.	*		.04
Liquid Shampoo	Breck	7	oz.	*		.27
Hair spray	Adorn	13	oz.	*		.21
Toothpaste	Close-up	6.4	oz.	*		.30
Mouthwash	Scope	12	oz.	*		.17
Deodorant	Right Grd.	7	oz.	*		.50
Antacids	Alka Seltz.	25's		*		.16

(continued)

Table B. 3, continued

Product	Nat'l. Brand	Size		Nat'l. Brand Weight	Pvt. Label Weight	Expenditure Weight
Cold med., Nyquil	Vicks	6	oz.	*		.15
Vitamins w/iron	One-A-Day	100's		*		.08
Trac II raz. bld.	Gillette	9's		*		.22
Aspirin	Anacin	100's		*		.20
Skin Bracer	Mennen	6	oz.	*		.05
Baby powder	J & J	9	oz.	*		.04
Swabs	Q-Tips	88's		*		.03
Skin cream	Noxzema	6	oz.	*		.14
"Day" disp. diapers	Pampers	30's		.90	.10	.18
"Nite" disp. diapers	Pampers	12's		.90	.10	.18

*Items where either national brands or private labels were included in the market basket and hence the total weight was assigned to only one category.

Sources: Company data provided to the Joint Economic Committee; "Supermarkets," Chain Store Age, 51, no. 7 (July 1975); Selling Areas Marketing, Inc.; National Commission on Food Marketing, Technical Study no. 10.

TABLE B. 4

Costs of Grocery Baskets and Private-Label/National-Brand Grocery Basket Ratios for 3 firms in 17 SMSAs not Included in Figures
4. 1 and 4. 2 and Tables B. 5 and B. 6

Company and SMSA	Weighted Grocery Basket (weighted dollars)	Private-Label/ National-Brand Ratio (percent)
Firm K		
City AA	93.09	88.0
City BB	93.09	88.0
City CC	95.67	87.0
Firm H		
City DD	94.57	92.0
City EE	91.22	91.0
City X	97.03	93.0
City FF	93.64	92.0
City Y	91.82	94.0
City Y	85.76	96.0
City HH	95.29	93.0
City II	96.77	91.0
City JJ	94.57	92.0
City KK	94.57	92.0
Firm D		
City DD	91.94	89.0
City S	93.34	88.0
City JJ	91.86	89.0
City LL	91.18	90.0

Source: Company data provided to the Joint Economic Committee.

TABLE B.5

Firm K: Private-Label Prices Relative to National-Brand Prices Weighted by Expenditure Weights, by Major Group and Market Basket, Seven SMSAs (percent)

| SMSA | Major Group | | | | Market Basket* |
	Frozen Foods	Dairy	Grocery	
City B	81.0	86.0	88.0	87.0
City F	80.0	81.0	82.0	82.0
City G	80.0	90.0	87.0	87.0
City H	85.0	88.0	88.0	87.0
City I	79.0	90.0	84.0	85.0
City J	87.0	92.0	90.0	90.0
City A	78.0	86.0	86.0	86.0
Mean	81.0	88.0	86.0	86.0

*The private-label/national-brand ratios for the market basket were calculated by dividing the sum of private-label prices across major groups by the sum of national-brand prices. A total of 63 national-brand items and their private-label counterparts were included in this market basket (126 in total). This compared with 173 items in the overall market basket for Firm K. The mean for the three major groups for any one SMSA will not necessarily equal the mean for the market basket as calculated above. Because some items have relatively higher prices than other items, this procedure reflects a bias toward the ratios of higher-priced items.

Source: Company data provided to the Joint Economic Committee.

190

TABLE B. 6

Firm H: Private-Lable Prices Relative to National-Brand Prices Weighted by Expenditure Weights, by Major Groups and Market Basket, 15 SMSAs
(percent)

SMSA	Major Group				Market Basket[a]
	Frozen Foods	Dairy	Grocery	Health and Beauty Aids	
City E	82.0	91.0	91.0	91.0	91.0
City K	76.0	90.0	91.0	86.0	90.0
City L	77.0	90.0	92.0	–	91.0[b]
City M	81.0	95.0	92.0	91.0	92.0
City N	90.0	90.0	92.0	86.0	91.0
City C	76.0	94.0	91.0	91.0	91.0
City O	86.0	89.0	92.0	91.0	91.0
City P	85.0	88.0	93.0	87.0	92.0
City Q	87.0	88.0	93.0	92.0	92.0
City R	78.0	92.0	93.0	91.0	92.0
City S	77.0	95.0	94.0	92.0	94.0
City T	90.0	88.0	93.0	–	92.0[b]
City U	85.0	90.0	94.0	76.0	92.0
City V	80.0	96.0	93.0	91.0	93.0
City D	79.0	97.0	93.0	95.0	93.0
Mean	82.0	92.0	92.0	89.0	92.0

[a]The private-label/national-brand ratios for the market basket were calculated by dividing the sum of private-label prices across major groups by the sum of national-brand prices. A Total of 56 national-brand items and their private-label counterparts were included in this market basket (112 in total). This compared with 183 items in the overall market basket for firm H shown in Table 3.2. The mean for the three major groups for any one SMSA will not necessarily equal the mean for the market basket as calculated above. Because some items have relatively higher prices than others, this procedure reflects bias toward the ratios of higher-priced items.

[b]The market basket private-label/national-brand ratios for City T and City L were calculated on a smaller number of observations because of missing health and beauty aid observations.

Source: Company data provided to the Joint Economic Committee.

TABLE B.7

Private-Label Prices as a Percent of National-Brand Prices in
Different Product Groups, Unweighted, Firms H and K, 1974

Grocery Products	Firm H[a]		Firm K[b]	
	No. of Items	Pvt. Label as Percent of Nat'l. Brand Prices	No. of Items	Pvt. Label as Percent of Nat'l. Brand Prices
Canned fruits, vegetables	13	92.1	14	89.5
Canned meat, prep. foods	5	92.8	5	89.7
Cereals, inst. breakfast	2	93.3	3	87.6
Pasta, dried veg- etables	1	89.5	1	90.9
Coffee, tea, soft drinks	2	97.3	5	87.9
Baking needs	8	92.0	6	91.2
Syrups, spreads	3	90.8	6	88.9
Baby prod., cond. milk	2	94.8	3	88.8
Pet foods	3	87.0	3	79.0
Cleaning products	4	84.7	8	77.2
Paper products	3	91.9	3	89.0
Grocery total	46	91.5	57	87.3
Health and beauty aids	2	89.9	—	—
Frozen foods	4	88.1	3	88.3
Dairy	4	91.1	3	87.2

[a]Private-label/national-brand price relationships are the
means of the relationships found in 16 SMSAs.

[b]Private-label/national-brand price relationships are the
means of the relationships found in 10 SMSAs.

Source: Company data provided to the Joint Economic Committee.

TABLE B. 8

Correlation Matrix for Regression Equations, Table 4. 3

	NPC	RFMS	CRFMS	CR₄	CCR₄	SS	MR	MG	MS	WR	FMS
NPC	1.000										
RFMS	.474	1.000									
CRFMS	.502	.989	1.000								
CR₄	.233	.180	.245	1.000							
CCR₄	.215	.159	.220	.978	1.000						
SS	-.066	.290	.312	.466	.484	1.000					
MR	-.520	-.133	-.111	.304	.296	.355	1.000				
MG	-.198	-.146	-.138	.193	.174	-.289	-.184	1.000			
MS	-.091	.080	.063	-.052	-.002	.584	-.090	-.219	1.000		
WR	.329	.313	.345	.173	.113	.478	-.126	-.342	.255	1.000	
FMS	.452	.915	.927	.534	.522	.450	.009	-.028	.076	.309	1.000

Source: Compiled by the authors.

TABLE B.9

Multiple-Regression Equations Explaining Cost of a Grocery Basket of 3 Chains in 36 SMSAs, 1972

Dependent Variable[a]	Intercept	Relative Firm Market Share (RFMS)[b]	Curvilinear Relative Firm Market Share (CRFMS)[b]	Four-Firm Concentration (CR_4)	Curvilinear Four-Firm Concentration (CCR_4)[b]	Mean Store Size (SS)	Market Growth (MG)	Market Size (MS)	Market Rivalry (MR)	$\bar{R}^2$	F-Value
a—NPC	87.81	5.094 †(1.678)					-0.079 *(-1.982)			0.26	**5.10
b—NPC	89.28	4.038 †(1.692)		12.932 **(3.393)			-.088 **(-2.808)		-0.433 **(-4.612)	.55	**11.57
1a—NPC	89.51	9.027 **(3.008)		10.995 *(2.407)		-0.005 *(-2.294)				.29	**5.69
1b—NPC	90.11	7.296 **(2.684)		17.973 **(3.893)		-.007 **(-3.366)	-.113 **(-3.133)			.44	**7.90
1c—NPC	90.45	5.627 *(2.417)		16.662 **(4.275)		-.004 *(-2.351)	-.108 **(-3.542)		-.351 **(-3.725)	.60	**11.72
1d—NPC	90.42	5.240 *(2.236)		15.073 **(3.652)		-.002 (-.843)	-.111 **(-3.639)	-0.903 (-1.128)	-.405 **(-3.845)	.61	**10.06
1e—NPC	90.11	4.636 *(2.088)		13.294 **(3.766)			-.107 **(-3.575)	-1.386 *(-2.490)	-.455 **(-5.207)	.61	**12.05
1f—NPC	95.61	4.552 *(2.066)			6.652 **(3.874)		-.112 **(-3.716)	-1.592 **(-2.862)	-.463 **(-5.337)	.62	**12.39
1g—NPC	96.00		2.433 *(2.168)		6.250 **(3.535)		-.109 **(-3.618)	-1.536 **(-2.787)	-.460 **(-5.332)	.62	**12.62
2c—NC	90.41	5.149 *(2.356)		13.555 **(3.902)			-.095 **(-3.236)	-.842 (-1.537)	-.474 **(-5.512)	.63	**13.00
2g—NC	96.42		2.813 **(2.800)		6.349 **(3.723)		-.097 **(-3.328)	-.996 †(-1.875)	-.478 **(-5.748)	.66	**14.41

Notes: Figures in parentheses are t-values. The statistical significance of the regression coefficients for RFMS, CRFMS, CR_4, CCR_4, SS, and MR were tested by means of a one-tailed t-test; MG and MS were tested by means of a two-tailed t-test. The adjusted coefficients of multiple determination were tested by means of F-ratio.

†, *, and ** indicate that the regression coefficients are statistically significant at the 10, 5, and 1 percent levels, respectively.

[a] The dependent variable (NPC) in equations 1a–1h is the cost of a grocery basket of national-brand and private-label products. The dependent variable (NC) in equations 2e and 2h is the cost of a grocery basket of only national-brand products. Equations 1a–1d have 36 observations, equations 1e–1h have 35 observations (one observation was omitted for lack of union wage data).

[b] CRFMS and $CCR_4 = (x + \alpha)^3 / (1 - 3[x + \alpha] + 3[x + \alpha]^2)$, where x equals RFMS or CR_4. Values for each variable were expressed in decimals between 0 and 1. The function of CRFMS and CCR_4 has a positive slope and is symmetric about an inflection point. The inflection point occurs at the point that satisfies the equation $I = .5 - \alpha$, where I equals the inflection point. For CRFMS, the inflection point for each of the above equations was .35 (that is, $\alpha = -.15$). For CCR_4, the inflection point for each of the above equations was .63 (that is, $\alpha = -.13$).

Source: Compiled by the authors.

TABLE B.10

Correlation Matrix for Regression Equations, Table 3.5

	Avg. P/S 1970-74	P/S 1970	P/S 1971	P/S 1972	P/S 1973	P/S 1974	RFMS	CR$_4$	CCR$_4$
Avg. P/S 1970-74	1.000								
1970 P/S	.781	1.000							
1971 P/S	.862	.710	1.000						
1972 P/S	.921	.582	.736	1.000					
1973 P/S	.881	.470	.636	.866	1.000				
1974 P/S	.786	.338	.494	.786	.900	1.000			
RFMS	.507	.548	.515	.390	.315	.277	1.000		
CR$_4$	.225	.182	.211	.184	.150	.206	.156	1.000	
CCR$_4$	.266	.291	.280	.161	.147	.185	.245	.833	1.000
SS	-.157	-.111	-.250	-.142	-.106	-.031	-.171	.259	.101
E	-.380	-.557	-.448	-.254	-.132	-.043	-.439	.193	.007
FG	.389	.122	.138	.446	.522	.556	-.263	.174	.128
LNFG	.444	.094	.185	.518	.606	.644	-.192	.180	.114
MG	.367	.179	.315	.450	.351	.319	-.054	.307	.187
MG^2	.359	.212	.306	.411	.339	.291	-.029	.312	.170
MS	-.139	-.183	-.206	-.057	-.040	-.039	-.196	-.308	-.515
MS^2	-.085	-.120	-.159	-.022	-.009	-.023	-.210	-.343	-.558
API	-.128	-.154	-.008	-.175	-.109	-.088	.064	.056	.070

(continued)

Table B.10 continued

	SS	E	FG	LNFG	MG	MG²	MS	MS²	API
SS	1.000								
E	.244	1.000							
FG	.146	.311	1.000						
LNFG	.152	.289	.963	1.000					
MG	-.076	.123	.344	.350	1.000				
MG²	-.049	.069	.303	.305	.938	1.000			
MS	.317	-.006	.018	.063	-.371	-.275	1.000		
MS²	.292	-.064	.013	.049	-.380	-.274	.968	1.000	
API	-.481	-.109	-.456	-.436	-.216	-.164	-.210	-.191	1.000

Source: Compiled by the authors.

TABLE B.11

Correlation Matrix for Regression Equations, Table 3. 6

	Avg. P/S 1970-74	P/S 1970	P/S 1971	P/S 1972	P/S 1973	P/S 1974	RFMS	CR$_4$	CCR$_4$
Avg. P/S 1970-74	1.000								
1970 P/S	.908	1.000							
1971 P/S	.931	.945	1.000						
1972 P/S	.937	.873	.920	1.000					
1973 P/S	.859	.628	.645	.686	1.000				
1974 P/S	.854	.620	.649	.679	.939	1.000			
RFMS	.565	.529	.508	.515	.494	.498	1.000		
CR$_4$	.170	.102	.194	.201	.104	.145	.012	1.000	
CCR$_4$	.170	.128	.207	.200	.090	.125	-.013	.824	1.000
FG	.609	.475	.487	.577	.615	.579	.083	.112	.136
LNFG	.638	.480	.501	.601	.651	.630	.157	.148	.146
MG	.455	.428	.474	.480	.313	.330	.071	.292	.170
MG^2	.412	.391	.410	.422	.305	.308	.042	.273	.152
MS	-.145	-.101	-.187	-.144	-.078	-.140	-.070	-.122	-.245
MS^2	-.096	-.039	-.134	-.112	-.035	-.107	-.045	-.188	-.323
APC	-.521	-.417	-.466	-.629	-.400	-.368	-.299	-.112	-.018
API	-.280	-.202	-.225	-.336	-.226	-.243	-.207	-.029	.102

(continued)

Table B.11 continued

	FG	LNFG	MG	MG^2	MS	MS^2	APC	API
FG	1.000							
LNFG	.964	1.000						
MG	.268	.285	1.000					
MG^2	.278	.286	.961	1.000				
MS	.040	.031	-.308	-.248	1.000			
MS^2	.045	.041	-.308	-.245	.963	1.000		
APC	-.385	-.336	-.198	-.187	-.055	-.038	1.000	
API	-.244	-.273	-.329	-.284	.012	-.015	.347	1.000

Source: Compiled by the authors.

TABLE B.12

Correlation Matrix for Regression Equations, Table 3.7

	Avg. P/S 1970–74	P/S 1970	P/S 1971	P/S 1972	P/S 1973	P/S 1974	RFMS	CR₄	CCR₄
Avg. P/S 1970–74	1.000								
1970 P/S	.916	1.000							
1971 P/S	.936	.917	1.000						
1972 P/S	.972	.856	.902	1.000					
1973 P/S	.953	.800	.814	.917	1.000				
1974 P/S	.935	.765	.794	.892	.942	1.000			
RFMS	.483	.475	.457	.500	.426	.419	1.000		
CR₄	.161	.057	.197	.171	.146	.182	.049	1.000	
CCR₄	.297	.208	.332	.285	.276	.299	.117	.825	1.000
FG	.604	.487	.486	.596	.656	.600	-.040	.080	.161
LNFG	.669	.516	.533	.680	.720	.682	.069	.125	.170
MG	.431	.380	.414	.446	.410	.380	.036	.272	.169
MG²	.400	.374	.367	.410	.385	.345	-.001	.261	.166
MS	-.273	-.213	-.305	-.242	-.217	-.316	-.220	-.107	-.186
MS²	-.208	-.139	-.239	-.187	-.161	-.262	-.202	-.166	-.254
API	-.145	-.088	-.098	-.206	-.121	-.156	-.128	.012	.133

(continued)

Table B. 12 continued

	FG	LNFG	MG	MG²	MS	MS²	API
FG	1.000						
LNFG	.960	1.000					
MG	.237	.264	1.000				
MG²	.246	.261	.965	1.000			
MS	.024	.015	-.354	-.282	1.000		
MS²	.040	.036	-.354	-.279	.965	1.000	
API	-.128	-.177	-.316	-.257	.039	-.003	1.000

Source: Compiled by the authors.

TABLE B.13

Multiple-Regression Equations Explaining Profit-Sales Ratios for 28 Divisions of A&P

Dependent Variable Profit-Sales Ratio	Intercept	Independent Variable					R²	F-Value
		Relative Firm Market Share (RFMS)	Curvilinear Four-Firm Concentration (CCR4)	Market Growth Squared (MG²)	Market Size (MS)	Market Size Squared (MS²)		
1a 1970-74 average	-7.875	.135 (4.190)**	5.299 (1.214)	.108 (2.049)*	-1.265 (.965)	.297 (.749)	.526	4.88**
1b 1970-72	-15.598	.166 (3.760)**	13.002 (2.167)*	.203 (2.797)**	-2.629 (1.459)†	.698 (1.277)	.538	5.12**
1c 1973-74	3.710	.088 (1.925)*	-6.256 (1.013)	.034 (.454)	.781 (.421)	-.305 (.542)	.287	1.77
2 1970	-14.237	.168 (3.834)**	12.724 (2.147)*	.176 (2.450)**	-2.694 (1.514)†	.820 (1.519)†	.529	4.95**
3 1971	-12.092	.155 (3.604)**	10.038 (1.717)†	.210 (2.972)**	-2.414 (1.375)†	.614 (1.154)†	.533	5.03**
4 1972	-20.465	.176 (3.399)**	16.244 (2.312)*	.223 (2.265)*	-2.779 (1.317)†	.660 (1.032)	.509	4.56**
5 1973	4.903	.082 (1.602)†	-7.593 (1.090)	-.072 (.859)	.053 (.025)	-.120 (.189)	.274	1.66
6 1974	2.516	.093 (2.212)*	-4.919 (.863)	.005 (.066)	1.510 (.882)	.490 (.943)	.302	1.91

Significance levels: ** = 1 percent; * = 5 percent; † = 10 percent.
Source: Compiled by the authors.

TABLE B.14

Correlation Matrix for Regression Equations, Table 2.2

	HM	EDN	FEX	NFC	CEM	CR$_4$	MG	MS	CHCR$_4$	SAP	PCHCR$_4$	PHM
HM	1.000											
EDN	-.163	1.000										
FEX	.119	.120	1.000									
NFC	.140	.082	.282	1.000								
CEM	.012	.223	.239	.251	1.000							
CR$_4$	-.182	-.292	-.288	.099	-.030	1.000						
MG	-.195	.165	-.161	.020	-.007	.258	1.000					
MS	.188	-.036	.046	.245	.267	.113	-.164	1.000				
CHCR$_4$	.218	.337	.363	.356	.391	-.205	-.056	.050	1.000			
SAP	-.021	-.410	-.181	-.136	-.192	.222	-.234	.091	-.370	1.000		
PCHCR$_4$	.234	.391	.354	.335	.367	-.292	-.082	.057	.981	-.384	1.000	
PHM	.991	-.141	.119	.133	.008	-.218	-.181	.182	.228	-.043	.251	1.000

Source: Compiled by the authors.

TABLE B.15

Comparison of Market Structure-Profit Models Using Grocery Store and Supermarket Measures of Concentration and Relative Market Share, 1972

Dependent Variable: Profit-Sales Ratio	Intercept	Grocery Store Relative Firm Market Share (RFMS)	Grocery Store Four-Firm Concentration (CR₄)	Grocery Store Curvilinear Four-Firm Concentration (CCR₄)	Mean Store Size (SS)	Entry (E)	Firm Growth (FG)	Log Firm Growth (LNFG)	Market Growth (MG)	Market Growth Squared (MG²)	Market Size (MS)	Market Size Squared (MS²)	A&P Impact (API)	R²ᶜ	F-Value
1970-74 average	-3.116	.063 (5.808)**	.026 (1.846)†		-1.005 (-1.650)†	-.042 (-5.559)**	.045 (6.965)**		.032 (3.046)**		.272 (1.448)†			.824	36.73**
1970-74 average	-.446	.065 (6.830)**		3.119 (2.323)**	-.284 (-.480)	-.034 (-5.455)**		1.832 (7.548)**		.044 (3.494)**	-1.720 (-2.971)**	.547 (3.364)**	.544 (2.010)*	.889	48.82**

Dependent Variable: Profit-Sales Ratio	Intercept	Supermarket Relative Firm Market Share (SRFMS)	Supermarket Four-Firm Concentration (SCR₄)	Supermarket Curvilinear Four-Firm Concentration (SCCR₄)	Mean Store Size (SS)	Entry (E)	Firm Growth (FG)	Log Firm Growth (LNFG)	Market Growth (MG)	Market Growth Squared (MG²)	Market Size (MS)	Market Size Squared (MS²)	A&P Impact (API)	R²ᶜ	F-Value
1970-74 average	-3.641	.064 (6.795)**	.022 (1.871)*		-.609 (-1.050)	-.042 (-5.297)**	.046 (7.115)**		.033 (3.068)**		.273 (1.440)†			.811	33.70**
1970-74 average	-.862	.064 (6.717)**		3.136 (2.545)**	.259 (.454)	-.035 (-5.417)**		1.822 (7.808)**		.044 (3.341)**	-1.906 (-3.205)**	.614 (3.589)**	.482 (1.749)†	.880	44.92**
1970-74 average	-.581	.064 (6.781)**		3.074 (2.526)**		-.034 (-5.500)**		1.813 (7.850)**		.044 (3.389)**	-1.871 (-3.193)**	.609 (3.590)**	.429 (1.732)*	.380	50.55**

Notes: SCR₄ was expressed in percentages, whereas SCR₄ was calculated in decimals, with the estimated regression coefficients multiplied by 100. One-tailed tests were used in all cases. Figures in parentheses are t-values. Significant levels: ** = 1 percent; * = 5 percent; † = 10 percent.

[a] P/S, RFMS, CR₄, and FG are expressed as percentages. LNFG is the natural logarithm of FG expressed in decimals. MG is expressed in percentages; MG² is expressed in percentages; MG² is the percentage of market growth squared and divided by 100. MG is expressed in billions of dollars. SS is expressed in million dollar sales per store. E is expressed in percentage.

[b] CCR₄ = (CR₄ + α)³/1 - 3(CR₄ + α) + 3(CR₄ + α)². This function of CR₄ has positive slope and is symmetric about an inflection point. The inflection point of the curve occurs at the concentration ratio that satisfies the equation CR₄ = 0.5 - α. For all equations in this table α = 0.20, so the inflection point of the curve is CR₄ = 0.30.

[c] Because of computation procedures, R² values are not comparable with those in Table 4.3. For care needed in interpretation, see footnote on p. 81.

Source: Compiled by the authors.

APPENDIX C
FOOD EDITORS' STUDY
OF FOOD PRICES, 1977

A national market basket survey conducted early in June 1977 placed Washington supermarket food prices at the top of 17 cities in the continental United States. Prices were higher only in Anchorage, Alaska, and Honolulu, Hawaii.

The price of the 34-item market basket in Washington was $34. 93. This was 9. 2 percent over the national average and 7. 8 percent higher than the price of the same items one year ago.

Food editors in each city shopped in three chain stores on June 2. The lowest price they found for an item in each category was used to compile their market basket. Editors in five Canadian cities conducted a simultaneous survey. The cost of the market basket was higher than Washington's in every Canadian city.

Washington led the American survey with its price for canned tuna fish (17 cents above the average) and was highest in the continental United States for instant coffee (a whopping 91 cents above the average), evaporated milk, canned peaches, and canned pineapple. The sugar price, $1. 15 for five pounds of granulated white, was equaled only in Portland, Oregon and Denver, Colorado.

Anchorage, participating in the survey for the first time, was not factored into the averages. Market baskets were not compiled in two cities that participated last year, Philadelphia and Detroit.

On a national basis, the market basket reflected the effect of the cold winter on fruit and vegetable supplies and improved supplies of meat and poultry. Prices were down from 1976 for eggs, flour, sugar, beans, rice, rump roast, ground beef, pork chops, wieners, and chicken. The items that had increased most sharply in price were instant coffee (up 52. 9 percent), mayonnaise (up 20 percent), ice cream (up 20. 2 percent), frozen orange juice (up 20 percent), frozen broccoli (up 23. 6 percent), carrots (up 47. 3 percent), cabbage (up 23 percent), lettuce (up 26. 5 percent), and oranges (up 16. 7 percent).

Washington was below the average for eight items: cheese, bread, cereal, beans, ham, cabbage, bananas, and tomatoes. The ham price, 69 cents for one pound of smoked butt end, was the lowest in the survey, 35 cents less than the average.

First published as William Rice, "Food Prices: Washington Tops the List," Washington Post, June 30, 1977.

On the other hand, District prices were significantly above the average for ten items in addition to tuna fish and coffee. Among them: mayonnaise (39 cents above the average), rump roast, pork chops, and wieners (all more than 20 cents above the average), and oranges (20 cents above).

Last year orange and orange juice prices here, as well as ham, were well below the average.

Boston, another city in the "Northeast Corridor," where operating costs for supermarkets are traditionally high, had a market basket valued at $34.04, trailing Washington by 89 cents. But New York City, with a $32.85 market basket, was well down the list.

Industry experts cite numerous factors that result in the high price of food here, including labor costs, distance from centers of production of meat, fruits, and vegetables, local demand for high quality and service. They also point out deficits in this and other market baskets. The 34 items are only a minute sampling of the 10,000 or more items stocked by large supermarkets. The survey is done only on a single day, is subject to error, and is not weighted. (For example, a ten-ounce jar of instant coffee will last a family some time; one pound of steak will disappear during a single meal.)

Paul Forbes, assistant to the president of Giant Food, said the consumer should realize supermarket pricing is not similar to automobile pricing. "There is not a fixed wholesale and a fixed markup," he said. "It all depends on the ever-changing merchandise mix and you can determine that only by looking at the total market basket."

But the food editors' market basket is a snapshot of food prices and Washington has consistently been near the top. Other studies, more thorough and more extensive, tend to support this finding.

One charge raised consistently by consumerists is that food prices are high in Washington because it is a concentrated market, with more than 60 percent of sales divided between only two chains, Safeway and Giant. The chains refute this, contending there is considerable competition.

According to Bruce Marion, a University of Wisconsin professor who helped prepare a study on prices and profits in the supermarket industry for the Joint Economic Committee of the Congress, "there is pretty strong evidence" that lack of competition "tends to lead to high prices.

"When a market is dominated by two chains, as is the case in Washington, two things happen. The firms tend to shy away from head-on price competition and move toward nonprice competitive factors (such as advertising and games) and prices go up enough to result in increased profits."

Marion discounted transportation and rent or building costs as not significant enough to explain price differences in a market such as Washington. Labor, he said, is a "real biggie," but Washington labor costs are not the industry's highest, he said. He cited "softer competition" as a potential cause of looser cost controls and internal inefficiency.

The Joint Economic Committee study said of City B, since identified as Washington: "Little, if any, price competition existed between these two [dominant] firms." The result, the study concluded, was that consumers here paid an additional 6.9 percent for groceries in 1974.

Even if the market basket is small, the survey findings have been consistent. But for explanations, the industry and its critics will have to look elsewhere.

TABLE C.1

Cost of a 35-Item Market Basket, 19 Cities, June 2, 1977

Item	1976 Average	1977 Average	Percent Difference	San Diego	Tampa	San Francisco	Des Moines	Phoenix	Milwaukee	Atlanta	Dallas
Milk, homogenized, 1/2 gal.	$0.78	$0.81	+3.8	$0.64	$0.88	$0.69	$0.81	$0.71	$0.80	$0.97	$0.85
Eggs, 1 doz. grade A, large	.70	.62	-11.4	.63	.48	.73[a]	.59[a]	.69	.63	.58	.53
Cheese, 10 ozs., sharp, Cracker Barrel	1.36	1.42	-4.4	1.39	1.29	1.43	1.39	1.47	1.45	1.44	1.43[b]
Margarine, 1 lb., 4 sticks, Blue Bonnet or Parkay	.47	.55	+17.0	.49	.62	.44	.49	.55	.50	.44	.55
Bread, white, sliced, 24-oz. loaf	.46	.50	+8.7	.25	.38[d]	.49	.63	.43	.45	.45	.53
Flour, 5 lbs., all-purpose, Gold Medal or Pillsbury	.83	.78	-6.0	.63	.68	.67	.57	.67	.79	.79	.85
Special K, 11 oz. package	.78	.88	+12.8	.80	.85	.93[c]	.83	.80	.81	.89	.86
Sugar, 5 lbs., white granulated	1.12	.92	-17.9	.96	.87	1.10[c]	.99	.93	1.13	.58[c]	.99
Instant coffee, 10 ozs., Nescafe or Maxwell House	2.80	4.28	+52.9	3.39[c]	3.39	3.69	3.49	3.69	4.32	3.78	4.19
Great Northern beans, dry, 1 lb.	.43	.36	-16.3	.32	.36[d]	.35	.31	.32	.37	.37	.29
Rice, 2 lbs., Uncle Ben's converted	1.09	1.04	-4.6	.99	.95	1.05	.99	1.05	.99	1.04	.99
Mayonnaise, 1 qt., Best Foods, Hellman's, or Kraft	1.10	1.32	+20.0	.98	1.18	1.27	1.19	.95	1.19	1.29	1.47
Peanut butter, 18-oz. jar, smooth, Jif, Peter Pan, Planters, or Skippy	.94	.95	+1.0	.89	1.02	.99	.89	1.02	.79	.79	.99
Tuna, 6-1/2-oz. can, light chunk meat in oil, Chicken of the Sea or Starkist	.57	.64	+12.3	.58	.49[c]	.59	.67	.63	.65	.68	.69
Evaporated milk, 14.5-oz. can (13 fl. ozs.), Carnation, Golden Key, or Pet	.33	.36	+9.0	.31	.30	.35	.30[c]	.32	.39	.34	.35
Cling peach halves, 29-oz. can, heavy syrup, Del Monte, Hunt, Libby, or Stokely	.56	.61	+13.0	.51	.59	.45	.63	.59	.67	.59	.59
Pineapple, 20-oz. can, sliced, heavy syrup or own juice, Del Monte or Dole	.56	.61	+8.9	.56	.60	.59	.59	.56	.63	.61	.57

(continued)

207

Table C.1 continued

Item	1976 Average	1977 Average	Percent Difference	San Diego	Tampa	San Francisco	Des Moines	Phoenix	Milwaukee	Atlanta	Dallas
Ice Cream, 1/2 gal., any brand	.89	1.07	+20.2	.69[c]	.77[c]	1.19	.98	1.09	1.05	.78	1.39
Frozen orange juice concentrate, grade A or fancy, 6-oz., can, any brand	.25	.30	+20.0	.23	.26	.34[c]	.25	.31	.31	.30	.35
Broccoli spears, frozen, 10-oz. package, grade A or fancy	.38	.47	+23.6	.43	.49	.51	.53	.39	.49	.45	.61
Rump roast, boneless, choice, 1 lb.	1.60	1.43	-10.6	1.19	1.78	1.39	1.49	1.69	1.19[c]	1.18[c]	1.38
Sirloin steak, bone-in, choice, 1 lb.	1.77	1.80	+1.7	1.48[e]	1.88	1.49[e]	1.79	2.09	1.89	2.19[c]	1.48
Ground beef, regular, 1 lb.	.81	.79	-2.5	1.19	.78	.68	.69	.69	.79	.88	.68
Pork loin chops, 1 lb., 1/2 to 3/4-in. thick, with tenderloin	1.83	1.75	-4.3	1.88	1.78	1.79	1.59	1.79	1.69	1.79	1.79
Ham, smoked, butt end, 1 lb.	1.01	1.04	+3.0	1.18	.88	.89	.89	.98	.79	.78[c]	1.09
Bacon, regular slice, 1 lb., Armour, Cudahy, Hormel, Oscar Mayer, Rath, Swift, or Wilson	1.68	1.38	-17.9	1.18	1.19	1.63	1.25	1.33	1.19	1.39	1.65
Wieners, all meat, 1 lb., Armour, Cudahy, Hormel, Oscar Mayer, Rath, Swift, or Wilson	1.08	1.07	-.93	.89	1.09	.79	1.24	.95	1.29	.89[c]	.133
Chicken, whole, broiler-fryer, never frozen, grade A, 1 lb.	.54	.50	-7.4	.49	.48	.45	.49	.49	.39[c]	.38[c]	.45
Potatoes, 5 lbs., regular, all-purpose, US1	.87	.90	+3.4	.50	.79	.49	.98	.69	.89	.99	.89
Carrots, whole, 1 lb., US1	.19	.28	+47.3	.20	.23	.25	.30[d]	.20	.34	.29	.29
Cabbage, 1 lb., US1	.13	.16	+23.0	.08	.14	.12	.19	.12	.14	.10[c]	.10
Lettuce, 1 head, US1	.34	.43	+26.5	.29	.34	.29	.49	.39	.39	.34	.33
Bananas, 1 lb., yellow	.24	.26	+8.3	.19	.23	.29	.25	.29	.29	.23	.20
Tomatoes, 1 lb., vine-ripened, 3-in. diameter	.45	.46	+2.2	.39	.35	.39	.59	.20	.69	.59	.39
Oranges, 5 lbs., juice fruit	.90	1.05	+16.7	.87[d]	.98	.79	.86[d]	1.00	1.19	1.39	.99
Subtotal	29.82	31.75		27.67	29.38	29.58	30.21	29.90	31.57	30.57	32.09
Percentage tax on food	0	0		0	0	0	0	0	0	0	0
Amount tux on food	0	0		0	0	0	0	0	0	0	0
Total	30.45	32.29	+6.0	27.67	29.38	29.58	30.21	31.40	31.57	31.79	32.09
Percent difference from average				-14.3	-9.0	-8.4	-6.4	-2.8	-2.2	-1.5	-.61

[a] Grade AA eggs.
[b] Extra sharp cheese.
[c] Special.
[d] Price adjusted.
[e] Boneless sirloin steak price-adjusted 50 cents per pound to compare with bone-in steak price.

Table C.1

Item	New York	Salt Lake City	Chicago	Port-land, Ore.	Cleve-land	St. Louis	Denver	Boston	Wash-ington, D.C.	Hono-lulu	An-chor-age
Milk, homogenized, 1/2 gal.	$0.73	$0.74	$0.84	$0.72	$0.78	$0.82	$0.85	$0.73	$0.83	$1.11	$1.36
Eggs, 1 doz. grade A, large	.83	.50[a]	.595	.485	.495	.575	.59	.79	.67	.73	.72[a]
Cheese, 10 ozs., sharp, Cracker Barrel	1.43	1.49	1.52	1.395	1.39	1.29	1.40	1.25	1.29	1.75	1.78
Margarine, 1 lb., 4 sticks, Blue Bonnet or Parkay	.65	.47	.50[b]	.57	.39[b]	.59	.65	.69	.63	.65	.79
Bread, white, sliced, 24-oz. loaf	.73[c]	.50	.49	.27[b]	.595	.50	.53	.54	.49	.69[b]	.96
Flour, 5 lbs., all-purpose, Gold Medal or Pillsbury	.83[c]	.87	.90	.99	.85	.69	.775	.89	.99	.60[b]	1.25
Special K, 11 oz. package	.88	.91	.83	.91	.89	.87	.91	.89	.87	1.17	1.05
Sugar, 5 lbs., white granulated	.89[b]	.99	.69[d]	1.15	.79[b]	.29[b]	1.15	1.05	1.15	.895[b]	1.32
Instant coffee, 10 ozs., Nescafe or Maxwell House	4.29	4.59	4.70[b]	4.99	4.79[b]	4.98	4.58	4.19	5.19[b]	4.79	5.49
Great Northern beans, dry, 1 lb,	.43	.34	.35	.35	.39	.33	.29	.43	.29	.55	.41
Rice, 2 lbs., Uncle Ben's converted	1.09	1.15	.99	1.12	1.05	1.15	.89	1.05	1.09	1.12	1.29
Mayonnaise, 1 qt., Best Foods, Hell-man's, or Kraft	1.47	1.27	1.47	1.49	1.49	1.29	1.52	1.55	1.49	1.19[b]	1.79
Peanut butter, 18-oz. jar, smooth, Jif, Peter Pan, Planters, or Skippy	.89	1.06	.955	1.09	.79[b]	.97	1.05	.99	1.00	.89[b]	1.33
Tuna, 6-1/2-oz. can, light chunk meat in oil, Chicken of the Sea or Starkist	.71	.54	.55[b]	.68	.49	.67	.67	.79	.81	.71[c]	.75
Evaporated milk, 14.5-oz. can (13 fl. ozs.), Carnation, Golden Key, or Pet	.38	.34	.39	.39	.40	.34	.37	.38	.41	.35	.43
Cling peach halves, 29-oz. can, heavy syrup, Del Monte, Hunt, Libby, or Stokely	.61	.67	.49[b]	.62[b]	.71	.55	.66	.65	.69	.62	.73
Pineapple, 20-oz. can, sliced, heavy syrup or own juice, Del Monte or Dole	.64	.63	.65	.63	.63	.59	.62	.63	.69	.56	.73
Ice Cream, 1/2 gal., any brand	1.19	1.16	.79[b]	1.19	1.29	.99[d]	1.22	.99	1.29	1.23	1.69
Frozen orange juice concentrate, grade A or fancy, 6-oz. can, any brand	.30	.20[b]	.35	.25[b]	.35	.33	.29	.34[b]	.30	.35	.49
Broccoli spears, frozen, 10-oz. package, grade A or fancy	.49	.43	.47	.39	.53	.45	.40[b]	.47	.50	.49	.45
Rump roast, boneless, choice, 1 lb.	1.19[b]	1.19[b]	1.19[b]	1.34	1.48	1.59	1.48[b]	1.39[b]	1.69	1.89	1.85

(continued)

209

Table C.1 continued

Item	New York	Salt Lake City	Chicago	Portland, Ore.	Cleveland	St. Louis	Denver	Boston	Washington, D.C.	Honolulu	Anchorage
Sirloin steak, bone-in, choice, 1 lb.	1.49	1.98[b]	1.38[b]	2.57[e]	1.58	1.69	1.58	1.99	1.94	1.99	2.79[e]
Ground beef, regular, 1 lb.	.95	.55[b]	.79	.74[c]	.72	.69	.69	.99	.79	.95	.85
Pork loin chops, 1 lb., 1/2 to 3/4-in. thick, with tenderloin	2.09	1.78	1.09[f]	1.88	1.58	1.89	1.75	1.79	1.98	1.19	2.45
Ham, smoked, butt end, 1 lb.	1.25	1.19	.99	.89	1.38	.77	1.15	1.69	.69	1.19	1.09
Bacon, regular slice, 1 lb., Armour, Cudahy, Hormel, Oscar Mayer, Rath, Swift, or Wilson	.89	1.29[b]	1.19	1.09	1.68	1.69	1.55	1.59	1.39	1.59	1.93
Wieners, all meat, 1 lb., Armour, Cudahy, Hormel, Oscar Mayer, Rath, Swift, or Wilson	1.19		.79	.99[b]	1.19	1.35	.92[b]	1.09	1.29	1.09	1.59
Chicken, whole, broiler-fryer, never frozen, grade A, 1 lb.	.45	.88[b]	.38[b]	.49[b]	.58	.49	.62	.55	.57	.69	.95
Potatoes, 5 lbs., regular, all-purpose, US1	.89	.45[b]	1.59	.60	1.29	1.09	.95	.98	.99	1.09	1.25
Carrots, whole, 1 lb., US1	.29	.20	.34[c]	.25	.33	.33	.29	.34	.34	.25[b]	.49
Cabbage, 1 lb., US1	.19	.15	.25	.15[b]	.25	.19	.12	.23	.14	.13	.29
Lettuce, 1 head, US1	.59	.30	.59	.39	.49	.59	.49	.34	.49	.61[c]	.69
Bananas, 1 lb., yellow	.19	.30	.25	.34	.16	.27	.29	.30	.25	.33	.45
Tomatoes, 1 lb., vine-ripened, 3-in. diameter	.49	.49	.39[g]	.39	.57[h]	.39	.39	.39	.45	.79	.69
Oranges, 5 lbs., juice fruit	.98[c]	1.00	1.39	.99[c]	1.12	.99	1.00[b]	1.09	1.25	1.00	1.89
Subtotal	32.58	31.09	31.11	32.80	33.48	32.27	32.68	34.04	34.93	35.52	44.11
Percentage tax on food	0	5.0	5.0	0	0	4.5	3.5	0	0	4.0	0
Amount tax on food	0	1.55	1.55	0	0	1.45	1.14	0	0	1.42	0
Total	32.58	32.64	32.66	32.80	33.48	33.72	33.82	34.04	34.93	36.94	44.11
Percent difference from average	+.89	+1.1	+1.1	+1.6	+3.7	+4.4	+4.7	+5.4	+8.2	+14.4	+36.6

[a] Grade AA eggs.
[b] Special.
[c] Price adjusted.
[d] With coupon.
[e] Boneless sirloin steak price adjusted 50 cents per pound to compare with bone-in steak prices.
[f] Combination of cuts from pork loin.
[g] Small salad tomatoes.
[h] Hothouse tomatoes.
Source: William Rice, "Food Prices: Washington Tops the List," Washington Post, June 30, 1977.

APPENDIX D
CONCENTRATION OF GROCERY STORE AND SUPERMARKET SALES BY FOUR, EIGHT, AND TWENTY LARGEST FIRMS, 263 SMSAs, 1954-72

TABLE D.1

Concentration of Grocery Store and Supermarket Sales by Four, Eight, and Twenty Largest Firms, 263 SMSAs, 1954–72

Standard Metropolitan Statistical Area	Percentage of Grocery Store Sales Accounted for by															Percentage of 1972 Supermarket Sales by Top	
	Top 4 Grocery Store Companies					Top 8 Grocery Store Companies					Top 20 Grocery Store Companies					4 Firms	8 Firms
	1954	1958	1963	1967	1972	1954	1958	1963	1967	1972	1954	1958	1963	1967	1972		
Abilene, TX	44.0	54.3	54.4	52.2	48.1	52.9	65.5	68.4	66.2	69.8	68.0	79.3	83.7	84.8	83.5	81.9R	100.0
Akron, OH	48.5	61.0	62.1	52.6	53.4	55.3	70.8	71.2	72.7	70.9	63.2	76.6	78.3	80.7	80.7	67.9	(D)
Albany, GA	45.5	49.3	51.7	50.3	44.9	60.3	63.1	66.1	67.5	67.0	75.4	80.7	80.3	82.5	85.1	67.9	82.3
Albany–Schenectady–Troy, NY	39.3	47.5	47.8	44.4	53.2	50.8	54.9	57.7	58.5	64.8	57.7	62.9	66.3	68.5	73.6	67.5	(D)
Albuquerque, NM	49.8	60.3	68.7	69.5	66.3	62.3	71.9	74.0	79.5	84.2	74.4	81.8	82.7	88.5	90.0	84.4	99.1
Alexandria, LA	n.a.	n.a.	n.a.	n.a.	44.0	n.a.	n.a.	n.a.	n.a.	52.2	n.a.	n.a.	n.a.	n.a.	62.5	92.2	100.0
Allentown–Bethlehem–Easton, PA–NJ[b]	49.1	54.7	52.3	51.1	40.3	53.5	60.9	58.4	62.6	51.5	58.3	68.3	67.6	73.1	70.8	52.5	67.8
Altoona, PA	65.9	67.8	64.2	61.3	56.4	68.8	71.2	76.8	76.5	74.8	74.4	77.7	83.1	85.0	86.9	75.7	100.0
Amarillo, TX	62.5	68.9	62.8	60.9	62.7	72.3	75.7	70.9	74.6	82.1	83.1	86.9	86.4	89.3	94.8	74.9	(D)
Anaheim–Santa Ana–Garden Grove, CA	39.6	47.1	43.2	38.6	54.1	54.1	63.0	61.8	58.8	67.3	66.8	77.2	79.6	83.2	88.6	49.0	(D)
Anchorage, AK	n.a.	n.a.	n.a.	n.a.	70.3	n.a.	n.a.	n.a.	n.a.	84.4	n.a.	n.a.	n.a.	n.a.	95.3	80.8	(D)
Anderson, IN	38.6	38.4	42.1	49.8	61.8	58.2	63.8	63.6	67.5	77.7	77.6	85.8	87.4	91.3	95.1	73.5R	(D)
Ann Arbor, MI	55.5	59.7	61.0	66.0	65.2	62.6	67.7	70.9	77.9	80.7	72.8	79.5	81.9	87.4	92.3	74.4X	91.1
Appleton–Oshkosh, WI	n.a.	n.a.	n.a.	n.a.	26.6	n.a.	n.a.	n.a.	n.a.	41.4	n.a.	n.a.	n.a.	n.a.	69.1	34.6	53.9
Asheville, NC	n.a.	67.9	64.1	67.4	72.8	62.7	73.8	70.8	77.5	82.3	70.4	80.0	79.3	85.1	88.4	89.0A	100.0
Atlanta, GA[c]	53.9	55.6	60.5	60.0	54.6	60.3	61.5	67.0	67.9	68.4	66.1	67.3	72.1	73.1	73.0	74.5	88.9
Atlantic City, NJ	57.0	62.3	56.7	58.5	63.1	62.8	69.5	71.8	72.5	75.0	69.3	75.7	79.5	83.0	86.7	82.6X	96.8X
Augusta, GA–SC	48.8	48.8	55.2	48.0	47.2	59.1	60.6	63.5	60.9	66.5	68.0	70.2	72.3	73.8	78.6	68.4R	93.6
Austin, TX	44.6	46.1	45.6	47.2	51.8	60.6	63.4	61.6	64.5	70.7	77.7	82.6	84.8	86.7	86.5	76.5	(D)
Bakersfield, CA	31.1	31.4	35.8	35.5	40.8	39.4	39.8	46.1	45.7	51.4	50.3	53.4	60.5	61.3	67.2	61.0	76.9
Baltimore, MD	47.9	49.9	53.9	55.0	57.0	50.2	55.4	61.3	64.5	67.6	54.8	60.5	67.3	70.0	72.7	71.3X	83.2
Baton Rouge, LA[c]	52.9	61.8	61.0	45.7	57.2	59.4	70.7	71.6	62.1	62.7	67.0	76.7	80.0	74.0	72.8	73.4X	87.2
Battle Creek, MI	n.a.	n.a.	n.a.	n.a.	52.6	n.a.	n.a.	n.a.	n.a.	(D)	n.a.	n.a.	n.a.	n.a.	84.2	68.4A	92.0
Bay City, MI	38.3	48.0	52.2	65.0	68.0	46.7	61.9	66.9	76.3	81.0	57.5	72.9	77.5	84.7	88.6	86.0	100.0
Beaumont–Port Arthur–Orange, TX	37.0	41.1	41.6	38.1	34.2	44.5	46.8	48.5	46.4	46.4	56.6	57.4	59.2	61.3	64.1	56.8	76.1
Billings, MT	49.6	47.9	51.6	42.4	54.9	63.1	64.5	66.2	63.6	(D)	77.9	80.8	86.2	88.6	94.0	72.0	(D)

City	1	2	3	4	5	6	7	8	9	10	11	12	13	14	15	16	17	18	19
Biloxi-Gulfport, MS[c]	n.a.	n.a.	n.a.	51.0	60.1	n.a.	n.a.	n.a.	n.a.	70.0	71.2	n.a.	n.a.	n.a.	n.a.	n.a.	80.1	75.7A	100.0
Binghamton, NY-PA	53.8	51.4	52.0	50.6	41.8	64.2	67.3	67.9	67.2	67.0	69.7	77.3	77.6	80.0	81.0	—	—	(D)	(D)
Birmingham, AL	42.1	46.1	42.0	37.7	47.7	47.1	55.9	53.7	53.9	47.2	58.4	55.7	63.6	58.3	67.1	64.4R	78.5		
Bloomington-Normal, IL	n.a.	n.a.	n.a.	48.6	57.0	59.8	n.a.	n.a.	n.a.	62.8	72.6	74.8	76.4	83.9	91.5	80.5X	100.0		
Boise, ID	47.1	40.7	63.9	48.6	57.0	65.2	59.8	55.5	74.2	77.8	80.8	74.8	76.4	87.4	90.5	91.5	92.2	85.7	100.0
Boston, MA	56.2	47.6	52.3	49.0	63.6	60.0	57.2	64.4	66.7	76.7	63.1	64.4	66.2	71.3	60.6	88.0A			
Bridgeport, CT	n.a.	n.a.	n.a.	43.5	45.4	57.1	64.6	67.6	72.4	64.7	69.4	74.5	77.0	81.5	55.1A	88.0A			
Bristol, CT	46.0	61.8	59.0	62.0	63.9	72.5	74.3	77.5	74.0	80.8	83.4	83.7	87.9	97.0	63.7	96.1			
Brockton, MA[c]	30.7	33.0	39.3	68.5	44.0	48.0	53.4	58.6	58.4	61.2	81.1	71.5	77.0	91.7	81.7	(D)			
Brownsville-Harlingen-San Benito, TX	n.a.	n.a.	n.a.	57.9	47.1	41.3	53.3	48.0	63.1	58.4	77.2	80.2	58.8A	(D)					
Bryan-College Station, TX	59.8	56.4	56.4	41.0	57.9	62.0	57.9	77.2	65.3	77.2	87.1	(D)							
Buffalo, NY	n.a.	n.a.	n.a.	38.2	41.0	62.0	58.7	53.7	53.3	49.9	73.1	65.3	63.1	62.9	61.5	45.7	60.4		
Burlington, NC	30.0	39.2	39.0	54.8	54.8	58.7	51.7	73.1	53.9	65.7	63.3	65.8	74.5	80.4	72.8	96.6			
Canton, OH	45.1	55.9	55.9	33.7	33.7	42.2	53.5	52.0	59.6	65.7	53.9	59.2	65.8	80.4	43.9	67.7			
Cedar Rapids, IA	58.2	61.0	50.5	51.5	66.1	66.8	71.9	65.6	67.4	86.2	90.0	77.1	87.4	89.9	93.2	95.3	96.5	92.7A	100.0
Champaign-Urbana-Rantoul, IL	28.8	35.6	35.2	66.8	33.7	57.4	66.8	71.9	67.9	80.7	80.7	87.4	89.9	95.3	78.3X	(D)			
Charleston, SC[b]	54.4	59.1	56.8	26.3	45.4	51.7	50.9	53.7	58.5	48.1	48.1	64.8	72.0	71.6	36.1A	64.1A			
Charleston, WV	50.1	58.4	57.0	51.1	58.4	71.1	65.5	57.6	66.2	57.6	66.6	73.6	70.4A	(D)					
Charlotte-Gastonia, NC[c]	38.2	35.6	43.8	48.6	48.6	65.9	65.9	65.6	72.9	66.6	65.6	75.1	76.2	77.7	65.5	(D)			
Chattanooga, TN-GA[b]	49.0	51.9	51.9	43.9	51.1	47.6	54.9	58.6	57.7	61.4	55.1	69.6	73.0	72.3	56.6	(D)			
Chicago, IL	49.7	51.4	51.9	57.7	57.2	59.3	61.4	63.0	62.7	59.3	66.4	65.5	68.0	70.6	68.5R	71.3			
Cincinnati, OH-KY-IN	51.1	53.0	56.0	49.9	51.7	61.6	61.8	56.2	58.4	63.3	63.3	59.2	65.8	70.6	70.0A	79.3			
Cleveland, OH	58.1	66.2	69.8	58.4	59.4	61.6	61.8	68.1	66.8	60.8	65.8	66.8	73.3	72.3	67.8	85.8			
Colorado Springs, CO	n.a.	n.a.	n.a.	64.3	45.7	80.8	88.7	83.3	82.4	85.6	85.6	89.8	96.2	96.3	76.6	(D)	98.1		
Columbia, MO	49.1	47.7	48.1	45.7	48.1	45.7	57.2	54.8	69.0	68.5	68.5	63.4	67.3	95.2	53.9	(D)			
Columbia, SC	36.4	41.3	37.3	42.9	34.0	42.9	50.3	45.2	59.4	53.7	53.7	62.7	67.4	73.4	59.3A	73.7			
Columbus, GA-AL	54.9	56.9	53.2	50.7	52.9	32.6	61.9	66.4	59.4	46.1	46.1	69.1	67.5	69.9	53.4R	73.4			
Columbus, OH[b]	42.9	51.8	53.4	54.3	50.7	58.6	63.2	67.7	62.9	67.7	67.7	71.5	83.3	74.2	66.1	81.9			
Corpus Christi, TX	n.a.	n.a.	n.a.	46.6	54.3	51.0	69.7	61.9	61.4	67.3	67.3	75.7	80.0	81.1	78.4X	89.5X			
Dallas-Fort Worth, TX[a]	53.1	47.1	45.7	60.0	51.0	63.4	63.2	60.4	61.4	65.6	65.6	66.2	74.6	65.2	87.4				
*Dallas, TX	49.6	46.4	37.1	59.7	62.0	61.4	58.3	69.5	60.4	69.9	n.a.	67.6	72.2	74.6	n.a.	n.a.			
*Fort Worth, TX	n.a.	n.a.	n.a.	n.a.	59.7	49.5	55.4	69.5	49.5	69.9	n.a.	68.8	78.6	n.a.	n.a.	n.a.			
Danbury, CT	n.a.	n.a.	n.a.	55.3	57.2	55.3	n.a.	n.a.	n.a.	76.7	76.7	72.9	n.a.	91.6	67.0	91.0			
Davenport-Rock Island-Moline, IA-IL	50.2	55.1	54.1	67.0	67.0	63.3	65.1	71.4	80.6	80.6	72.6	76.3	80.9	88.4	81.4	(D)			
Dayton, OH	45.9	45.2	43.2	37.0	40.8	54.9	51.0	46.2	51.4	51.4	63.6	61.3	60.8	71.0	50.6	65.0			
Daytona Beach, FL	n.a.	n.a.	n.a.	65.4	n.a.	56.7	n.a.	n.a.	n.a.	77.8	77.8	n.a.	n.a.	86.7	(D)	(D)			
Decatur, IL	54.2	64.5	63.2	73.0	63.3	67.6	74.6	76.5	75.6	87.7	79.0	85.6	90.1	96.9	87.9A	100.0			

(continued)

Table D. 1 continued

Standard Metropolitan Statistical Area	Percentage of Grocery Store Sales Accounted for by															Percentage of 1972 Supermarket Sales by Top	
	Top 4 Grocery Store Companies					Top 8 Grocery Store Companies					Top 20 Grocery Store Companies						
	1954	1958	1963	1967	1972	1954	1958	1963	1967	1972	1954	1958	1963	1967	1972	4 Firms	8 Firms
Denver–Boulder, CO	67.1	66.9	70.4	66.0	80.5	72.9	72.3	75.7	74.9	88.3	77.9	77.9	81.3	84.2	91.9	90.5X	96.5
Des Moines, IA	36.9	41.4	33.9	44.4	69.4	44.8	51.3	49.3	59.1	81.3	56.0	66.3	71.3	80.4	89.4	80.4	(D)
Detroit, MI	38.5	49.9	52.1	49.4	49.8	45.5	57.9	62.1	69.8	(D)	50.5	62.3	66.6	73.4	75.0	62.4X	(D)
Dubuque, IA	43.8	54.6	65.5	57.7	69.4	54.0	65.4	75.2	74.3	87.9	66.9	79.1	88.0	86.5	95.4	89.8	100.0
Duluth–Superior, MN–WI	28.1	33.4	34.5	34.4	43.2	33.9	39.4	44.8	47.0	55.8	44.3	51.8	60.8	65.6	72.9	(D)	(D)
El Paso, TX	53.9	53.5	53.0	48.1	54.1	60.4	63.0	61.7	59.7	66.0	70.6	76.1	75.9	78.1	81.3	78.8	(D)
Elmira, NY	n.a.	n.a.	n.a.	n.a.	46.5	n.a.	n.a.	n.a.	n.a.	73.9	n.a.	n.a.	n.a.	n.a.	89.2	59.8	94.1
Erie, PA	52.0	58.2	49.3	48.0	43.9	58.9	63.3	57.9	58.2	57.4	66.8	71.3	71.0	72.6	75.3	60.2A	(D)
Eugene–Springfield, OR	39.0	54.7	59.4	55.3	46.9	50.7	63.6	69.6	67.5	58.0	64.1	74.7	80.0	79.7	76.9	62.3	77.1
Evansville, IN–KY[b]	42.4	43.8	42.7	40.1	41.4	54.4	55.5	55.0	62.6	53.5	64.6	70.6	71.9	80.7	71.4	52.1	(D)
Fall River, MA–RI	53.7	54.6	56.4	61.2	57.9	59.2	68.6	67.8	76.3	(D)	67.8	75.6	76.6	87.1	90.7	72.7	97.5
Fargo–Moorhead, ND–MN	42.1	44.1	49.9	55.2	53.6	53.8	60.9	65.2	72.2	71.3	65.7	74.9	78.9	84.7	87.3	70.3	(D)
Fayetteville, NC	n.a.	n.a.	n.a.	56.4	48.9	n.a.	n.a.	n.a.	63.4	64.2	n.a.	n.a.	n.a.	73.8	77.0	(D)	(D)
Fayetteville–Springdale, AR	n.a.	n.a.	n.a.	n.a.	42.2	n.a.	n.a.	n.a.	n.a.	(D)	n.a.	n.a.	n.a.	n.a.	79.4	(D)	80.8
Fitchburg–Leominster, MA	43.4	41.6	37.1	42.4	44.4	50.6	66.7	58.9	67.4	65.9	n.a.	81.8	82.6	89.5	91.5	55.5	82.4
Flint, MI	n.a.	53.6	53.1	60.6	45.5	n.a.	62.4	63.4	67.6	61.8	60.0	71.9	72.6	77.4	75.2	57.1X	(D)
Florence, AL	n.a.	n.a.	n.a.	n.a.	41.4	n.a.	n.a.	n.a.	n.a.	59.8	n.a.	n.a.	n.a.	n.a.	73.2	77.8	100.0
Fort Lauderdale–Hollywood, FL	72.3	70.5	65.5	68.6	69.4	78.8	78.7	79.7	81.0	(D)	84.2	87.5	88.9	89.0	91.2	85.6	97.2
Fort Myers, FL	n.a.	n.a.	n.a.	n.a.	62.8	n.a.	n.a.	n.a.	n.a.	76.4	n.a.	n.a.	n.a.	n.a.	88.7	83.3	97.7
Fort Smith, AR–OK	39.1	48.3	34.6	43.8	39.5	56.4	65.7	47.4	55.5	49.0	75.4	80.5	63.9	66.1	65.4	67.6	83.8
Fort Wayne, IN[c]	55.0	60.8	57.8	62.9	56.5	63.7	81.8	79.4	83.5	72.3	71.3	88.3	87.4	93.3	86.5	66.3A	82.7
Fresno, CA	22.7	27.7	23.5	24.6	27.2	33.4	37.1	37.2	36.7	38.3	46.1	51.8	55.6	54.4	57.5	41.8A	59.2A
Gadsden, AL	35.8	44.6	37.5	38.9	44.8	41.8	55.9	51.3	55.1	61.9	51.7	68.5	65.2	70.3	80.1	(D)	(D)
Gainesville, FL	n.a.	n.a.	n.a.	n.a.	61.8	n.a.	n.a.	n.a.	n.a.	75.7	n.a.	n.a.	n.a.	n.a.	89.4	85.4	97.6
Galveston–Texas City, TX	27.0	34.2	40.3	37.7	44.2	39.9	46.9	51.9	51.2	53.1	59.3	68.0	70.8	71.8	73.2	67.7	78.1
Gary–Hammond–E. Chicago, IN	38.9	34.4	29.3	33.9	35.8	43.7	43.4	47.8	52.3	57.4	53.0	59.0	68.2	73.7	76.5	40.0A	(D)
Grand Rapids, MI	40.3	44.9	44.0	52.0	67.8	46.8	52.0	56.3	62.5	74.4	55.9	61.8	65.4	74.3	82.5	79.0	86.7
Great Falls, MT	48.4	63.0	75.6	69.1	67.6	60.4	71.4	82.6	80.2	82.1	79.0	82.4	92.6	90.6	93.6	86.7	100.0
Green Bay, WI	45.2	50.1	56.5	57.6	67.2	59.0	67.5	68.0	68.3	76.5	72.3	82.0	84.3	86.7	92.5	83.7X	94.0X

214

	1	2	3	4	5	6	7	8	9	10	11	12	13	14	15	16	17	18
Greensboro-Winston-Salem-High Point, NC[c]	n.a.	n.a.	n.a.	n.a.	37.9	36.5	n.a.	n.a.	n.a.	n.a.	54.4	52.7	n.a.	n.a.	65.5	67.6	53.4A	76.3
Greenville-Spartanburg, SC[c]	49.1	57.7	55.6	57.4	57.9	63.4	68.8	67.3	66.3	78.3	70.3	72.8	77.2	76.7	80.3	80.5	85.9A	95.5
Hamilton-Middletown, OH	37.6	55.0	50.5	45.1	46.6	51.6	62.8	66.2	60.5	72.2	63.9	69.5	54.4	72.2	79.0	82.7	71.7A	91.2
Harrisburg, PA	49.7	48.1	50.9	56.3	56.0	51.1	58.6	60.5	63.8	69.6	68.5	64.9	62.4	69.6	78.2	77.6	69.0X	84.3X
Hartford, CT	n.a.	48.6	48.4	36.8	47.9	40.9	60.7	63.8	65.3	61.8	65.7	64.9	64.7	61.8	75.3	69.6	48.6A	(D)
Honolulu, HI	29.7	37.8	52.1	42.3	48.5	53.6	49.1	65.3	63.6	61.8	42.0	67.8	54.0	63.6	75.1	81.0	66.2	(D)
Houston, TX	35.5	33.2	35.1	42.3	32.2	34.7	41.5	42.3	53.6	46.6	42.0	44.3	49.4	49.3	52.0	58.7	50.1X	63.1
Huntington-Ashland, WV-KY-OH[b]	37.2	47.5	38.8	44.1	32.0	29.2	53.6	46.6	44.9	44.9	41.8	61.1	53.2	62.9	60.2	58.9	42.0	(D)
Huntsville, AL[c]	30.8	34.3	49.9	42.4	55.4	48.6	50.1	58.6	66.1	66.1	53.0	61.1	64.7	71.0	78.4	74.2	72.8A	90.1A
Indianapolis, IN	48.5	55.6	60.0	56.8	59.3	52.7	64.5	64.1	69.4	74.5	68.5	65.7	71.0	70.8	78.8	80.0	61.7	(D)
Jackson, MI	46.8	54.0	52.5	53.4	56.8	63.0	65.2	65.1	74.5	65.3	78.5	64.1	76.2	77.8	85.3	88.3	78.7A	97.9
Jackson, MS	51.5	48.9	55.9	60.8	51.8	55.9	64.6	66.0	65.3	65.3	69.1	67.9	73.9	75.8	75.6	78.8	(D)	95.9
Jacksonville, FL[b]	52.0	62.7	61.3	67.5	61.0	56.2	74.9	74.7	78.6	78.0	78.0	74.7	81.2	82.2	85.2	82.2	82.5	(D)
Jersey City, NJ	54.3	52.0	52.0	60.8	43.2	44.2	59.0	54.8	58.6	58.4	61.6	56.7	66.4	66.9	73.2	74.9	58.5A	(D)
Johnstown, PA	n.a.	55.8	56.8	52.5	56.3	53.4	60.7	63.9	64.3	64.3	64.6	64.6	58.4	71.3	74.4	75.5	74.3A	92.7A
Kalamazoo-Portage, MI[c]	33.4	41.9	56.7	45.8	72.2	64.9	59.6	70.6	87.1	63.0	78.5	63.0	74.8	82.8	93.3	89.7	76.1A	(D)
Kansas City, MO-KS	48.1	49.8	49.1	52.7	41.8	41.8	57.3	55.4	49.6	56.7	56.7	59.6	66.1	65.0	63.5	68.4	59.2	67.6
Kenosha, WI	45.3	44.6	49.3	54.0	46.5	54.5	58.3	65.3	67.0	73.7	73.7	64.0	73.8	78.4	82.6	85.9	73.7	100.0
Killeen-Temple, TX	n.a.	n.a.	n.a.	n.a.	n.a.	40.1	n.a.	n.a.	n.a.	56.8	56.8	56.8	n.a.	n.a.	n.a.	75.8	67.8A	88.2
Kingsport-Bristol, TN-VA	48.3	55.5	60.1	54.2	56.2	53.9	59.4	65.4	63.8	49.3	49.3	61.3	66.5	72.6	72.9	67.7	56.8	(D)
Knoxville, TN	n.a.	n.a.	n.a.	54.2	n.a.	47.7	n.a.	n.a.	n.a.	n.a.	68.1	n.a.	n.a.	72.6	n.a.	70.5	76.3A	89.7
La Crosse, WI	38.1	52.2	55.7	45.4	55.7	41.0	59.3	63.2	62.3	86.4	61.0	58.6	70.7	76.3	73.4	87.2	68.2	97.4
Lafayette, LA	n.a.	n.a.	n.a.	41.0	n.a.	72.1	n.a.	n.a.	n.a.	n.a.	(D)	n.a.	n.a.	n.a.	n.a.	(D)	69.8	100.0
Lafayette-W. Lafayette, IN	33.4	44.9	41.7	42.7	50.8	45.0	56.7	56.8	65.6	65.6	62.2	55.9	69.4	71.2	78.7	78.2	82.8	100.0
Lake Charles, LA	n.a.	n.a.	n.a.	48.3	n.a.	57.5	n.a.	n.a.	n.a.	n.a.	70.7	n.a.	n.a.	71.2	n.a.	78.7	73.7	96.8
Lakeland-Winter Haven, FL	42.4	45.7	48.1	56.5	49.2	45.8	52.2	55.0	56.3	56.3	55.8	62.3	64.4	64.4	68.2	70.6	85.9	(D)
Lancaster, PA	48.2	36.1	32.1	62.6	41.1	42.8	48.4	47.3	55.0	59.7	59.7	66.2	62.9	61.5	68.2	74.2	73.1	85.1
Lansing-E. Lansing, MI[b]	48.5	48.8	45.1	65.0	53.4	56.6	63.2	60.5	71.3	71.3	73.9	81.5	81.7	81.6	87.6	74.2	59.3X	78.4
Laredo, TX	46.4	46.6	52.8	62.6	61.2	57.5	64.5	60.5	83.6	81.6	73.9	85.9	86.6	90.1	94.2	(D)	78.0	100.0
Las Vegas, NV	43.0	46.6	43.0	52.4	51.7	55.7	55.2	60.1	64.1	69.8	69.8	81.6	67.0	75.1	80.7	93.3	67.2	94.3
Lawrence-Haverhill, MA-NH	54.0	48.9	50.0	60.9	52.0	58.9	62.0	64.3	68.0	73.7	73.7	61.1	82.9	82.9	87.2	85.7	67.8X	83.8
Lawton, OK	n.a.	30.8	32.7	46.8	38.9	60.0	50.2	56.3	69.9	69.9	73.3	72.9	78.6	82.9	74.3	87.3	88.5A	100.0
Lewiston-Auburn, ME	47.1	54.9	61.2	54.3	59.0	60.4	70.6	72.8	56.3	69.9	69.9	77.1	62.9	81.9	82.3	81.9	91.3A	95.4
Lexington, KY[c]	50.4	52.2	72.1	60.8	56.4	52.1	68.1	70.6	72.8	65.4	68.5	78.9	81.7	87.6	79.4	78.6	82.1X	93.2
Lima, OH[c]	44.2	50.8	54.2	54.1	51.9	57.3	62.6	66.7	62.7	72.4	70.5	79.0	83.9	81.4	83.9	(D)	79.1	82.7

(continued)

Table D.1 continued

Standard Metropolitan Statistical Area	Percentage of Grocery Store Sales Accounted for by															Percentage of 1972 Supermarket Sales by Top	
	Top 4 Grocery Store Companies					Top 8 Grocery Store Companies					Top 20 Grocery Store Companies					4 Firms	8 Firms
	1954	1958	1963	1967	1972	1954	1958	1963	1967	1972	1954	1958	1963	1967	1972		
Little Rock, AR	51.4	n.a.	55.1	62.7	61.8	54.9	59.3	62.1	67.3	67.2	60.8	66.4	70.0	75.4	77.3	86.4A	93.1A
Long Branch–Asbury Park, NJ	n.a.	n.a.	n.a.	n.a.	53.4	n.a.	n.a.	n.a.	n.a.	73.2	n.a.	n.a.	n.a.	n.a.	89.8	60.0	82.9
Lorain–Elyria, OH	44.5	54.6	53.9	45.6	42.5	53.5	62.4	62.8	61.2	64.8	63.7	72.4	74.3	78.7	83.1	56.2	79.7
Los Angeles–Long Beach, CA	29.6	24.6	30.3	28.5	35.6	40.6	39.6	43.1	46.3	53.8	53.0	54.8	60.5	67.8	71.9	41.4X	62.6
Louisville, KY-IN	51.2	57.7	60.3	55.8	54.8	55.1	62.2	65.0	62.1	61.3	59.7	67.5	71.3	69.4	68.4	76.0X	84.5
Lowell, MA-NH	40.0	38.8	37.2	58.5	71.6	52.0	58.6	58.8	71.7	81.5	64.8	72.4	77.8	86.4	89.5	89.4A	100.0
Lubbock, TX	58.0	60.1	62.7	64.5	69.4	62.8	65.8	71.0	77.2	81.9	71.5	75.1	81.7	86.4	89.9	84.3	97.9
Lynchburg, VA	38.7	39.5	40.9	39.4	40.9	43.6	49.0	51.4	53.6	56.8	54.2	60.8	63.8	69.3	73.4	(D)	(D)
Macon, GA	38.0	43.1	47.6	48.8	50.3	53.2	58.0	62.8	65.2	63.8	66.3	71.2	76.1	78.9	78.0	79.1A	94.5A
Madison, WI	41.5	43.2	40.6	40.4	47.4	52.6	54.6	55.9	52.8	62.5	62.6	66.4	70.1	70.1	77.4	64.0	(D)
Manchester, NH[b]	41.6	46.4	43.7	47.1	33.5	51.1	54.4	61.4	60.0	52.0	61.5	66.8	73.3	75.0	73.3	48.8	75.7
Mansfield, OH	n.a.	n.a.	n.a.	54.6	50.8	n.a.	n.a.	n.a.	70.7	73.9	n.a.	n.a.	n.a.	87.9	91.7	65.2A	94.7A
McAllen–Pharr–Edinburg, TX	n.a.	n.a.	n.a.	37.9	41.7	n.a.	n.a.	n.a.	46.1	50.4	n.a.	n.a.	n.a.	61.8	65.9	83.5	96.5
Melbourne–Titusville–Cocoa, FL	n.a.	n.a.	n.a.	n.a.	79.0	n.a.	n.a.	n.a.	n.a.	89.4	n.a.	n.a.	n.a.	n.a.	94.8	97.3X	100.0
Memphis, TN-AR-MS	23.1	32.7	28.9	35.9	41.4	30.8	40.0	42.8	49.3	54.5	40.2	50.3	55.9	59.6	64.2	61.8	(D)
Meriden, CT	57.4	60.8	67.1	68.2	67.5	65.9	70.9	78.9	79.6	86.3	80.0	84.0	91.2	91.8	94.2	85.2	100.0
Miami, FL	55.5	62.6	53.3	60.5	62.8	69.4	73.0	73.6	74.1	72.3	76.7	79.3	80.2	80.6	78.1	84.9X	90.5X
Midland, TX	51.0	49.9	56.5	50.6	63.6	66.2	66.4	66.9	66.3	78.8	89.3	89.6	85.8	88.2	90.8	93.6	100.0
Milwaukee, WI	42.6	46.7	39.9	31.6	57.4	47.5	51.7	47.3	41.6	66.9	55.3	60.6	56.6	52.5	73.5	67.4	77.9
Minneapolis–St. Paul, MN-WI	31.4	38.5	39.3	43.7	42.4	38.1	44.3	48.7	54.3	55.4	46.9	52.6	60.7	63.7	65.4	54.4X	(D)
Mobile, AL	43.6	48.0	46.2	50.6	42.0	56.8	59.2	61.7	66.3	62.1	66.1	73.7	72.8	78.6	74.9	60.9	(D)
Modesto, CA	n.a.	n.a.	n.a.	n.a.	42.5	n.a.	n.a.	n.a.	n.a.	58.9	n.a.	n.a.	n.a.	n.a.	79.2	57.0R	78.8
Monroe, LA	37.5	39.1	55.0	51.0	46.6	52.4	52.1	69.7	65.0	68.3	64.8	68.4	84.1	78.7	86.5	(D)	(D)
Montgomery, AL[b]	49.9	62.5	53.7	55.8	56.0	58.8	68.4	63.7	68.2	70.2	67.0	75.9	73.2	78.2	82.0	75.4	(D)
Muncie, IN	39.4	60.4	44.6	61.0	68.2	55.4	71.5	65.5	77.1	84.3	75.4	85.1	85.8	93.5	94.6	79.9A	97.6
Muskegon–Muskegon Heights, MI[b]	40.1	47.5	49.7	60.2	56.6	47.7	56.3	59.3	69.5	78.8	58.1	67.5	81.2	81.2	81.4	75.0	(D)
Nashua, NH	n.a.	n.a.	n.a.	n.a.	51.8	n.a.	n.a.	n.a.	n.a.	70.2	n.a.	n.a.	n.a.	n.a.	87.9	64.9	87.9
Nashville–Davidson, TN[c]	50.4	59.0	52.1	58.2	47.5	59.2	67.1	56.2	62.2	52.3	66.8	74.0	62.4	69.2	60.6	72.1A	(D)
Nassau–Suffolk, NY	n.a.	n.a.	n.a.	n.a.	45.7	n.a.	n.a.	n.a.	n.a.	70.8	n.a.	n.a.	n.a.	n.a.	82.7	54.1A	(D)

New Bedford, MA	38.4	44.0	40.5	51.5	60.2	54.5	59.9	63.9	71.9	(D)	66.7	69.8	74.5	81.1	87.5	79.7	100.0
New Britain, CT	51.8	46.4	50.6	47.8	44.2	59.9	60.3	71.1	68.8	66.6	69.1	74.0	84.4	85.1	89.7	52.6X	79.8X
New Brunswick–Perth Amboy–Sayreville, NJ	n.a.	n.a.	n.a.	n.a.	45.9	n.a.	n.a.	n.a.	n.a.	64.8	n.a.	n.a.	n.a.	n.a.	85.4	52.4X	(D)
New Haven–W. Haven, CT[b]	38.4	44.0	48.2	54.4	51.3	47.1	52.9	60.8	66.4	64.9	56.2	64.5	71.3	76.2	76.6	72.3A	(D)
New London–Norwich, CT–RI[b]	n.a.	n.a.	53.8	58.1	51.2	n.a.	66.3	66.3	74.6	70.5	n.a.	n.a.	77.8	85.0	88.3	(D)	84.1
New Orleans, LA	36.0	44.8	52.0	54.4	59.6	41.7	55.2	58.6	61.6	67.1	50.5	64.2	67.5	71.4	75.2	75.6X	84.0
New York, NY–NJ[b]	41.1	36.7	34.5	33.0	30.9	47.6	45.4	47.6	45.0	45.6	54.7	54.4	56.9	58.7	56.7	39.7A	58.7
Newark, NJ[b]	52.8	47.9	40.2	42.5	44.2	60.1	56.4	51.5	57.7	57.6	66.1	65.8	65.1	72.0	73.5	50.2	(D)
Newport News–Hampton, VA[c]	62.0	63.6	60.1	60.5	56.7	70.2	76.4	76.2	82.0	78.4	77.3	84.3	88.5	92.7	90.2	70.8	(D)
Norfolk–Va. Beach–Portsmouth, VA–NC	48.7	39.1	46.1	51.6	48.7	55.5	49.8	56.3	67.3	67.6	63.9	65.6	71.6	83.4	84.3	60.5	78.6
*Northeast Pennsylvania[a]	n.a.	n.a.	n.a.	n.a.	53.0	n.a.	n.a.	n.a.	n.a.	62.0	n.a.	n.a.	n.a.	n.a.	70.1	74.2A	(D)
*Scranton, PA	50.2	47.6	50.6	55.2	n.a.	53.7	62.3	61.6	67.2	n.a.	58.8	69.4	69.0	75.1	87.5	75.3	100.0
*Wilkes-Barre, PA	49.1	54.9	55.7	58.5	n.a.	52.7	61.3	61.6	65.1	n.a.	57.4	66.8	67.5	73.0	85.8	53.8	79.5
Norwalk, CT	n.a.	n.a.	65.0	59.4	56.9	n.a.	n.a.	77.8	79.8	78.6	n.a.	n.a.	n.a.	87.5	88.3	71.2A	97.5
Odessa, TX	50.2	49.8	51.8	52.1	47.2	68.5	66.9	71.6	77.4	75.8	86.3	82.4	92.3	90.8	92.2	64.9	100.0
Oklahoma City, OK	40.3	40.0	40.2	38.8	35.8	45.5	46.7	46.9	46.7	44.6	56.7	59.1	58.9	60.3	58.0	45.5	55.5
Omaha, NE–IA	38.9	45.1	53.5	55.7	62.0	43.9	51.7	61.7	69.7	73.0	54.1	62.8	71.1	80.4	84.0	73.1X	99.0
Orlando, FL	63.2	62.5	63.8	61.0	65.7	68.1	70.6	75.6	76.2	80.5	76.1	79.0	83.8	86.8	89.4	83.5A	(D)
Owensboro, KY	n.a.	n.a.	n.a.	n.a.	54.8	n.a.	n.a.	n.a.	n.a.	72.8	n.a.	n.a.	n.a.	n.a.	87.5	75.3	100.0
Oxnard–Simi Valley–Ventura, CA	n.a.	n.a.	n.a.	46.4	54.8	n.a.	62.8	62.8	68.4	68.4	n.a.	n.a.	82.1	82.1	85.8	61.4	79.5
Parkersburg–Marietta, WV–OH	n.a.	n.a.	n.a.	n.a.	45.6	n.a.	n.a.	n.a.	n.a.	62.4	n.a.	n.a.	n.a.	n.a.	82.0	82.0	78.3
Paterson–Clifton–Passaic, NJ[c]	64.2	60.6	48.6	51.1	46.6	68.4	66.9	59.3	61.6	63.2	73.8	73.6	71.9	77.0	87.6	52.5A	(D)
Pensacola, FL	37.4	49.7	43.1	42.7	40.4	48.3	60.5	59.7	58.3	64.8	60.5	72.6	76.7	76.5	82.1	61.0A	(D)
Peoria, IL	38.4	45.8	37.9	36.2	50.2	45.6	52.8	52.8	51.4	55.9	57.5	66.5	67.7	67.9	72.9	47.7	(D)
Petersburg–Colonial Hts–Hopewell, VA	52.6	60.3	60.7	59.8	54.1	56.9	63.3	63.7	67.4	64.6	59.0	65.9	67.1	71.7	73.4	77.7	97.2
Philadelphia, PA–NJ	45.4	46.1	46.6	39.8	47.8	50.9	57.9	63.5	62.7	72.2	60.6	70.1	78.0	83.8	71.7	69.7A	82.9
Phoenix, AZ	39.7	48.7	43.5	58.6	58.0	60.7	60.7	54.6	67.5	67.4	63.9	73.4	71.8	79.4	86.7	61.4	(D)
Pine Bluff, AR	45.0	53.2	51.7	58.6	50.6	51.2	60.7	54.0	54.0	49.5	63.9	66.7	65.0	60.8	81.7	91.5	100.0
Pittsburgh, PA	45.0	61.3	69.7	66.7	61.9	50.6	73.1	81.0	83.0	82.0	79.6	84.2	90.0	92.4	91.9	55.5	57.1
Pittsfield, MA[b]	57.5	61.3	69.7	66.7	61.9	73.1	73.1	81.0	83.0	82.0	79.6	84.2	90.0	92.4	91.9	76.1	(D)
Portland, OR–WA	43.1	41.2	49.3	40.1	50.1	49.6	53.6	63.6	57.0	62.9	60.5	67.1	81.7	75.2	77.2	68.4A	99.0
Portland, ME[b]	39.6	43.1	35.3	40.7	53.7	45.8	48.7	48.5	55.6	63.5	55.1	57.1	58.4	66.4	74.9	66.3X	83.1
Poughkeepsie, NY	n.a.	n.a.	n.a.	n.a.	73.0	n.a.	n.a.	n.a.	n.a.	84.9	n.a.	n.a.	n.a.	n.a.	90.9	83.2X	78.0
Providence–Warwick–Pawtucket, RI–MA	48.7	48.9	50.9	58.5	59.1	54.0	58.5	65.9	74.9	75.9	60.3	67.2	72.2	80.5	83.7	74.9X	97.3X
Provo–Orem, UT	40.6	39.4	49.8	50.3	51.3	52.0	52.4	62.7	69.2	73.5	70.8	73.3	82.8	87.5	90.2	62.3	(D)
Pueblo, CO	50.1	53.4	60.2	60.2	70.3	60.1	66.4	75.1	75.6	86.2	74.1	82.1	86.0	90.8	95.3	91.6X	100.0

(continued)

Table D. 1 continued

Percentage of Grocery Store Sales Accounted for by

Standard Metropolitan Statistical Area	Top 4 Grocery Store Companies					Top 8 Grocery Store Companies					Top 20 Grocery Store Companies					Percentage of 1972 Supermarket Sales by Top	
	1954	1958	1963	1967	1972	1954	1958	1963	1967	1972	1954	1958	1963	1967	1972	4 Firms	8 Firms
Racine, WI	38.5	51.2	52.9	43.0	51.9	50.0	63.2	64.9	62.0	69.3	62.2	77.4	77.1	81.0	87.1	65.0	86.9
Raleigh-Durham, NC[a] [c]	47.9	56.8	58.8	61.1	63.5	54.2	64.0	62.7	65.6	68.7	63.3	72.8	69.7	73.5	74.7	93.5A	98.2
Reading, PA	46.9	44.8	48.0	46.7	42.5	55.2	53.4	60.3	57.6	56.2	63.4	64.7	70.3	70.8	71.5	60.0	(D)
Reno, NV	48.2	54.4	65.6	76.1	59.7	63.2	72.5	79.4	89.9	(D)	83.2	88.2	92.9	96.5	94.0	68.3	(D)
Richland-Kennewick, WA	n.a.	n.a.	n.a.	n.a.	57.1	n.a.	n.a.	n.a.	n.a.	n.a.	n.a.	n.a.	n.a.	n.a.	92.6	70.3A	100.0
Richmond, VA	50.5	47.9	49.9	50.4	45.2	57.7	57.7	60.4	62.2	65.9	65.2	69.7	72.4	77.8	81.1	58.0A	83.9
Riverside-San Bernardino-Ontario, CA	29.8	37.2	38.1	41.6	45.5	36.9	46.5	55.9	62.2	62.4	52.8	59.0	68.3	71.2	74.4	59.1	77.9
Roanoke, VA[c]	58.8	62.7	66.8	69.2	62.9	63.6	68.6	75.9	78.6	73.1	72.0	76.9	82.2	86.1	83.4	89.0	98.6
Rochester, MN	n.a.	n.a.	n.a.	n.a.	76.6	n.a.	n.a.	n.a.	n.a.	91.3	n.a.	n.a.	n.a.	n.a.	98.2	91.8	100.0
Rochester, NY	58.5	65.7	55.5	56.2	59.3	62.0	69.2	61.9	64.2	67.7	66.0	73.5	67.6	72.0	74.6	73.2	(D)
Rockford, IL	43.9	50.8	41.0	42.1	50.7	52.2	60.1	57.4	64.2	66.8	62.6	74.0	76.6	82.4	85.5	62.1A	(D)
Sacramento, CA	40.6	44.5	36.3	40.1	48.5	54.5	51.3	47.4	58.4	66.0	65.6	63.2	65.1	72.2	78.7	59.8X	(D)
Saginaw, MI	29.9	37.0	46.9	51.3	58.3	36.6	50.2	58.1	64.0	69.0	47.9	61.5	68.8	76.1	79.3	76.7A	90.9A
St. Cloud, MN	n.a.	n.a.	n.a.	n.a.	40.6	n.a.	n.a.	n.a.	n.a.	58.8	n.a.	n.a.	n.a.	n.a.	81.9	59.6A	(D)
St. Joseph, MO	42.7	45.8	51.7	50.6	51.2	53.0	61.2	69.4	70.8	73.7	66.8	76.5	83.6	87.0	91.2	63.3	91.1
St. Louis, MO-IL	34.6	42.7	42.9	39.3	46.2	44.7	49.1	50.6	51.3	53.1	49.3	54.2	56.8	59.9	63.2	57.6A	(D)
Salem, OR	n.a.	n.a.	n.a.	50.2	53.4	n.a.	n.a.	n.a.	63.2	64.4	n.a.	n.a.	n.a.	79.4	82.7	63.6	77.6
Salinas Seaside-Monterey, CA	n.a.	n.a.	n.a.	42.4	47.4	n.a.	n.a.	n.a.	56.9	57.4	n.a.	n.a.	n.a.	70.4	71.1	71.4	(D)
*Salt Lake City-Ogden, UT[a]	52.0	61.5	60.2	(D)	59.2	65.8	72.1	78.8	(D)	66.4	80.7	86.0	90.5	(D)	82.5	71.2	79.6
*Ogden, UT	37.4	42.2	50.3	54.4	n.a.	44.6	50.3	56.8	64.5	n.a.	56.3	62.6	67.3	74.1	n.a.	n.a.	n.a.
*Salt Lake City, UT	65.5	66.3	59.8	56.2	58.6	72.6	75.2	71.0	74.3	75.8	83.3	87.6	83.5	90.4	89.5	90.6R	100.0
San Angelo, TX	50.0	47.9	54.4	53.5	55.1	72.6	75.2	71.0	74.3	75.8	83.3	87.6	83.5	90.4	89.5	n.a.	n.a.
San Antonio, TX	50.0	40.6	54.4	53.5	55.1	75.2	55.3	61.9	61.8	66.1	70.0	66.1	70.0	72.6	78.4	90.6R	87.5
San Diego, CA	41.1	28.6	33.0	40.4	46.0	49.0	35.3	42.9	49.3	56.3	40.8	44.5	55.2	62.6	68.6	70.1X	(D)
San Francisco-Oakland, CA	27.1	30.7	33.0	40.4	46.0	33.5	35.3	42.9	49.3	56.3	40.8	44.5	55.2	62.6	68.6	59.3	70.9
San Jose, CA	28.4	30.7	33.9	37.8	46.0	40.4	35.3	43.7	49.6	60.3	52.4	55.9	59.2	66.3	79.8	54.8X	71.9X
Santa Barbara-Santa Maria-Lompoc, CA	47.0	45.7	52.6	60.0	62.0	57.2	56.9	64.2	72.0	74.8	69.8	75.0	80.8	85.2	87.3	75.9R	(D)
Santa Cruz, CA	n.a.	n.a.	n.a.	n.a.	49.5	n.a.	n.a.	n.a.	n.a.	61.7	n.a.	n.a.	n.a.	n.a.	82.2	63.1	78.6
Santa Rosa, CA	n.a.	n.a.	n.a.	n.a.	51.7	n.a.	n.a.	n.a.	n.a.	62.9	n.a.	n.a.	n.a.	n.a.	76.7	65.9	80.2

Sarasota, FL	n.a.	n.a.	n.a.	n.a.	73.2	n.a.	n.a.	n.a.	n.a.	84.7	n.a.	n.a.	n.a.	n.a.	96.3	87.9	98.4
Savannah, GA	33.7	32.1	34.7	41.2	42.3	46.9	48.1	52.6	55.4	56.0	61.3	65.5	74.3	73.6	74.4	63.8	(D)
Seattle-Everett, WA	39.7	38.4	41.1	41.5	49.0	45.1	46.4	51.8	56.0	62.2	52.6	54.9	61.0	67.5	74.4	60.9A	76.6
Sherman-Denison, TX	n.a.	n.a.	n.a.	50.5	57.7	n.a.	n.a.	n.a.	64.0	(D)	n.a.	n.a.	n.a.	76.4	(D)	100.0	100.0
Shreveport, LA[b]	48.6	57.1	54.4	51.8	45.5	52.7	62.2	64.6	64.8	62.3	59.6	70.7	75.6	73.8	(D)	59.4	(D)
Sioux City, IA-NE	42.8	46.3	44.1	49.3	45.9	58.9	60.0	56.2	65.0	64.8	68.9	74.8	75.3	81.4	84.2	(D)	86.8
Sioux Falls, SD	67.2	62.3	70.9	72.3	79.4	73.8	72.7	80.9	84.8	87.2	85.6	86.7	94.7	97.4	97.0	100.0	100.0
South Bend, IN	41.2	46.6	42.4	46.7	47.3	47.3	56.3	56.2	59.3	60.4	55.6	67.4	72.8	74.8	78.1	60.5	77.9
Spokane, WA	38.4	47.0	54.7	56.3	62.4	51.1	59.1	65.4	68.1	70.3	65.1	70.1	75.6	78.6	82.6	78.2	(D)
Springfield, IL	46.5	51.7	47.2	49.4	55.6	54.9	63.7	62.6	68.6	71.8	64.7	75.9	78.0	85.2	87.2	68.3X	(D)
Springfield, MO	46.3	50.5	54.8	60.5	58.8	57.6	62.4	69.1	78.0	75.3	69.2	73.6	82.4	87.3	89.6	78.9	100.0
Springfield, OH[b]	50.5	58.9	49.6	56.6	44.2	63.7	69.9	63.6	74.1	62.3	72.9	79.6	79.7	89.2	83.6	64.2	(D)
Springfield-Chicopee-Holyoke, MA-CT	45.2	45.4	43.5	44.4	47.0	54.1	59.2	63.2	66.6	65.8	62.4	70.0	72.7	77.6	78.8	63.0X	80.8
Stamford, CT	53.8	59.9	45.9	46.2	43.4	65.0	73.8	62.1	59.5	(D)	75.4	83.8	84.5	82.3	90.8	49.4X	76.3
Steubenville-Weirton, OH-WV	n.a.	59.5	55.2	57.3	43.2	n.a.	62.4	63.6	68.5	(D)	n.a.	67.8	71.3	76.5	76.3	66.3	84.1
Stockton, CA	23.8	25.4	26.1	28.3	34.0	34.8	37.9	38.2	43.3	(D)	50.4	56.9	59.5	65.3	70.2	51.8	74.3
Syracuse, NY	39.5	42.7	40.2	33.8	29.9	49.5	57.3	53.3	50.0	45.8	59.7	64.9	63.8	63.5	63.8	37.5	(D)
Tacoma, WA	33.7	39.5	41.3	46.0	49.1	43.8	53.1	56.9	62.9	67.7	57.6	66.0	72.8	78.9	82.5	64.5	(D)
Tallahassee, FL	n.a.	n.a.	n.a.	63.1	70.7	n.a.	n.a.	n.a.	77.1	82.4	n.a.	n.a.	n.a.	89.7	90.9	100.0	100.0
Tampa-St. Petersburg, FL	51.1	60.4	62.3	63.1	63.5	60.1	70.1	75.1	77.3	78.0	65.3	74.8	81.1	84.4	86.5	82.5X	94.5X
Terre Haute, IN	60.5	60.9	52.5	54.2	56.1	64.1	67.0	60.8	67.1	69.2	70.4	76.3	71.0	77.0	82.0	74.4X	92.2X
Texarkana, TX-Texarkana, AR	27.3	47.9	41.0	39.4	41.1	34.7	54.8	51.0	53.3	55.5	46.1	65.1	66.0	67.5	68.8	81.5R	(D)
Toledo, OH-MI	47.8	52.6	59.4	62.5	55.0	58.1	62.6	67.8	74.9	68.2	67.1	74.1	76.2	81.8	76.8	68.0X	84.5X
Topeka, KS[b]	31.5	32.6	32.3	49.3	35.7	46.7	52.0	52.9	65.4	53.5	64.3	75.0	82.6	86.3	76.9	49.1	(D)
Trenton, NJ	63.9	61.3	59.9	53.6	50.1	67.7	70.0	72.3	73.7	73.0	72.1	76.5	79.8	84.4	87.3	60.0A	88.2A
Tucson, AZ	53.6	54.8	48.6	48.4	45.8	60.9	66.5	65.1	66.7	69.4	70.1	76.3	78.6	82.7	86.1	57.9	82.9
Tulsa, OK[b]	45.4	46.3	47.8	50.6	52.5	53.9	53.7	54.3	62.2	66.1	62.2	66.8	65.0	73.6	75.9	70.1A	82.5
Tuscaloosa, AL	36.1	41.7	39.3	45.7	65.6	44.8	54.9	54.1	64.9	75.8	57.4	68.5	69.3	80.6	85.2	96.8	100.0
Tyler, TX	40.0	47.5	61.3	57.4	67.0	56.9	64.5	73.3	71.5	75.4	73.6	78.6	83.5	84.7	84.6	94.8	100.0
Utica-Rome, NY	37.5	42.3	38.3	41.4	39.4	49.7	61.8	58.9	64.6	63.1	59.3	70.4	70.3	75.4	76.1	53.8	78.8
Vallejo-Fairfield-Napa, CA	n.a.	n.a.	36.9	41.6	49.4	n.a.	n.a.	51.5	56.2	65.3	n.a.	n.a.	73.6	78.6	85.5	60.1X	81.8
Vineland-Millville-Bridgeton, NJ	n.a.	n.a.	n.a.	64.1	62.3	n.a.	n.a.	n.a.	75.6	(D)	n.a.	n.a.	n.a.	84.2	86.2	83.6A	100.0
Waco, TX	42.4	50.4	48.8	48.3	61.6	54.8	59.6	59.8	60.2	68.3	67.0	69.9	70.9	72.8	76.2	95.3A	100.0
Washington, DC-MD-VA	56.0	59.7	67.3	70.3	76.3	64.2	70.2	78.0	82.5	86.2	69.9	77.5	83.7	86.9	89.3	88.9X	96.3
Waterbury, CT	39.0	39.9	46.0	50.6	46.8	52.9	54.9	59.2	65.2	70.1	63.1	71.0	73.8	77.1	81.6	63.9A	94.4
Waterloo-Cedar Falls, IA	42.6	38.5	42.9	48.7	65.0	60.2	55.3	62.9	67.5	80.0	71.1	78.1	83.7	87.4	93.7	77.9	(D)
West Palm Beach-Boca Raton, FL	63.6	61.2	66.2	63.1	64.7	72.3	70.9	75.9	74.2	79.0	80.9	79.1	84.9	86.5	89.8	83.1	95.4

(continued)

Table D. 1 continued

| | Percentage of Grocery Store Sales Accounted for by | | | | | | | | | | | | | | | Percentage of 1972 Supermarket Sales by Top | |
| | Top 4 Grocery Store Companies | | | | | Top 8 Grocery Store Companies | | | | | Top 20 Grocery Store Companies | | | | | | |
Standard Metropolitan Statistical Area	1954	1958	1963	1967	1972	1954	1958	1963	1967	1972	1954	1958	1963	1967	1972	4 Firms	8 Firms
Wheeling, WV-OH	46.6	56.4	56.6	54.8	46.1	52.6	61.9	65.2	64.5	62.2	57.1	67.4	72.0	75.9	78.3	63.8A	86.3
Wichita, KS	52.7	47.5	41.9	42.4	40.5	60.8	56.9	54.4	58.0	56.4	73.2	71.8	70.4	74.2	74.3	47.6	67.8
Wichita Falls, TX	52.2	52.8	57.5	55.4	65.8	60.1	65.1	68.9	70.6	77.1	72.0	80.0	81.1	82.4	(D)	94.6	100.0
Williamsport, PA	n.a.	n.a.	n.a.	n.a.	73.4	n.a.	n.a.	76.5	79.3	82.8	71.0	79.4	81.7	85.3	90.2	93.7A	100.0
Wilmington, DE-NJ-MD	59.6	63.7	66.1	68.4	63.9	65.2	74.5	76.5	79.3	77.8	71.0	79.4	81.7	85.3	86.7	77.6	93.5
Wilmington, NC	n.a.	n.a.	n.a.	54.3	32.9	n.a.	n.a.	n.a.	68.8	70.0	n.a.	n.a.	n.a.	82.4	83.1	73.9	97.5
Worcester, MA	42.2	39.6	27.0	30.9	44.5	48.2	51.0	40.4	47.3	51.5	59.5	66.2	63.5	70.3	74.4	38.9A	61.5A
Yakima, WA	n.a.	n.a.	n.a.	n.a.	44.4	n.a.	n.a.	n.a.	n.a.	57.9	n.a.	n.a.	n.a.	n.a.	76.8	61.6A	(D)
York, PA	36.1	45.8	44.3	47.1	44.4	40.3	54.0	55.9	62.0	61.2	47.0	61.2	65.6	71.7	76.3	60.6A	82.3
Youngstown-Warren, OH	44.0	50.1	51.8	44.0	32.1	49.2	56.2	57.3	56.0	46.8	55.3	63.5	66.2	67.5	63.1	44.8R	59.3R
Simple average	45.5	49.3	50.1	51.1	52.4	54.4	59.9	62.0	64.8	67.3	64.5	71.0	74.3	77.7	80.7	69.5	100.0

n. a. = not available.

(D) = Withheld to avoid disclosing figures for individual companies.

*SMSAs that were combined in 1972 and for which 1954–67 data are shown for the previous components.

Notes: Averages for all years reflect SMSAs as defined at the time. Composition change between 1967 and 1972, due to the inclusion of new SMSAs and the combination of older SMSAs, is not significant. The simple average of four-firm concentration ratios for 39 completely new SMSAs in 1972 was 52.8 percent. This is just slightly higher than the all-SMSA average concentration ratio in 1972 (52.4 percent). Considering, further, that the average for all new SMSAs includes five newly defined combinations of SMSAs that, when reported on an uncombined basis in 1967, had a higher average concentration level than the 1972 average level of the combinations, composition change probably has less than 0.10 percent effect on the 1972 average concentration ratio compared with the average 1967 concentration ratio. The four-firm supermarket concentration ratio average is adjusted for SMSA composition differences between the sample of SMSAs with supermarket concentration ratios and the universe of all SMSAs. This is done in order to make the average supermarket concentration ratio of 69.6 comparable with the average 1972 four-firm grocery store ratio of 52.4 percent.

In addition to new SMSAs, the Census Bureau has changed the definitions of many SMSAs over time. These changes generally reflect the growth in market areas. For example, of the 231 SMSAs defined in 1967, 88 (38 percent) were redefined for the 1972 census by adding smaller geopolitical units to the 1967 definitions. In five instances units were dropped, but usually others were added at the same time. In addition to the 88 changed definitions, 10 of the 231 SMSAs of 1967 were dropped and merged to form five new SMSAs in 1972. The effect of definitional changes varied considerably. In 52 SMSAs redefinitions altered grocery store sales by less than 10 percent; in 21 SMSAs grocery store sales were changed by 10–20 percent; and in 15 SMSAs grocery store sales were altered by over 20 percent. SMSAs that were combined or experienced 1972 definitional changes affecting sales by over 10 percent are marked as follows:

^aSMSAs created by the merger of two previously separate SMSAs.

^bRedefinition resulted in a change of 10–20 percent in 1972 SMSA grocery store sales.

^cRedefinition resulted in a change of over 20 percent in 1972 SMSA grocery store sales.

Supermarkets are defined as grocery stores with $1 million or more in annual sales. In several instances where Census Bureau disclosure rules prevented the reporting of precise concentration ratios, concentration ratio ranges are reported. In such instances concentration ratios are expressed in whole numbers followed by letters to indicate the range within which the true value lies.

X—The maximum and minimum values of the observation lie within $\pm.5$ percentage point of the indicated value.

A—The maximum and minimum values of the observation lie within ±1.5 percentage points of the indicated value.

R—The maximum and minimum values of the observation lie within ±2.0 percentage points of the indicated value.

Source: Special tabulation prepared by the Bureau of the Census for the Bureau of Economics of the Federal Trade Commission and the Economic Research Service of the U. S. Department of Agriculture.

INDEX

inflation, 32
Intriligator, M., 92

Johnson, O., Jr., 150, 160
Joint Economic Committee, 44, 61, 95

K-Mart, 46
Kantor Markets, Inc., 38
Kimbell Grocery Co., 146-47
Kmenta, J., 106
Kohl's Food Stores, 46-47, 147
Kroger, Inc., 43

labor, 31, 77, 113
Lewis & Coke Super Markets, 44
Liebenstein, H., 133, 141
LIFO (last in—first out), 63, 134
Loblaw, Inc., 31-32
Lowe's Food Stores, 146
Lucky, Inc., 22, 38, 43, 61, 144, 146-50

Machlup, R., 35, 54
Mallen, B., 111, 132-33, 135
March, J., 141
Marion, B., 111
Marion, D., 94
market: basket, 95-96; bill, 1, 3-4; definition, 58; expansion by chains, 36-39; growth, 48-49, 52, 72-73, 83, 87, 106; power, 14-18, 67, 144-45; prices, 96-99; relevant, 57-58; rivalry, 76-77, 100-01, 104, 107; share, 5-9, 39, 64-65, 67, 69-70, 110-11; size, 49, 52, 73, 83, 87, 104, 106; structure variables, 56-58, 67-72
Mather, L., 160
McCowan, F., 149, 159-60
merger(s): activity, 19-26, 38; conglomerate, 23-24, 46-47,

50-53, 147; enforcement policy, 19, 22, 144-52; horizontal, 23-26, 40, 45, 145-51; market extension, 23-24, 38-39, 145-48, 151; structural influence of, 19-26, 42-43, 52, 145-50
models: change in concentration, 49; price, 100-01, 117; profit, 78-79
monopoly overcharge, 137-41
Mori, H., 111
Mountain States Whsle. Co., 147
Mueller, W., 34, 55, 93

Nat'l Ass'n of Food Chains, 28
national brands, 96-100, 107, 109
National Commission on Food Marketing (NCFM), 13-15, 34, 19, 28, 55, 58-59, 70, 92-93, 116, 129, 135-37
National Tea, 19, 39, 40, 42-43, 54, 144-45, 150-51, 159
Nourse, E., 38, 53, 54, 55

Olson, M., 149, 160
operating: costs, 28-29, 31, 58, 106-07, 112-13, 133; profit, 29, 31; results, 29-32
Operating Results of Food Chains, 28
Operations Review, 28

Penn Fruit, 31
Pic-n-Pay, 40
price: analysis, 101-10; comparisons, 95-96, 110, 113-14; controls, 63, 65; limitations, 109-10; models, 100-01, 117; patterns, 96-98, 120-29; price/profit results, 130-36; price/structure relationships, 99-110, 114-15; spreads, 115-20

224

private label, 107, 109
product-service mix, 57, 120–22
profit(s): analysis, 79–91 [divisional, 64–67, 85–90; SMSA, 80–85]; firm, 61; models, 78–79; operating, 31; performance, 30–32, 61–67, 135–36; strategies, 70; structure relationship, 90–91
Progressive Grocer, 4, 33–34, 57, 92

Red & White, 10
relative firm market share, 71, 85, 88, 90–91, 104
retail: food sales, 4; food stores, 4; grocery sales, 4–5; grocery stores, 4
retailers: affiliated, 10, 12; chain, 6–10; independent, 5, 10, 12; unaffiliated, 10, 12
Rhoades, S., 54, 55, 76
Rhodes, R., 149–50, 160
Rice Markets, 43–44
Robinson-Patman Act, 144

SMI (See Super Market Institute)
Safeway Stores, Inc., 5, 43–44, 63, 65, 67, 143–44, 149, 159, 160
Scherer, F., 92, 141
Shepherd, W., 54, 71
Sherman Act, 144
Shop Rite (Foodarama), 143
Shopping Bag, 38, 148

Smith Co., C. F., 42–43
Stigler, G., 48, 54, 55, 92
Sultan, R., 54
Super Market Institute (SMI), 28, 31
Super Value, 10
supermarket: concentration, 5, 72, 101, 108–10; definition, 33; general, 5, 57
Supermarket News, 43, 47, 55, 146, 159
Supermarkets General, 38

Time, Inc., 92–93

vertical integration, 10
Von's Grocery Co., 145, 147–48 151, 159

wage: price controls, 63, 65; rates, 77, 104, 106–07
Wakefern Coop., 38
Wall Street Journal, 40
WEO (See A&P)
Weekly Digest, 33
Weingarten, 43–44, 55
Weiss, L., 92
wholesaler(s): concentration, 11–14; cooperative, 11–13; mergers by, 23; voluntary, 11–13
Winn-Dixie, 63, 65, 67, 75, 134, 144, 146

X-inefficiency, 133, 137, 141

ABOUT THE AUTHORS

BRUCE W. MARION has been Adjunct Professor of Agricultural Economics at the University of Wisconsin-Madison since 1974. He is also Agricultural Economist with the U.S. Department of Agriculture. He was Assistant Professor-Professor at Ohio State University from 1963 to 1974, and a Visiting Research Fellow, Harvard University, 1969-70. He has received awards for outstanding research from the American Agricultural Economics Association and the American Council on Consumer Interests. He is the author of numerous articles and monographs on topics dealing with food retailing and public policy.

WILLARD F. MUELLER is William F. Vilas Professor of Agricultural Economics, Professor of Economics, and Professor in the Law School, University of Wisconsin-Madison, 1969 to present. He was Chief Economist, Federal Trade Commission, from 1961 to 1968, and taught at the University of California-Davis, University of Maryland, and Michigan State University. He is a Fellow, American Agricultural Economic Association, and author of numerous articles and monographs on subjects dealing with industrial organization and public policy.

RONALD W. COTTERILL is Assistant Professor of Marketing and Public Policy in the Department of Agricultural Economics at Michigan State University. After graduating with Honors and Distinction from Cornell University in 1970 he was a Marshall Fellow in Economics at the University of Copenhagen, Denmark from 1971 to 1972. His contribution to this book was a component of graduate studies at the University of Wisconsin-Madison. Mr. Cotterill received a joint Ph.D. in Agricultural Economics and Economics from Wisconsin in June of 1977.

FREDERICK E. GEITHMAN received a B.A. in Economics in 1973 and an M.S. in Agricultural Economics in 1975 from New Mexico State University. He is currently a Research Specialist in the Department of Agricultural Economics at the University of Wisconsin-Madison. He held that same position during the time the research of this book was completed.

JOHN R. SCHMELZER received his B.A. in 1974 and his M.S. in 1976, both in Agricultural Economics, from Ohio State University.

He was a Research Specialist in the Department of Agricultural Economics at the University of Wisconsin-Madison during the time the research of this book was completed. He is currently a doctoral candidate in the Department of Agricultural Economics at Michigan State University.

DATE DUE

DEC 19 1982			
MAY 9 1983			
JAN 1 1984			
1988			
APR 1994			

30 505 JOSTEN'S